COMPETITIVENESS
FORGING AHEAD

*Presented to Parliament by the President of the Board of Trade and the Chancellor of the
Exchequer, the Secretaries of State for Transport, Environment and Employment, the Chancellor
of the Duchy of Lancaster, and the Secretaries of State for Scotland, Northern Ireland, Education
and Wales by Her Majesty May 1995*

Cm 2867 LONDON HMSO £19 50 net

INTRODUCTION BY THE PRIME MINISTER

Our economic ambition is to enable this country to double its living standards within twenty five years.

Unless we can create the conditions for strong and sustainable growth no Government will be able to improve education and health, maintain strong defence, increase pensions, or provide care in the community. So we are working for long term growth, for a stronger more prosperous country.

This time last year, the Government published "Competitiveness: Helping Business to Win". This was the first comprehensive national survey of Britain's competitive position against that of our leading trading rivals. We promised then to update this national survey each year, as a hard-headed assessment of our competitive position.

There is much that has happened in the last year in which Britain can justifiably take pride: exports are at record levels as we win markets across the world; manufacturing industry is expanding again and so, too, is employment in it; inflation remains at the lowest level most people can remember. As a result, Britain's economy grew by 4 per cent last year and we are set to outpace our main competitors again this year.

But there are areas where, for many decades, Britain has been behind other countries; and our rivals will not wait for us to catch up and overtake them. The pace of change is increasing year by year. Many of the old hugely labour-intensive industries are no more, right across Western Europe. By the turn of the century, perhaps half of Britain's workforce will be employed in relatively small firms. These are the new businesses on which our future jobs and prosperity will depend. This White Paper sets out a programme of further action to help small businesses to expand and export.

We also live in an increasingly knowledge-based economy. The education and skills of all our people are crucial to our prosperity and national success. We have endorsed the demanding new national education and training targets. The White Paper sets out the steps we are taking, in partnership with industry, to realise our ambition that Britain should have the best qualified workforce in Europe.

John Major

CONTENTS

Substantive references to Deregulation (Cutting Red Tape), Business Links and Small Firms/SMEs in the text are highlighted as shown. There is a Glossary at the end of the White Paper. Publications referred to in the White Paper are identified in footnotes.

For information on the data in the textual charts please contact Steve Leighton, Competitiveness Division, DTI. Tel. 0171 215 6397; Fax. 0171 215 6984.

Two complementary documents were published at the same time as the White Paper. These are:-

Competitiveness: Forging ahead - A Summary
Competitiveness: Helping Smaller Firms.

These documents are available free of charge from DTI Publications. Tel. 0171 510 0174; Fax. 0171 510 0197

This White Paper is available from HMSO outlets and can be found on the Internet at http://www.op en.gov.uk/

SETTING THE SCENE

1.1 Our commercial success, and ultimately our standard of living, depend on continuously improving all aspects of our performance across the whole economy. As the Prime Minister said in his introduction to the 1994 Competitiveness White Paper[1], higher living standards for our families, better schools and hospitals, strong defence, a cleaner environment, and a thriving artistic and cultural national life all depend on wealth creation.

The 1994 White Paper analysed our competitive position.

1.2 The 1994 White Paper was the first comprehensive Government audit of the UK's competitive position. It showed that a competitiveness gap between the UK and other major economies had opened up over the best part of a century and had been particularly marked since 1945. The UK fell from third in real income per head in Europe in 1950 to tenth by 1979. In 1950, our productivity in manufacturing industry was, on average, over 10 per cent higher than in Germany, and over twice that of Japan: by 1979, German productivity was 50 per cent higher than ours, and Japanese productivity a third higher. Over the same period, the UK's share of world trade in goods fell from 10.5 per cent to 5.3 per cent.

1.3 The 1994 White Paper reported major improvements in our competitive position during the 1980s, which were continuing in the 1990s, but said that much remained to be done. For example, manufacturing productivity grew faster in the UK than in the US, France and Germany but average productivity levels still fell short of those achieved by our main competitors. Our share of the volume of world trade in manufactures stabilised after decades of decline, but we continued to lose share of world trade in services. Our overall growth rate was similar to that in France, Germany and Italy – whereas we had grown significantly more slowly in previous economic cycles – but our GDP per head remained below that of those and many other advanced countries.

1.4 The 1994 White Paper identified ten main factors influencing competitiveness. These were the macroeconomy, education and training, the labour market, innovation, management, fair and open markets, finance for business, communications and infrastructure, the commercial framework and the business of government and public purchasing. It contained more than 300 commitments and plans and underlined the determination of the whole of Government to improve the long run performance of the economy.

1.5 The Commons Trade and Industry Select Committee reported last year on the competitiveness of manufacturing industry[2]. The Government welcomed that report as a contribution to the debate on the ways in which the UK could improve its relative economic performance. Although confined to the manufacturing sector, the report shared much of the analysis in the White Paper and reached many of the same conclusions about the UK's relative position and the improvements needed.

[1]*Competitiveness: Helping Business to Win* Cm 2563 [HMSO] (1994)
[2]*Competitiveness of UK Manufacturing Industry* [Second Report, Trade and Industry Committee] (Session 1993-94)

WHAT IS COMPETITIVENESS?

For a firm, competitiveness is the ability to produce the right goods and services of the right quality, at the right price, at the right time. It means meeting customers' needs more efficiently and more effectively than other firms.

For a nation, the OECD defines competitiveness as:

"...the degree to which it can, under free and fair market conditions, produce goods and services which meet the test of international markets, while simultaneously maintaining and expanding the real incomes of its people over the long term."

A sustained improvement in our competitiveness requires further underlying improvement in long term productivity, control of costs, and a performance in many aspects of national life that compares favourably with others.

Trade has been a major engine of world growth. An open world economy provides the opportunities to specialise and reap economies of scale. It also provides the stimulus of competition. There are prizes in world markets for all.

It was generally well received .....

1.6 The decision to publish an audit of the UK's competitive position was widely welcomed by business. The recognition that competitiveness depended on many factors and that there was no single quick solution was widely acknowledged, as was the involvement of the whole of Government and the emphasis given to education and training. The 1994 White Paper was seen as an important first step in improving our competitiveness. The Confederation of British Industry (CBI), Institute of Directors (IoD), Association of British Chambers of Commerce (ABCC), and Engineering Employers' Federation (EEF) amongst others called for the exercise to be repeated.

..... although there were criticisms.

1.7 The EEF thought the 1994 White Paper too complacent about the improvement in our competitiveness during the 1980s, arguing that our manufacturing base was too small and that there had been insufficient new investment in manufacturing. The ABCC thought that a franker appraisal of our competitive position was needed. The CBI argued that public investment needed to rise in education and training and in transport, although total public spending should be kept under tight control. They also urged a wider consideration of the relationship between environmental policies and competitiveness.

1.8 Others criticised the absence of significant increases in public expenditure, ignoring the importance to competitiveness of keeping public spending down. Those who criticised the 1994 White Paper because it contained too few new announcements overlooked the point that the White Paper was a "snapshot" of progress.

There is now widespread recognition of the importance of competitiveness.

1.9 The Government welcomed the request that the 1994 White Paper be updated. This publication is the result. The Government also welcomes the wide-ranging debate in both the wealth-creating sector and in the public sector about the importance of competitiveness and of the measures needed to improve it.

The need for improved performance is as pressing as ever.

1.10 The UK economy performed strongly last year. Both total output and manufacturing output rose by 4 per cent. Unemployment fell by nearly 300,000 and manufacturing productivity grew by over 4 per cent. The current account deficit fell sharply. Underlying inflation was at the lowest sustained level for 30 years.

1.11 We must not let this short-term progress, in which the economic cycle is playing a part, mask the need for continued improvement. It is an enormous task to correct a century of relative decline. The search for increased competitiveness must continue.

1.12 The Prime Minister has declared his aspiration of doubling living standards in 25 years. This will need further, sustained, action to raise the economy's long run rate of growth. It will require business and Government to work in partnership to build on strengths and tackle weaknesses. Sustained investment in people and ideas, as well as in machines and buildings, will be needed.

The economic landscape continues to change .....

1.13 Our companies face the most competitive environment they have ever seen. Barriers to the movement of goods and services continue to fall, many emerging nations are achieving rapid growth, and advances in technology are opening new markets and transforming existing industries. These changes present enormous opportunities to us where we are competitive. They are a threat wherever we are not.

..... and others are seeking to improve their performance.

1.14 A prime purpose in publishing White Papers on competitiveness is to focus attention on our absolute performance and to put that alongside that of our main competitors. The pressure is for continual change. Targets set today may no longer be world class when they are achieved. There is no winning post in the search for competitiveness. Governments throughout the world are now committed to a competitiveness agenda. Many have published analyses of their performance and set out strategies for improvement. Germany, the US, Canada, Australia, New Zealand, the Netherlands, Sweden, Belgium, Ireland and Finland have all published such work in the last three years. Like the 1994 White Paper, these have emphasised the importance of creating the right climate for business to prosper and of initiatives to help business to help itself.

SOME RECENT COMPETITIVENESS INITIATIVES

Australia

In May 1994, the Australian Government published a White Paper "Working Nation - Employment and Economic Growth", covering innovation, science and technology, management, access to finance, government purchasing, export promotion, business costs and deregulation.

Canada

In December 1994, the Canadian Government published a White Paper "Building a More Innovative Economy" as part of its action plan "Agenda: Jobs and Growth". It set out the challenges facing Canada as a result of structural changes in the world economy, focusing on small businesses, trade policy, infrastructure and technology.

Spain

In February 1995, the Spanish Government published "An Industrial Policy for Spain - A Proposal for Discussion". It sought to provoke a debate about the future competitiveness of Spanish industry. It identified strengths and weaknesses and indicated the progress sought by Government in each area. The paper was in favour of markets and gradually reducing the state sector.

United States

The Competitiveness Policy Council, a 12 member bipartisan national commission, provides a forum for the analysis of competitiveness issues and the development of recommendations for long-term strategies for sectors of the US economy and specific policy on competitiveness issues. In May 1994, the Council made its third report to the President and Congress. The areas covered included education, training, technology, public infrastructure, trade policy, improving the policy process, social policy and private investment. It acknowledged that there were no quick fixes for competitiveness, and that the changes proposed would take many years to implement.

Europe

The European Commission followed up its 1993 White Paper "Growth, Competitiveness and Employment" with a separate Communication on industrial competitiveness. The Commission came forward in March 1995 with a work programme to implement the Communication and will also be presenting an annual report to the Industry Council on the competitiveness of European industry. The first report is expected around the end of 1995.

In parallel, the Commission has invited 13 high level experts on European competitiveness to participate in a new Competitiveness Advisory Group. The Group will report, prior to each European Council, on the state of EU competitiveness and advise on appropriate political priorities and policy changes. The first report is expected in time for the European Council in June 1995.

OECD

The OECD has identified a range of factors which influence the performance of individual firms. These include skills, taxation, corporate governance, management and the macroeconomy. The OECD is to hold a Forum on Industrial Competitiveness in October 1995.

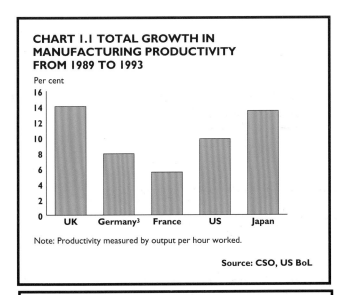

CHART 1.1 TOTAL GROWTH IN MANUFACTURING PRODUCTIVITY FROM 1989 TO 1993

Per cent

Note: Productivity measured by output per hour worked.

Source: CSO, US BoL

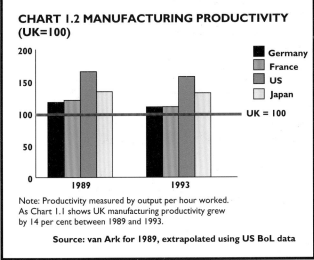

CHART 1.2 MANUFACTURING PRODUCTIVITY (UK=100)

Germany
France
US
Japan

UK = 100

Note: Productivity measured by output per hour worked.
As Chart 1.1 shows UK manufacturing productivity grew by 14 per cent between 1989 and 1993.

Source: van Ark for 1989, extrapolated using US BoL data

We are moving rapidly in the right direction although there is still much room for improvement.

1.15 This White Paper seeks to update wherever possible the international comparisons included in the 1994 White Paper and to focus on changes over the past year. This has often proved difficult because of the lack of reliable and timely international data. Comparisons between countries are also affected by the timing of the economic cycle.

1.16 We have continued to improve our manufacturing productivity compared with our main rivals (Chart 1.1) although German manufacturing productivity rose extremely rapidly last year. International comparisons of the level of productivity are difficult to make with precision, but it appears that a significant gap remains overall (Chart 1.2). We also appear to lag behind the US, Germany and France in some areas of service sector productivity, although the gap is less than in manufacturing.

³*Unless otherwise specified Germany refers to the former West Germany*

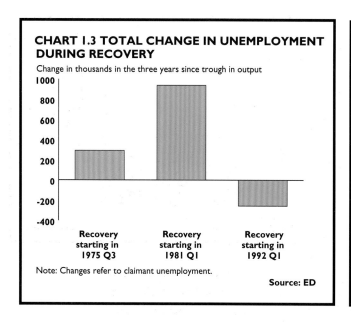

CHART 1.3 TOTAL CHANGE IN UNEMPLOYMENT DURING RECOVERY

Change in thousands in the three years since trough in output

Recovery starting in 1975 Q3

Recovery starting in 1981 Q1

Recovery starting in 1992 Q1

Note: Changes refer to claimant unemployment.

Source: ED

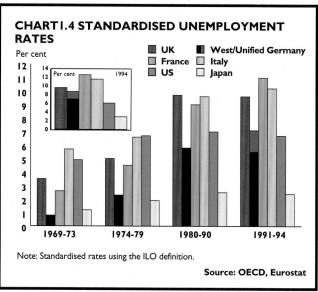

CHART 1.4 STANDARDISED UNEMPLOYMENT RATES

Per cent

UK · West/Unified Germany
France · Italy
US · Japan

1969-73 1974-79 1980-90 1991-94

Note: Standardised rates using the ILO definition.

Source: OECD, Eurostat

1.17 Increased flexibility in the labour market has led to unemployment falling sooner in the present recovery than in the previous two recoveries (Chart 1.3). But unemployment remains too high (Chart 1.4). Recent evidence suggests that our unit labour costs in manufacturing are lower than those in Germany, Japan and France, although German unit labour costs fell sharply last year. Inflation has continued to fall but there is still some way to go to match the best of our competitors (Chart 1.5).

1.18 The profitability of industry is higher than at the comparable point in the two previous recoveries (Chart 1.6) and is expected to have risen further last year.

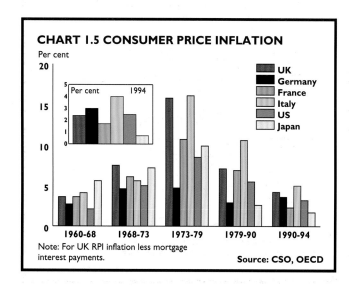

CHART 1.5 CONSUMER PRICE INFLATION

Per cent

UK
Germany
France
Italy
US
Japan

1960-68 1968-73 1973-79 1979-90 1990-94

Note: For UK RPI inflation less mortgage interest payments.

Source: CSO, OECD

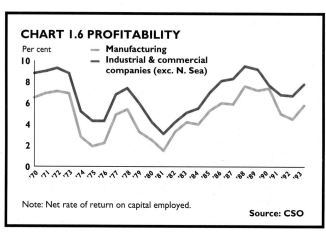

CHART 1.6 PROFITABILITY

Per cent

Manufacturing
Industrial & commercial companies (exc. N. Sea)

Note: Net rate of return on capital employed.

Source: CSO

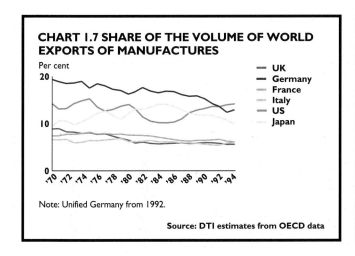

CHART 1.7 SHARE OF THE VOLUME OF WORLD EXPORTS OF MANUFACTURES

Per cent

— UK
— Germany
— France
— Italy
— US
— Japan

Note: Unified Germany from 1992.

Source: DTI estimates from OECD data

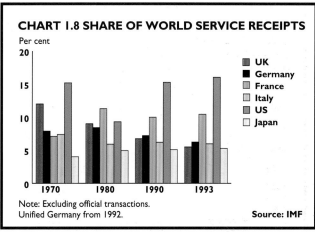

CHART 1.8 SHARE OF WORLD SERVICE RECEIPTS

Per cent

■ UK
■ Germany
■ France
□ Italy
■ US
□ Japan

Note: Excluding official transactions.
Unified Germany from 1992.

Source: IMF

1.19 Exports rose by 11 per cent in volume last year and we have continued to hold our share of world trade in manufactures despite increased competition in world markets (Chart 1.7). Although we have continued to lose our share of world trade in services (Chart 1.8), trade shares alone can be a misleading indicator of performance because effective competition in many service industries requires local delivery.

1.20 Despite its recent rapid growth, GDP has grown more slowly than in most of our major competitors since 1990, reflecting the timing of the economic cycle (Chart 1.9). Our GDP per head remains below that of other major industrial countries such as France and Germany (Chart 1.10). Some of the economies of the Far East – such as Hong Kong and Singapore – have overtaken us on this measure.

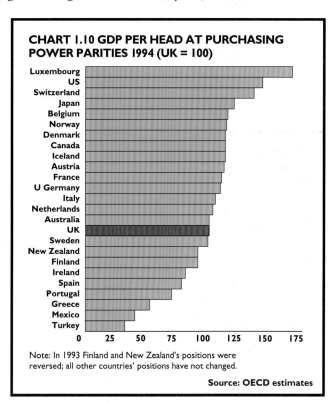

CHART 1.10 GDP PER HEAD AT PURCHASING POWER PARITIES 1994 (UK = 100)

Note: In 1993 Finland and New Zealand's positions were reversed; all other countries' positions have not changed.

Source: OECD estimates

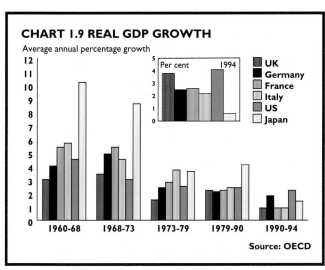

CHART 1.9 REAL GDP GROWTH

Average annual percentage growth

■ UK
■ Germany
■ France
□ Italy
■ US
□ Japan

Source: OECD

THE UK'S INVESTMENT PERFORMANCE

Investment in its widest sense, including investment in "intangibles" such as innovation, training, marketing and supply chains, as well as in machines and buildings, must be sustained if the UK is to increase its underlying rate of growth.

The Government believes that it can best encourage investment through the creation of a stable, low inflation environment and a favourable regulatory and tax regime that allows companies to spend money how they, rather than the Government, think best. Academic research and business surveys show that expected demand and rates of return are the main factors influencing fixed investment (Chart 1.11).

Capital Investment

The UK has consistently invested a smaller proportion of GDP than its major competitors, with the exception of the US. However, this largely reflects the relatively low share of housing investment in total investment in the UK. Business sector investment and investment in machinery and equipment have been similar as a proportion of GDP to those of other members of the G7 (apart from Japan) since 1980. Manufacturing invested a similar proportion of its output to Germany and the US over the last complete economic cycle (Charts 1.12, 1.13, and 1.14).

Studies have found that the use to which investment is put is at least as important as its quantity. For example, one recent study[4] suggests that differences in the quantity of capital explain only around one-half of the gap in manufacturing productivity between the UK and Germany, one-third of the gap between the UK and France, and one-eighth of the gap with Japan. Other key factors in explaining productivity differences include the skill level of the labour force and the quality of management.

Capital Stock

It is sometimes suggested that the UK has suffered from a relatively old capital stock. Direct evidence is limited and often dated, but suggests that the age of the UK capital stock is similar to that in other countries. One study found that the average age of the machine stock in metal working in the early 1980s was 10 years for Japan and 12 years for the UK, but 14 years for the US

continues...

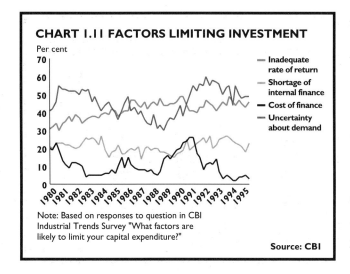

CHART 1.11 FACTORS LIMITING INVESTMENT

Per cent

— Inadequate rate of return
— Shortage of internal finance
— Cost of finance
— Uncertainty about demand

Note: Based on responses to question in CBI Industrial Trends Survey "What factors are likely to limit your capital expenditure?"

Source: CBI

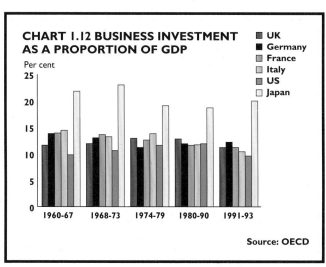

CHART 1.12 BUSINESS INVESTMENT AS A PROPORTION OF GDP

■ UK
■ Germany
■ France
□ Italy
■ US
□ Japan

Per cent

1960-67   1968-73   1974-79   1980-90   1991-93

Source: OECD

[4]*Mary O'Mahony: Capital Stock and Productivity in Industrial Nations* [National Institute Economic Review] (August 1993)

THE UK'S INVESTMENT PERFORMANCE *continued*

and Germany and 15 years for France[5]. Studies of matched plants carried out by the National Institute of Economic and Social Research (NIESR) also found the age of machinery in use to be similar in a range of industries in the 1980s. However, there are exceptions: NIESR found that the average age of machines in the UK engineering industry was 12 years, whereas it was only 8 years in the Netherlands[6]. There is also some evidence from these studies that UK capital equipment may be less technologically advanced. For example, the proportion of Computer Numerically Controlled (CNC) machinery in engineering was much higher in the Netherlands than in the UK (35 per cent compared to the UK's 20 per cent).

Investment in Innovation

UK firms increasingly recognise the importance of innovation. A recent survey of over 600 firms found that 185 had brought forward either research and development investment or product innovation during the recession, and 110 of these had also brought forward process innovations[7]. Innovation held up well during the recession. Government policy towards innovation is set out at greater length in Chapter 11.

UK business has increased its spending on R&D over the last decade, but more slowly than its main competitors. Many medium and low tech sectors appear to underinvest in R&D relative to their competitors. However, companies can source their innovative ideas from the UK or overseas so that R&D figures alone may not be a reliable indicator of innovation.

Investment in Skills

A more highly skilled workforce can perform a wider range of tasks and is better able to meet and consistently maintain higher quality standards. Capital equipment is much more effectively selected and used in plants where managers are well supported by highly qualified technical staff. Chapter 7 contains a fuller account.

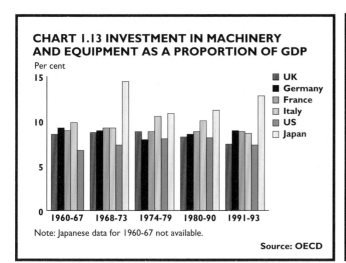

CHART 1.13 INVESTMENT IN MACHINERY AND EQUIPMENT AS A PROPORTION OF GDP

Per cent

UK, Germany, France, Italy, US, Japan

1960-67 1968-73 1974-79 1980-90 1991-93

Note: Japanese data for 1960-67 not available.

Source: OECD

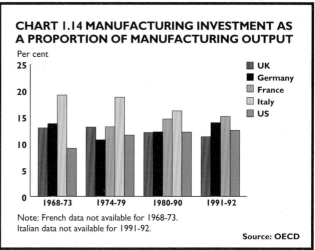

CHART 1.14 MANUFACTURING INVESTMENT AS A PROPORTION OF MANUFACTURING OUTPUT

Per cent

UK, Germany, France, Italy, US

1968-73 1974-79 1980-90 1991-92

Note: French data not available for 1968-73.
Italian data not available for 1991-92.

Source: OECD

[5]S Prais; *Some International Comparisons of the Age of the Machine Stock* [Journal of Industrial Economics] (1986)

[6]G Mason and B van Ark; *Productivity, Machinery and Skills in Engineering: an Anglo-Dutch Comparison* [NIESR Discussion Paper (New Series) No 36] (May 1993)

[7]P A Geroski and P Gregg; *Coping with the Recession* [National Institute Economic Review] (November 1993)

Improving competitiveness is primarily for business .....

1.21 In a market economy, the primary responsibility for improving competitiveness must lie with firms; this is recognised by business itself. There is considerable scope for companies to help themselves by adopting best practice in all activities, benchmarking against the best in the world and striving to surpass that standard. The vast majority of businesses prosper without public subsidy.

..... but all parts of Government have an important role to play .....

1.22 When market imperfections limit the scope for firms to improve competitiveness, the Government may need to intervene. The Government creates the climate within which business can improve its performance by:

- providing the stable macroeconomic environment, based on low inflation, sound public finances and competitive tax rates, which is essential to give business confidence to invest;

- maintaining and developing open and competitive world markets and fighting to bring down barriers to trade;

- removing unnecessary burdens on business through deregulation, aimed particularly at small and medium-sized enterprises (SMEs);

- making markets work better through liberalisation, sharpening incentives by the reform of personal and business taxation, and extending markets through privatisation;

- helping business help itself through better informed decision-making and the spread of best practice;

- ensuring a favourable environment for inward investment; and

- improving value for money and standards in services, such as education, which are best provided by the public sector.

..... with the Private Finance Initiative (PFI) in the forefront.

1.23 The PFI is creating new opportunities for businesses to develop as operators of public services (Chapter 10). It is turning the Government from a provider of services to the public into a purchaser of services on behalf of the public. It is injecting private sector skills and disciplines into public services.

The Government attaches the greatest importance to meeting the continuing challenge of competitiveness .....

1.24 This White Paper underlines the Government's determination to help business improve its performance. Following a discussion (Chapter 2) of the policies which the Government is following to maintain a stable, low inflation environment, the White Paper extends the analysis of competitiveness to individual sectors (Chapters 3 and 4) and regions (Chapter 5). Chapter 6 looks to the challenges and opportunities of the future. Chapters 7 to 15 show how the Government's approach is evolving in response to new challenges and set out a range of initiatives.

ECONOMIC FRAMEWORK

2.1 The most important contribution that the Government can make to improving competitiveness is the creation of a stable macroeconomic environment. This requires a disciplined approach with monetary and fiscal policy set to deliver permanently low inflation and sound public finances. Tax and spending policies must also help to make the economy work better.

Low inflation is essential for growth .....

2.2 Low inflation is not an end in itself, but one of the necessary conditions for sustained growth. Since 1945, the UK economy has been prone to higher and more variable rates of inflation than most of its major competitors, particularly in the 1970s. Economic performance worsened as a result.

2.3 Inflation hinders the working of markets by distorting price signals. It creates uncertainty for savers and business about future returns, pushing up interest rates and discouraging longer term investment. As inflation becomes entrenched, even those who may initially have benefited (such as debtors) eventually lose.

2.4 The Government aims to keep underlying inflation (as measured by the Retail Prices Index excluding mortgage interest payments) in a range of 1 to 4 per cent, and to get it into the lower half

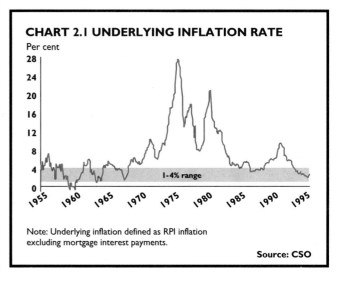

CHART 2.1 UNDERLYING INFLATION RATE

Note: Underlying inflation defined as RPI inflation excluding mortgage interest payments.

Source: CSO

of the range by the end of the present Parliament. Underlying inflation has been within this range for some 2¹/2 years – the best sustained performance for a generation (Chart 2.1).

2.5 Control of inflation is essential for sustainable recovery. Business and individuals need to be confident that low inflation is permanent if saving and investment are to be encouraged. To underline its commitment to low inflation, the Government has made the monetary framework one of the most open in the world. The Bank of England's quarterly Inflation Report is published independently of the Government and the minutes of the monthly monetary meetings between the Chancellor and the Governor have been published since the start of 1994.

.... as are sound public finances.

2.6 Permanently low inflation is just one element of the Government's macroeconomic policy. Sound public finances are also essential if business is to plan with confidence. A commitment to low inflation and sound public finance in all

European countries is the necessary foundation for sustainable exchange rate stability in Europe, and thus to obtaining the full benefits of the Single Market.

2.7 During the recession the budget deficit inevitably rose, but once the recovery was clearly under way the Government took action to reduce the deficit quickly. The Budgets of 1993 and 1994 put the necessary measures in place and helped to ensure a balanced recovery, which has increasingly been driven by exports rather than by consumer spending.

2.8 The ever-present scrutiny of world markets means that attempts to pursue imprudent budgetary policies undermine economic and financial stability, resulting in higher interest rates and more painful corrective measures than if prompt action had been taken. They also leave a legacy in high debt and debt interest burdens (Chart 2.2).

2.9 The public sector borrowing requirement (PSBR) fell sharply in 1994-95. A further rapid fall is in prospect. Borrowing in 1995-96 is forecast to be less that half that in 1993-94. The Government aims to bring the PSBR back to balance before the end of the decade (Chart 2.3). Borrowing will then be less than public sector net investment, meeting the "golden rule" that governments should borrow only to finance worthwhile investment.

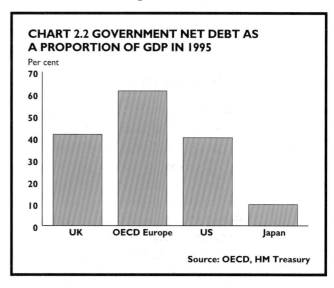

CHART 2.2 GOVERNMENT NET DEBT AS A PROPORTION OF GDP IN 1995

Per cent

Source: OECD, HM Treasury

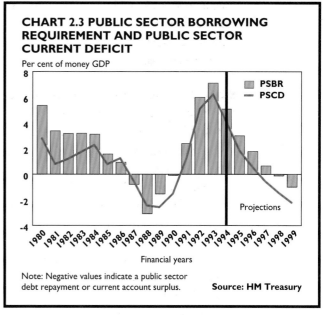

CHART 2.3 PUBLIC SECTOR BORROWING REQUIREMENT AND PUBLIC SECTOR CURRENT DEFICIT

Per cent of money GDP

Financial years

Note: Negative values indicate a public sector debt repayment or current account surplus.   Source: HM Treasury

Recent budgets have reduced public spending and reflected strategic priorities.

2.10 The Government's public spending policy has two strands:

◆ to reduce public spending as a share of national income. This helps competitiveness by contributing to sound public finances and a low tax burden; and

◆ within overall control of spending, to take a strategic view of priorities and to pursue reforms which will improve value for money, help the economy work better and thereby enhance competitiveness.

2.11 Under the new system for public spending control, introduced in 1992, the Government's spending objectives are reviewed each year by the Ministerial Committee on Public Expenditure (EDX). The Treasury's Departmental objectives, revised in the wake of its Fundamental Review, stress the twin aims of keeping total public spending to an affordable level and promoting policies and spending priorities which strengthen the long-term performance of the economy and the outlook for jobs.

2.12 The spending plans announced in the 1994 Budget were consistent with these aims:

- lower than expected inflation, tight control of administrative costs and increased efficiency meant that planned spending was cut by £29.5 billion over three years compared to previous plans. The ratio of public spending to national income is set to fall from 43.5 per cent in 1994-95 to 41 per cent in 1997-98;

- there were further reforms of social security, including a modification of housing benefit to encourage tenants to economise on housing costs and landlords to moderate rents on which benefit is paid. The work disincentives created by the current arrangements for paying income support on mortgage interest were reduced. In all, policy measures in the last two Budgets are expected to reduce social security expenditure by up to £4 billion a year at 1994-95 prices by the turn of the century;

- Training for Work, the Government's main training programme for long-term unemployed adults, was refocussed to increase the number of trainees who get jobs;

- ECGD average medium- and long-term premiums were reduced by around 10 per cent to help exporters; and

- in the light of the 1994 White Paper, resources were provided for the development of Business Links (in Scotland, Business Shops) and services delivered through them, including support for exports, innovation and good management practice.

2.13 In recent years the Government has placed greater emphasis on the distinction between capital and current spending in presenting the Budget. Capital spending is expected to remain at around £22 billion over the next two years, higher than the average during the 1980s (after stripping out the spending of industries now privatised). As the effect of measures taken during the recession unwinds, public sector capital spending is expected to fall back in real terms. However, the Private Finance Initiative has attracted private sector capital into areas previously funded exclusively by the public sector. Chapter 10 gives further details.

2.14 A wider definition of capital spending would include "human capital". This is treated as current spending under national accounting conventions but might be considered to produce future benefits in much the same way as physical assets. Chart 2.4 shows the recent trend for one measure of spending on human capital, bringing together total general Government spending on education, employment training and civil science and technology. The Government is encouraging business and individuals to invest more in these areas.

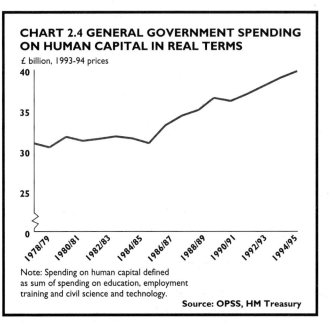

CHART 2.4 GENERAL GOVERNMENT SPENDING ON HUMAN CAPITAL IN REAL TERMS

£ billion, 1993-94 prices

Note: Spending on human capital defined as sum of spending on education, employment training and civil science and technology.

Source: OPSS, HM Treasury

2.15 "Better Accounting for the Taxpayer's Money"[1] explained how resource accounting would lead to improved management of capital resources by giving public sector managers new information about capital assets' value and depreciation, and linking these more closely to Departmental objectives and outputs. Resource accounting will be introduced in all Government Departments by 1 April 1998. This will allow better informed decisions.

2.16 The Unified Budget has encouraged the development of coordinated measures in tax and spending to help the supply side. For example, the work incentives package announced in 1994 (and discussed in more detail in Chapter 8) included social security measures, such as prompt payment of housing benefit and family credit for people taking jobs, as well as employment measures, and changes to employers' national insurance contributions (NICs).

Tax policy has a number of objectives.

2.17 The Government seeks to:

- keep the overall tax burden as low as possible, through firm control of public spending;

- reduce marginal tax rates on income and profits, to sharpen incentives to work and create wealth;

- maintain a broad tax base which helps to keep tax rates low and avoid distorting commercial decisions;

- shift the balance of taxation from taxes on income to taxes on spending;

- simplify the administration of the tax system and minimise the burdens of compliance on taxpayers;

- ensure that the tax system is applied fairly and evenly, closing loopholes so that commercial decisions are not distorted by attempts to avoid tax;

[1]*Better Accounting for the Taxpayer's Money* Cm 2626 [HMSO] (July 1994)

♦ use the tax system to make markets work better, for example by making decision makers aware of the external costs of their decisions; and

♦ ensure that revenue is raised in ways which do least harm to economic efficiency and take account of the competitive position of UK industry.

Despite recent increases, the overall tax burden remains low.

2.18 In reducing public borrowing, the Government looked first to public spending. Although taxation also had to be increased, the overall burden of tax in the UK remains significantly lower than the average for other EU countries. Preliminary estimates indicate that UK general government current receipts amounted to 36.5 per cent of GDP in 1994, compared with an EU average of 47 per cent.

2.19 Taxes on business – on corporate profits, payroll, and employers' social security costs – are lower than in any other G7 country apart from Canada. Business taxes amount to 6 per cent of GDP in the UK, compared to 9 per cent in Germany, 10 per cent in Japan and 14 per cent in France.

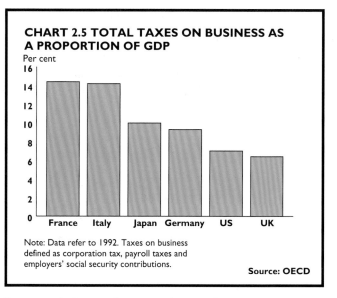

CHART 2.5 TOTAL TAXES ON BUSINESS AS A PROPORTION OF GDP

Note: Data refer to 1992. Taxes on business defined as corporation tax, payroll taxes and employers' social security contributions.

Source: OECD

2.20 Rates of tax are also very low by international standards. At 33 per cent, the UK has the lowest main rate of corporation tax among major industrial countries. It compares with rates of around 40 per cent in the US, 50 per cent in Japan and over 55 per cent (on undistributed profits) in Germany. The small companies' rate of corporation tax has been reduced from 42 per cent to 25 per cent since 1979.

2.21 The top rate of income tax and national insurance contributions combined in the UK is 40 per cent. This is the lowest in the EU, matched only by Greece. Low marginal rates of tax minimise the adverse effect of taxation on incentives and make the UK an attractive location for internationally mobile business.

Tax changes have promoted investment and employment ...

2.22 In recent Budgets the Government has cut the costs of employment and promoted investment in small businesses through a range of measures described in Chapters 8 and 13.

... and helped meet environmental objectives.

2.23 The tax system can contribute to meeting environmental objectives by helping to ensure prices reflect external costs. Economic instruments which work through the market will, where appropriate, be used in place of regulation:

◆ the duty differential in favour of unleaded petrol, first introduced in 1987, has played an important part in helping to reduce potentially damaging airborne lead;

◆ the Chancellor's commitment to raise road fuel duties by at least 5 per cent a year in real terms in future Budgets will help dampen the growth of carbon dioxide emissions from transport; and

◆ the landfill tax, announced by the Chancellor in the 1994 Budget, will discourage the production of waste and encourage recycling.

2.24 In considering tax changes to meet environmental objectives, the Government seeks to avoid damaging competitiveness. The UK has opposed a Europe-wide carbon tax which would raise business costs. In announcing the landfill tax, the Chancellor made clear his determination not to impose additional costs on business overall, and to seek offsetting reductions in employer NICs.

DEREGULATING TAX AND NICs

◆ *Quarterly instead of monthly payment of PAYE/NICs introduced for an additional 100,000 small employers*

◆ *De minimis exemption for personal incidental expenses for tax and NICs and future flexibilities in NIC administration*

◆ *Customs formalities in the Single Market reduced, abolishing ten million forms a year*

◆ *Tax and compliance cost burdens eased by raising the VAT registration threshold*

◆ *A pilot scheme to give rulings on the tax treatment of transactions undertaken before tax returns are completed*

for the future

◆ *Over the next two years closer working between Customs and Excise, Inland Revenue and the Contributions Agency will improve customer service, simplify systems and reduce compliance costs*

◆ *A single point of registration for new business for tax, national insurance and, where appropriate, VAT will be piloted in the next two years*

◆ *Customs and Excise is consulting on proposals to introduce annual rather than quarterly VAT payments for firms with a turnover of less than £100,000, with the changes to be phased in between December 1995 and December 1996, saving an estimated £85 million a year*

◆ *The Inland Revenue is reviewing ways to reduce the complexity of tax legislation*

SECTORAL OVERVIEW OF THE ECONOMY

3.1 This chapter:

- describes the sectoral structure of the economy;

- identifies some key structural changes, both between and within sectors; and

- assesses the performance of sectors.

3.2 Since 1970 the structure of the British economy has changed in three principal ways (Chart 3.1). The share of financial and business services has grown from 12 per cent of GDP to around 20 per cent. The share of manufacturing has fallen from 34 per cent to just over 20 per cent. The share of North Sea oil production peaked at 7 per cent in 1984 and has since fallen back to around 2.5 per cent. Shifts in GDP shares since 1984 are largely explained by changes in relative prices: in volume terms, the composition of GDP has been quite stable.

3.3 North Sea oil apart, our economic structure is not out of the ordinary for an advanced industrial country. Services (including public services) have been steadily increasing in importance, and now account for over 60 per cent of GDP in all G7 countries, apart from Japan. Manufacturing's share of GDP ranges from around 20 per cent in the UK, the US, France and Italy to over 25 per cent in Germany and Japan.

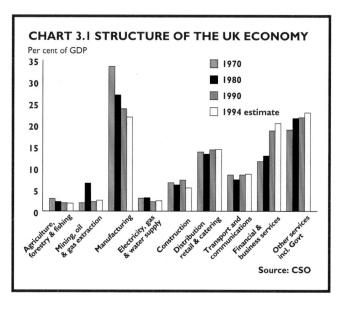

CHART 3.1 STRUCTURE OF THE UK ECONOMY

Per cent of GDP

- 1970
- 1980
- 1990
- 1994 estimate

Source: CSO

NORTH SEA OIL AND GAS

North Sea oil and gas production was at an all time high in 1994, but low world oil prices mean that North Sea oil's contribution to GDP is lower now than in the early 1980s (Charts 3.2 and 3.3).

The contribution of North Sea oil exports to the UK's balance of payments was over £4 billion in 1994. Even with low world oil prices this was the highest since 1987.

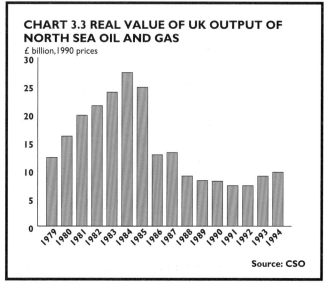

CHART 3.3 REAL VALUE OF UK OUTPUT OF NORTH SEA OIL AND GAS
£ billion, 1990 prices

Source: CSO

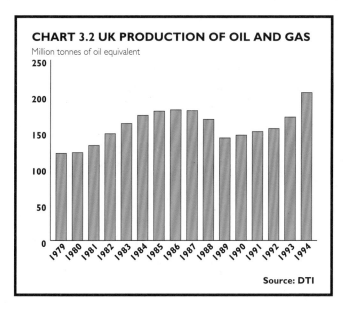

CHART 3.2 UK PRODUCTION OF OIL AND GAS
Million tonnes of oil equivalent

Source: DTI

3.4 Manufacturing industries are purchasing increasingly from service industries and from abroad. In 1963, 16 per cent of all inputs purchased by UK manufacturing industries were supplied by marketed services industries[1]. By 1990 this proportion had risen to 26 per cent, in part because of increasing contracting-out of services. In contrast, service sector industries are now purchasing less from manufacturing industries than in 1963, and more from each other.

	PURCHASES BY:			
	UK MANUFACTURING INDUSTRIES		UK MARKETED SERVICES INDUSTRIES	
Supplied by:	1963 per cent	1990 per cent	1963 per cent	1990 per cent
UK Manufacturing Industries	57	35	43	16
UK Marketed Service Industries	16	26	44	73
Other UK Industries	9	11	11	6
Imports	18	28	2	5
Total	100	100	100	100
Source: Derived from CSO, Input-Output Tables				

[1]Marketed services comprise all services, including those of the service sector public corporations, but exclude government services, such as public administration, defence, education, health and social services.

The international dimension

3.5 Manufacturing and marketed services accounted respectively for 64 per cent and 22 per cent of total UK exports of goods and services in 1994. When account is taken of contributions which each industry makes to exports indirectly, via supplies to other industries, the total direct and indirect contributions of manufacturing and services to the UK value added content of exports were respectively 46 per cent and 43 per cent.

3.6 Marketed services have consistently earned a current account surplus (on average 1 per cent of GDP since 1988). Financial and other business services have been consistently in surplus, offsetting the deficit in other services (Chart 3.4). The visible deficit has averaged about 2 per cent of GDP since 1991. Our share of world service receipts (not including earnings of interest, profits and dividends) has fallen from 9 per cent in 1970 to 5 per cent in 1993. We have lost share in sea transport, air transport, tourism and business travel. In part this may reflect the growing tendency to provide services from overseas locations.

3.7 In proportion to GDP, the UK is more actively engaged than other major industrial countries as an overseas investor and as a host for inward direct investment (Chart 3.5). This reflects the UK's traditionally international outlook, cultural accessibility, foreign exchange liberalisation in 1979 (earlier than in most other European countries), and its attractions as a location. The overseas stock of direct investment by UK service industries now exceeds that of UK manufacturing industries. The UK's earnings from its overseas direct investment exceed those of foreign direct investment in the UK, in both manufacturing and services (Chart 3.6).

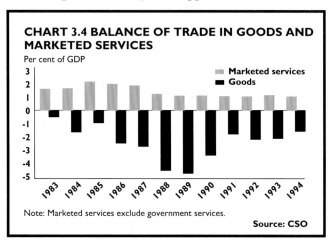

CHART 3.4 BALANCE OF TRADE IN GOODS AND MARKETED SERVICES

Per cent of GDP

Note: Marketed services exclude government services.

Source: CSO

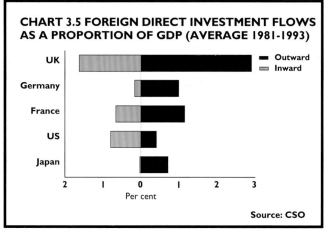

CHART 3.5 FOREIGN DIRECT INVESTMENT FLOWS AS A PROPORTION OF GDP (AVERAGE 1981-1993)

Source: CSO

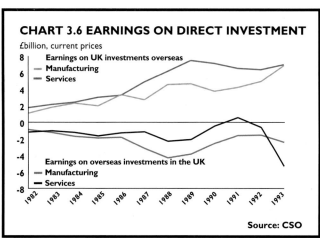

CHART 3.6 EARNINGS ON DIRECT INVESTMENT

£billion, current prices

Source: CSO

Productivity across the economy

3.8 It is important to improve the productivity of all resources, and to invest and trade profitably. Labour productivity is of particular interest. A rising standard of living tends to go hand in hand with increasing labour productivity. This is only a partial measure of performance, but can be estimated. We have also to recognise that the skills and abilities of the working population are diverse. A well-functioning labour market is needed to provide a wide range of employment opportunities, not all of which will necessarily be high value-added jobs.

3.9 In the last ten years, labour productivity has grown twice as fast in manufacturing as in distribution, retailing and catering, and faster than in services generally (Chart 3.7).

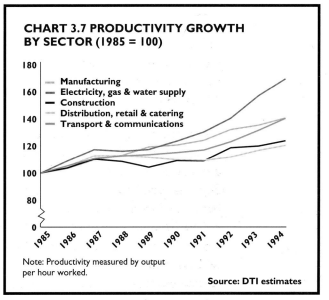

CHART 3.7 PRODUCTIVITY GROWTH BY SECTOR (1985 = 100)

- Manufacturing
- Electricity, gas & water supply
- Construction
- Distribution, retail & catering
- Transport & communications

Note: Productivity measured by output per hour worked.

Source: DTI estimates

Privatised utilities	Year in which privatised	Average annual increase in labour productivity[2] since privatisation
British Telecom	1984-85	7.0
British Gas	1986-87	3.7
Water	1989-90	1.7[3]
National Power	1990-91	20.7
PowerGen	1990-91	15.5
Regional Electricity Companies	1990-91	6.0

Public sector utilities	Reference year	Average annual increase in labour productivity since reference year
British Rail	1984-85	0.7
Royal Mail	1984-85	3.3
Nuclear Electric	1990-91	24.7

Source: Company accounts to 1993-4; for Gas, British Gas company accounts to December 1995 and Financial and Operation Statistics 1993; for water, *Waterfacts*, various years.

[2]Physical units delivered per employee: BT, connections; British Gas, temperature-adjusted Gwh; Water, litres/day supplied; electricty, Twh; British Rail, weighted sum of passenger miles and tonnes; Royal Mail, domestic and international letters.

[3]This figure takes no account of improvements in water quality and service provision, and demand management measures which have been reducing the amount of water being put into supply.

This is reflected in changes in the relative prices of manufactures and services; for example, since 1980 the price of a new car has increased by 70 per cent, whereas the price index for car maintenance has increased by 175 per cent. The fastest productivity growth has been achieved in the utilities sector, particularly by those exposed to competition. The Gas Bill, which is currently before Parliament, will introduce greater competition into that sector, too.

THE INCREASING ROLE OF SMALL FIRMS

There has been an economy-wide shift in favour of the smaller business. Between 1979 and 1993 the total number of businesses in the economy rose from 1.9 million to 2.8 million, largely due to an increase in the number of one- and two-person businesses. An increasing proportion of the non-government labour force is employed in companies with fewer than 100 people (40 per cent in 1979, 51 per cent in 1991). See Chart 3.8.

Small firms have played a leading role in job generation. Between 1985 and 1989, those employing fewer than 20 people created over a million extra jobs, twice as many as large firms. Between 1989 and 1991 small firms created 350,000 jobs at a time when private sector employment was falling. Some of these jobs will have been associated with a transfer of work from larger firms, rather than newly generated work.

Small firms are particularly important in the service sector. Thus two of the underlying structural changes identified in this chapter - towards services and towards smaller firms – are reinforcing each other, assisted by new technology (modems, personal computers – PCs – and facsimile machines) and encouraged by cultural and organisational changes (enterprise culture, self-employment, contracting out, franchising, management buy outs). Economies of scale are diminishing in some industries, as the emphasis shifts towards quality and meeting customer needs, and as flexible production methods become more widespread.

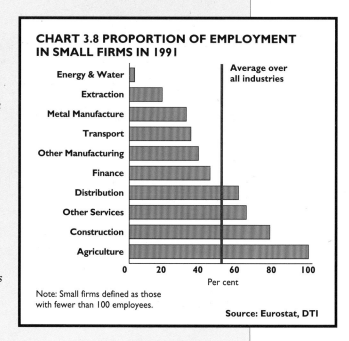

CHART 3.8 PROPORTION OF EMPLOYMENT IN SMALL FIRMS IN 1991

Note: Small firms defined as those with fewer than 100 employees.

Source: Eurostat, DTI

continues...

THE INCREASING ROLE OF SMALL FIRMS *continued*

There is also a shift towards smaller firms within manufacturing. The proportions of manufacturing employment in large and small business units have reversed over the last 20 years (Chart 3.9).

The relative size of the small firms sector is now much closer to that in other countries than at the start of the 1980s. The UK has more businesses with one to nine employees than, for example, Germany, but fewer with 10-200. The relative size and strength of the German Mittelstand rests largely on the higher proportion of start-ups which survive and grow. The priority for the Government's policy towards smaller firms is to give selective help to those with the management will and the business potential to grow.

In the coming year, the Government will invite private sector bodies representing small business to organise a UK conference on Small Firms, so as to involve the small business sector in generating policies to help them. The outcome will be considered in the competitiveness White Paper planned for 1996.

*The country-wide network of local Business Links (and equivalents in Scotland and Wales) will provide information and basic support services to **all** local businesses - and also offer selective counselling and help to those firms with growth potential.*

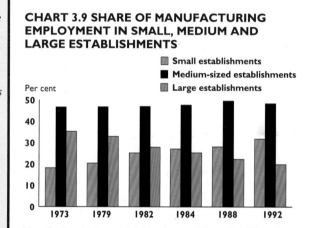

CHART 3.9 SHARE OF MANUFACTURING EMPLOYMENT IN SMALL, MEDIUM AND LARGE ESTABLISHMENTS

Note: Small establishments defined as those with fewer than 100 employees. Medium-sized establishments defined as those with between 100 and 1500 employees. Large establishments defined as those with more than 1500 employees.

Source: CSO

The service sector: structure and performance

3.10 Financial and business services are the fastest growing component of marketed services. They increased their

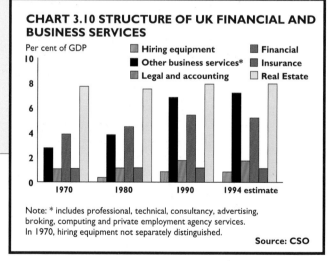

CHART 3.10 STRUCTURE OF UK FINANCIAL AND BUSINESS SERVICES

Note: * includes professional, technical, consultancy, advertising, broking, computing and private employment agency services. In 1970, hiring equipment not separately distinguished.

Source: CSO

share of GDP from 18 per cent in 1980 to around 25 per cent in 1994 and now employ nearly three million people. Law and accounting firms, advertising agencies, estate and land agents, have grown in importance (Chart 3.10). There is also a trend towards contracting out "non-core" activities such as maintenance, catering, transport and training. Equipment is increasingly hired, rather than owned, and if owned, maintained by contractors. Although as much as 30 per cent of the 3 million fall in manufacturing employment over the last two decades may have been due to contracting-out of services, this factor has become less important in recent years. Manufacturing employment fell by 33 per cent between 1980 and 1992. If manufacturing industries had not increasingly contracted-out services, manufacturing employment might have fallen in that period by about 31 per cent. There has been a marked increase in part-time working in services. Forty-three per cent of employees in distribution and catering and 18 per cent in financial and business services now work part-time. Services bought by private individuals to help them cope with their domestic responsibilities now provide around 2 million jobs, and is one of the fastest growing parts of the job market. This provides job opportunities (many part-time) and makes it easier for women to maintain their careers.

3.11 Service sector performance is important for the competitiveness of customer industries. For example, the cost of a standard bundle of five minute telephone calls is lower in the UK than in the US, Germany, France and Japan (see Chapter 14). International comparisons of productivity in services are always difficult. But one study[4] has suggested that in the late 1980s UK services lagged behind the US in productivity, except in air transport. According to that study, the UK achieved 80 per cent of US productivity in retailing, 60 per cent in banking and 50 per cent in telecommunications. The recently improved performance in UK service industries, such as retail banking and telecommunications, may well have closed these gaps.

3.12 The UK has a strong infrastructure in business services, with particular strengths in financial services, management consultancy (with 10 per cent of the world market), market research (with 9 per cent of the world market), design and advertising. Since 1981, UK advertising agencies have ranked either first or second in the number of awards won at the Cannes International Advertising festival. The

---

SERVICE SECTOR STATISTICS

Although marketed services industries are of growing importance to the UK economy, less is known about their size and performance than about manufacturing. In some service industries, like banking and consultancy, there are conceptual problems in measuring real output. Whereas basic information about value-added, investment, employment and trade is available for sectors of manufacturing such as textile machinery or aluminium production, such data are only available for service industries, if at all, at more aggregated levels, for example for insurance or communications. There is not yet enough information to measure progress in establishing the Single Market in services.

The Government is seeking to address these difficulties and deficiencies, particularly in respect of measures of productivity, prices and trade.

---

[4]*Service Sector Productivity*, [McKinsey Global Institute] (October 1992)

UK public relations industry has also grown spectacularly over the past ten years and is now the most highly developed in Europe. These industries not only win foreign business in their own right; they also enhance the competitive advantage of British products. Consultancy disseminates global best practice. Market research is the bridge between producer and client and also assists innovation. Advertising helps to build strong brands.

3.13 Popular music remains a British success, and so is fine art and antiques. The UK accounted for over half of total OECD exports of antiques over 100 years old in

THE COMPETITIVENESS OF THE CITY

The UK wholesale financial services sector ("the City") is more diverse and international than that of any other country. Its boundaries extend far beyond the City of London and include established and thriving businesses in Scotland and the English regions. The greatest concentration of services is nevertheless in the City of London which draws its strength from the liquidity of its markets, the range of institutions, innovation in products and the excellence of its business and professional skills.

The financial services sector (wholesale and retail) generates around 6.5 per cent of GDP and in 1993 its net overseas earnings from services and investment income are estimated to have been £15.6 billion.

The UK's percentage share of selected financial markets

	1989	1990	1991	1992	1993	1994
Foreign exchange turnover[1]	25	na	na	27	na	na
External bank lending[1]	17	17	16	16	16	17*
Foreign equities turnover[2]	na	na	65	64	58	59
International bond issues[3]	75	60	65	60	60	60
International bonds secondary trading[3]	80	75	70	70	75	75
Financial derivatives trading[4]	8	10	11	14	16	17
Insurance[5]						
Marine insurance	31	31	31	29	na	na
Aviation insurance	37	37	42	45	na	na

Compiled by British Invisibles.

Source: 1: *Bank for International Settlements*
2: *London Stock Exchange*
3: *Bank of England estimates*
4: *Futures Industry Association*
5: *Lloyd's of London (net of reinsurance ceded)*

na not available   * End-September

continues...

THE COMPETITIVENESS OF THE CITY *continued*

The City is the leading international financial centre in Europe and, with New York and Tokyo, is one of the three major international financial centres in the world. However, it will continue to face competitive pressures from elsewhere. There are initiatives to promote the attractions of established rival centres, such as Europlace for Paris and Finanzplatz Deutschland for Frankfurt, and new specialised financial centres are emerging (Bermuda for insurance, Piraeus for shipbroking). The City is relatively poorly placed geographically to compete with Tokyo, Hong Kong and Singapore in the rapid development of South-East Asia and the Pacific Rim.

The City's ability to create and trade innovative financial products has resulted in markets of great depth and diversity. To meet future challenges, the City will need to build on those strengths. Strong participation from practitioners in the UK regulatory regime will continue to be important. The Government, for its part, is committed to improving market efficiency by providing a regulatory regime which keeps in step with new developments and provides a proper framework for the industry in which free and fair competition can take place.

City-based institutions and markets are well placed to benefit from the General Agreement on Trade in Services (GATS). The Government is working with the Commission to secure a liberal outcome to the GATS financial services negotiations in Geneva, which should be concluded by June.

1992, drawing on a depth of expertise and a pool of secondary skills to facilitate dealing, security, financial services, and restoration. All these tradeable services derive support from the English language. Audio-visual products are not the clear success which our language and artistic talent seem to deserve. The UK has a range of artistic talents, but few entrepreneurs able and willing to exploit them effectively.

The manufacturing sector: structure and performance

3.14 Between 1979 and 1994 manufacturing output grew by 9 per cent. The principal changes within manufacturing over the last 15 years were in mechanical engineering and in office machinery (Chart 3.11). Demand for office machinery has been stimulated by the appearance of the PC and the dramatically falling cost of processing power. Whereas the price index for

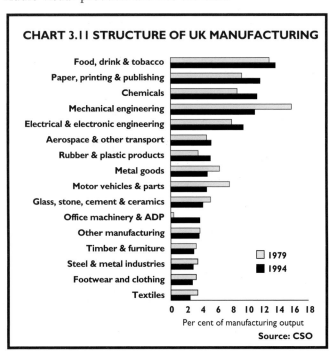

CHART 3.11 STRUCTURE OF UK MANUFACTURING

Food, drink & tobacco
Paper, printing & publishing
Chemicals
Mechanical engineering
Electrical & electronic engineering
Aerospace & other transport
Rubber & plastic products
Metal goods
Motor vehicles & parts
Glass, stone, cement & ceramics
Office machinery & ADP
Other manufacturing
Timber & furniture
Steel & metal industries
Footwear and clothing
Textiles

☐ 1979
■ 1994

0 2 4 6 8 10 12 14 16 18
Per cent of manufacturing output
Source: CSO

manufacturing has doubled over the last 15 years, the price index for computers and office machinery has halved. High-technology industries – aircraft, pharmaceuticals, office and computing equipment, radio, TV and communications equipment – accounted for an increasing proportion of manufacturing output in the 1980s. According to OECD estimates, high-technology industries accounted for roughly the same proportion of the UK's manufacturing employment in 1991 (19 per cent) as in the US, Japan, Germany and France. Computer software and services now employ as many people as the car industry. There are now more people employed in biotechnology SMEs than there are in cotton spinning.

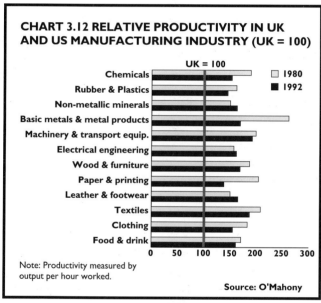

CHART 3.12 RELATIVE PRODUCTIVITY IN UK AND US MANUFACTURING INDUSTRY (UK = 100)

Note: Productivity measured by output per hour worked.

Source: O'Mahony

CHART 3.13 RELATIVE PRODUCTIVITY IN UK AND GERMAN MANUFACTURING INDUSTRY (UK = 100)

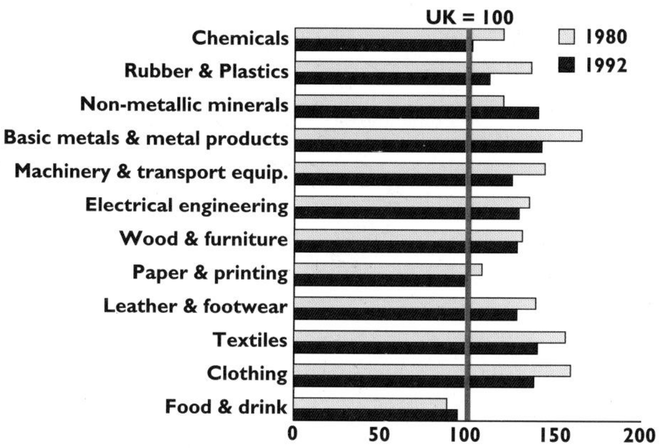

Note: Productivity measured by output per hour worked.

Source: O'Mahony

3.15 Labour productivity in manufacturing has grown by some 75 per cent since 1979. This was not due simply to the elimination of a tail of low-productivity capacity. The proportion of manufacturing employees in large plants, which have relatively high productivity, has declined faster than in smaller plants[5]. Nor was this increase in productivity due to any structural shift towards the higher productivity industries. It is a general phenomenon, driven by the economy's increased exposure to international competition and made possible by the supply side improvements of the 1980s.

3.16 The 1994 Competitiveness White Paper noted that US and German manufacturing productivity is significantly higher than the UK's. These comparisons of averages disguise significant sectoral differences. A comparison of productivity in 12 broad industry groupings in the UK, US and Germany reveal that none of these UK industries matched the labour productivity of its US counterpart (Charts 3.12 and 3.13). One UK industry - food and drink - achieved higher productivity than that of its German counterpart, and two others - chemicals, and paper and printing - matched it.

3.17 A number of UK industries made significant progress in catching up their US and German counterparts between 1980

[5]Nicholas Oulton; *Plant Closures and the Productivity Miracle in Manufacturing*, [National Institute Economic Review] (August 1987)

and 1992: in the case of the US, paper and printing, and metals; in the case of Germany, chemicals, rubber and plastics, and machinery and transport equipment.

3.18 Skill differences are important in understanding these productivity differentials. In detailed plant studies in the mid-1980s, the National Institute of Economic and Social Research found that the workforce in British plants was often less effective than its German counterparts in using, maintaining and choosing the most appropriate machinery because of weaknesses in skills, particularly at intermediate level. However, this and other research suggests that other factors, such as differences in capital equipment, are part of the explanation. Further, some companies achieve comparable levels of productivity with different skill mixes, which suggests that effective management skills may be equally important.

Sources of comparative advantage

3.19 When traded products were more basic, our trade pattern could be explained in geographical terms: we exported wool and imported wine. We still import wine, and export woollen textiles. However, trade patterns are now much more to do with the skills and capacities of people and whether, within a country's industrial and institutional structure, they are mutually supporting.

3.20 If those manufacturing industries producing products traded in significant quantities[6] are ranked by the ratio of sales to UK demand in 1992[7], the league leader, by a considerable margin, is spirit distilling (mainly Scotch whisky). In these terms, the most successful industries with the highest ratios of sales to UK demand in 1992 are ranked in the accompanying table.

TOP 20 MANUFACTURING INDUSTRIES, RANKED BY SALES TO UK DEMAND, 1992

	Industry Value Added	Ratio of Industry Sales to UK demand
	£ million	
Spirit distilling	850	8.80
Office machinery	130	4.30
Construction equipment	420	2.40
Pesticides	550	1.65
Tractors	210	1.58
Optical instruments	110	1.49
Wall coverings	120	1.46
Dyestuffs and pigments	310	1.45
Explosives	70	1.44
Refractory goods	180	1.43
Textile machinery	150	1.36
Internal combustion engines	450	1.35
Photographic materials	220	1.32
Aerospace	4,280	1.29
Synthetic rubber	80	1.28
Miscellaneous chemicals	1,330	1.25
Pharmaceutical products	4,400	1.25
Metal storage vessels	40	1.24
Organic chemicals	1,140	1.23
Perfumes and cosmetics	240	1.22

At the bottom of the list is motor cycles, with 1992 sales equivalent to only one-seventh of UK demand.

[6] Exports plus imports exceeding 15 per cent of UK demand.
[7] Equal to 1 + (exports - imports)/UK demand

3.21 A theme which runs through this diverse pattern is labour quality. Trade performance is quite strongly associated with the quality and performance of the labour force, as reflected, for example, in workforce qualifications, in the proportion of administrative, clerical and technical staff (whose average earnings are over 50 per cent higher than those of operatives, and whose proportion has increased since 1980 in three out of four manufacturing industries), the ratio of R&D to sales, and value added per employee. In the engineering industries, for example, trade performance is correlated with the proportion of operatives who are qualified craftsmen.

3.22 We have a relative advantage in R&D-intensive industries. Our share of total OECD exports of manufactures in 1992 was about 7 per cent – about the same as that of Italy, but less than that of France, Germany, the US and Japan. But in R&D-intensive industries our share was 9 to 10 per cent, higher than that of France, and over double that of Italy (Chart 3.14).

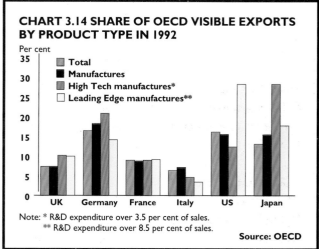

3.23 There is no automatic relationship between an industry's R&D expenditure and its trade performance. Competitiveness depends on how effectively R&D is conducted and brought to the market. Three sectors which illustrate R&D-based success are:

- the **chemicals** industry, where success factors include the quality of the research and the graduates produced by the chemistry, biology and bio-chemistry departments in UK universities, and the relationship established by chemical companies with the City, based on a record of commercially successful innovation;

- the **pharmaceutical** industry, where success factors include the quality of British medicine, university research in chemistry, pharmacology and biochemistry, and a price regulation scheme governing prices to the National Health Service, the industry's largest customer, which recognises the cost of R&D, while maintaining competitive pressure on the industry; and

The chemicals industry's trading success is based on commercially successful innovation and strong chemistry, biology and bio-chemistry departments in British universities

35

◆ the **aerospace** industry, where success factors include collaboration with overseas partners, for example on Eurofighter 2000 and Airbus, investment in training, R&D capabilities (supported by the Defence Evaluation and Research Agency and universities) and the presence of world class suppliers.

3.24 These three R&D-dependent industries illustrate how, assisted by supportive relationships with suppliers, universities and Government, industries can harness the nation's brain-power to create wealth and comparative advantage.

3.25 Despite the decline in the mechanical engineering sector, machine building remains an enduring UK strength, particularly in construction and earth-moving equipment, wheeled tractors, internal combustion engines, textile machinery, medical equipment, fork lift trucks, pumps and compressors. These industries illustrate the greatly changed commercial environment for manufacturing. The decline of the mining equipment industry's domestic market has forced it to expand exports, beyond its traditional anglophone markets. Having been the cradle of the industrial revolution and the principal supplier to the world textile industry in the first half of this century, the textile machinery industry has shrunk from 35,000 employees in 1975 to fewer than 8,000 in 1992. This has left gaps in the UK product range - there is now virtually no UK capability in spinning machinery - but a number of the UK companies which have survived are world leaders in their specialisms (for example, in electronic jacquard looms, carpet tufting and cotton carding machinery).

3.26 Thirty-five per cent of the PCs manufactured in Europe in 1994 were made in the UK, largely by foreign-owned companies. We may lack the ability to produce off-the-shelf packaged computer applications software for mass markets, but we excel in bespoke software production in specialist markets like artificial intelligence, computer-aided design, mathematical software, geographical information systems and data visualisation.

3.27 UK car production fell by about a million units between 1972 and 1982, to fewer than 900,000. It has since recovered to nearly 1.5 million (Chart 3.15). Much of the recent rise is due to the arrival of the Japanese-owned manufacturers – whose UK output has increased from nothing in 1987 to 330,000 in 1994 and may reach 600,000 by the turn of the century.

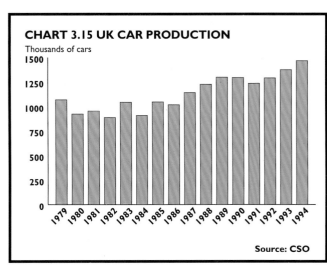

CHART 3.15 UK CAR PRODUCTION
Thousands of cars

Source: CSO

3.28 The UK has been less successful in less skilled, labour-intensive industries such as textiles, clothing, footwear, and toys, now being targeted by developing countries. In 1989, these UK industries had the highest proportion of employees – about 80 per cent – with no certified post-school qualifications. But even here there are outstanding companies pursuing successful niche strategies (quality footwear, woollen and worsted fabrics) or responding rapidly to market changes.

3.29 Some capital-intensive industries are highly competitive, successfully selling chemical products, man-made fibres, iron and steel. The UK has some of the lowest cost chemical, steel and aluminium plants in Europe. In petrochemicals, for example, the UK has strengths in ethylene production, access to raw materials and process technology.

3.30 Finally, we also succeed across a wide range of "lifestyle" products; whisky, quality foods, quality tableware, quality leather, racing cars and off-road vehicles, sporting guns and leisure craft.

Conclusions

The messages from this review are that:

- the last decade has brought significant shifts within sectors, in response to changes in relative productivity, markets and competitive performance;

- comparative advantage based on physical resources is now less important, but the inherited advantages based on traditions and relationships are as vital as ever, for example, in the City; and

- in manufacturing, the UK appears to have a perceptible comparative advantage in industries which employ those with above-average skills, and which exploit R&D effectively.

SPONSORSHIP

4.1 Sponsorship is the means by which the Government addresses the key factors of competitiveness in partnership with all sectors of industry and commerce.

4.2 Although ultimately competitiveness must lie in the efforts and performance of individual firms, companies in each sector share many of the same challenges and concerns. The Government has found that working with business on a sectoral basis is a particularly effective way of addressing competitiveness.

4.3 In carrying out its sponsorship role, the Government seeks to:

◆ understand the strengths, weaknesses and competitive position of each industry;

◆ work with industry to improve competitiveness;

◆ provide comprehensive support to help UK companies win in world markets;

◆ minimise unnecessary regulatory burdens, cutting out needless rules and paperwork and ensuring that enforcement is business friendly and meets the needs of the consumer; and

◆ ensure that the decisions of the Government, and those taken by the European Commission and by local authorities, take proper account of their impact on business.

4.4 The Government gains knowledge of industry in a number of ways: through intensive contact with companies and trade associations; from overseas visits; and, by sharing the Government's appreciation of industries' strengths, weaknesses, opportunities, and threats. Particularly helpful in developing this relationship has been the growing willingness of companies to second middle and senior managers, for a fixed period, to undertake sponsorship work in Government Departments. There are nearly 40 such managers in DTI and the practice is being adopted in other Departments. DTI intends attracting over 25 new secondees from companies, bringing significant additional industry expertise to the Department's sponsorship activities.

4.5 As the work of sponsorship develops, it is important to be clear what it is not. Sponsorship is not:

◆ acting as an uncritical mouthpiece for a particular sector or producer interest, since the Government must defend taxpayer and customer interests;

◆ "picking winners", since that is for customers and investors to decide;

◆ trying to direct business according to some centrally conceived "national plan", since planning should take place close to customers; or

◆ subsidising uncompetitive industries, or advocating special reliefs or grants in preference to market-based solutions.

4.6 At the suggestion of industry itself, sponsorship initiatives are increasingly being taken forward through partnerships involving the sponsoring Government Department, Government Offices in the regions of England, the Scottish and Welsh Offices and the Department of Economic Development in Northern Ireland, trade associations, TECs and Business Links, and the newly formed Regional Supply Offices. Common features are:

◆ spreading best practice;

◆ benchmarking;

◆ assisting the development of industry export strategies;

◆ initiatives aimed at small and medium sized firms;

◆ getting the right balance of regulation; and

◆ supply chain development.

4.7 These activities are illustrated in this chapter by examples from a variety of sectors, involving a wide range of Government Departments:

◆ manufacturing (pharmaceuticals, specialised organics, mechanical engineering, environmental industries, aerospace);

◆ oil and gas;

◆ services (tourism, fashion design, insurance, multimedia, freight transport);

◆ construction; and

◆ agriculture.

These activities are being replicated widely in other sectors.

PHARMACEUTICALS

4.8 There are about 300 pharmaceutical manufacturers established in the UK. Following strong growth of 8-9 per cent over the last two years, UK pharmaceutical production now accounts for almost 1 per cent of GDP. The UK is one of the world's four top exporters of high-quality modern medicines, accounting for about 12 per cent of the global market.

4.9 The UK industry is among the world's leaders in innovation, with nine of the top 35 prescribed medicines having been discovered and developed in this country. Over a quarter of the industry's 80,000 employees are engaged in R&D, the largest number in any country outside Japan and the US. Spending on R&D is equivalent to 50 per cent of the industry's revenue from sales in the UK and 8.5 per cent of world R&D is undertaken here.

Sponsorship activities

4.10 The Department of Health works closely with the pharmaceutical industry. Since 1957 there has been a voluntary agreement between the Department and The Association of British Pharmaceutical Industry (ABPI) to restrain profits from sales to the National Health Service whilst encouraging R&D.

4.11 In 1993, the Department set up a Government and industry Strategy Working Group to consider the future development of the industry and issues of common interest. One outcome was the development of guidelines for economic evaluation of pharmaceuticals[1], published last summer.

4.12 The Department and industry jointly mounted a successful campaign to bring to the UK the European Medicines Evaluation Agency, responsible for developing European licensing of medicines. The Agency was inaugurated at Canary Wharf in London in January 1995 and will employ 200 people when fully operational. It will provide a "one-stop shop" for the European market, helping to eliminate unnecessary duplication in approval of new medicines and reducing delay before products can be safely marketed. This will benefit the industry's competitive position in world markets and encourage companies to locate their regulatory offices here, as one international company has already done.

4.13 A joint Government and industry initiative entitled "Prescribe UK" was launched last December to encourage inward investment by Japanese pharmaceutical and US biopharmaceutical companies. This was promoted by a mission to Japan led by the Secretary of State for Health. Several companies are already showing interest in establishing European operations in the UK.

SPECIALISED ORGANIC CHEMICALS

4.14 Specialised organic chemicals are the molecular building blocks for pharmaceuticals, dyes, agrochemicals, biocides and fragrances. The UK's specialised organics industry has turned a trade deficit in 1970 into a current surplus of over £650 million. The last decade has seen employment rising, with productivity increasing at over 5 per cent a year. Our world market share now exceeds 7.5 per cent, making the UK the fourth largest producer in the world. Yet many of the companies involved are small; only half of the turnover comes from multinationals. The sector is characterised by entrepreneurial and highly educated managers, and a culture which favours innovation.

[1]*Guidelines for the Economic Evaluation of Pharmaceuticals* [DH] (1994)

Sponsorship activities

4.15 A DTI study revealed a world class industry faced with a number of opportunities and threats which had not been fully recognised. The Specialised Organics Sector Association (SOCSA), in partnership with DTI, has drawn up a plan to address these issues. Activities to date include:

- benefiting from an approach by the Health and Safety Executive to implementation of the EU Directive on Dangerous Substances, which better reflects the structure of the sector;

- development of export strategies for Japan, Germany and Switzerland, markets whose high potential had not been sufficiently appreciated before the study;

- a benchmarking club to spread best practice in marketing and other activities. Twenty companies are taking part in a pilot study; and

- a research programme on chiral synthesis, involving 22 companies and 40 academic groups, is under way, following the identification of the industry's ability to make "chiral" (left or right handed) molecules as a leading-edge technology in the Technology Foresight report.

DEREGULATION: CHEMICALS AND BIOTECHNOLOGY

The Government is committed to the development of a regulatory regime that encourages growth and innovation in the chemicals and biotechnology industries. Recent highlights include:

- *a simpler procedure for the notification of new substances – of particular value to the UK specialised organics sector*

- *more customer-focussed enforcement of Integrated Pollution Control*

- *progress on less burdensome application of EU rules on contained use of genetically modified organisms*

- *improvements to EU proposals on solvents, detergents and ECO-labelling*

MECHANICAL ENGINEERING

4.16 The mechanical engineering sector makes equipment for the manufacture of other products. Products range from construction equipment to textile machinery. The sector contains around 24,000 firms, employing over 470,000 people. Most companies have fewer than 100 employees. Collectively, they accounted for 2.4 per cent of GDP in 1992. Productivity within the sector rose by 14 per cent between 1991 and 1994 to the EU average. The sector exported £14.2 billion in 1994, generating a trade surplus of £2.6 billion.

Sponsorship activities

4.17 A recent DTI study highlighted some challenges facing the sector:

- customer-supplier relationships. Many firms lacked a clear idea of their market and the needs of customers. Trade associations and DTI launched "Successful Business Development: The Seven Steps", a marketing guide for the sector. The

Department is supporting a marketing challenge to identify up to four projects to improve marketing. The aim is to establish new, permanent trade association services or facilities;

◆ improving skills. The machine tool and spring trade associations, MTTA and SRAMA, have identified skills in their industries as a critical competitiveness factor. They have been working with DTI to benchmark education and training levels against the National Education and Training Targets. The aim is to bring skills to the required levels by encouraging employers through TECs, ITOs and, where appropriate, trade associations to establish skills action plans for their industries, with group training associations playing a particularly important role for smaller firms;

◆ benchmarking. In the gauge and tool industry, more than 100 firms are now using the "World Class Toolmaker" standards produced in collaboration with DTI; and

◆ strengthening representation. In May 1994, 15 business representative bodies in the process engineering sector formed the Process Plant Industry Forum (PPIF). This is working with DTI to improve competitiveness and the export performance of the sector. The Forum is sponsoring a series of conferences on Far East markets. These will permit companies to share experience and so enhance their export prospects.

OPPORTUNITIES IN ENVIRONMENTAL IMPROVEMENT

A range of equipment and services is used to measure, prevent, correct or limit environmental damage. The industry's world market is now comparable in size to aerospace or pharmaceuticals (around £200 billion in 1992). Strong growth is predicted, driven by growing awareness of the need for sustainable development.

The UK's environmental industry is performing well. In 1992 exports exceeded imports by 70 per cent, although our share of OECD exports was only half that of Germany. The UK's principal strengths lie in water and waste water treatment, monitoring and instrumentation, and environmental consulting.

The Joint DOE/DTI Environmental Markets Unit (JEMU) has been established to ensure that UK firms are briefed on worldwide commercial opportunities. Customers are increasingly demanding coordinated solutions to environmental problems requiring industry to bring together expertise in environmental technologies, engineering contracting, consulting and finance. This is a challenge for an industry which is spread across several traditional sectors. In response, JEMU will take on the lead sponsorship role for the environmental industry in Government. It will develop new inititatives to assist the industry to make the coordinated responses sought by world markets.

AEROSPACE

4.18 In 1992, the UK aerospace industry contributed £4.3 billion to UK GDP (0.8 per cent). Of the 543 core aerospace companies, only 9 companies employ 2,500 people or more, while two-thirds of companies employ fewer than 50. Every year since 1985 the aerospace industry has produced a significant contribution to the country's trade balance. In 1994, exports were worth £7.5 billion.

Sponsorship activities

4.19 DTI is working in partnership with the Society of British Aerospace Companies (SBAC) and with companies to identify strategic issues affecting the sector. Initiatives include:

- working closely with companies which are developing new joint ventures, and supporting moves to improve competitiveness within the Airbus consortium;

- consultation on implementation of the National Strategic Technology Acquisition Plan for civil aeronautics. To ensure best use of available resources, DTI and industry fund Technology Co-ordinators from industry to liaise between public and private sector organisations which undertake research on technology access;

- supporting benchmarking and spread of best practice by contributing funds to the SBAC Competitiveness Challenge, launched in November 1994. This is primarily aimed at encouraging interaction between SMEs and prime contractors. In addition, both SBAC and the General Aviation and Manufacturers Trade Association have started benchmarking programmes for member companies;

- supporting major export campaigns and the development of key overseas markets; and

- contributing to MOD's appreciation of the industrial implications of procurement decisions.

OIL AND GAS

4.20 Oil and gas from the UK Continental Shelf (UKCS) accounted for nearly 2 per cent of GDP in 1994. The sector invested some £3.6 billion in 1994, around one-sixth of UK industrial investment. In addition, nearly £1 billion was spent on exploration and appraisal. Research suggests that the UK leads the world in oil yield from exploration. Production is dominated by around ten large multinationals, with just four controlling some 40 per cent, but the offshore supply industry has several thousand companies.

Sponsorship activities

4.21 Remaining UKCS reserves will be more difficult to exploit. Minimising cost is therefore the key challenge if the industry is to maximise recovery and secure opportunities in export markets. DTI is working with the industry to meet this challenge by:

- supporting the work of the pan-industry best practice forum, CRINE (Cost Reduction Initiative for the New Era). Implementation of CRINE recommendations on inter-company co-operation and streamlined working practices has substantially reduced project costs. For example, one company has made a 33 per cent saving by giving its suppliers greater responsibility for the design of the equipment needed for a major field development, cutting the company's in-house design costs and allowing its suppliers to develop products that can be used across a number of different projects;

- contributing £100,000 to help SMEs participate in CRINE;

- establishing a supply chain group in the important niche market for floating production systems. The aim is to give vessel construction firms a better understanding of customer requirements and project-management best practice, and to improve bidding opportunities for UK equipment suppliers;

- helping UK suppliers to win overseas contracts by mounting overseas missions and facilitating oil company procurement seminars;

- supporting R&D. Recent successes include a sub-sea control system sold to Brazil and seismic acquisition software sold to the US; and

- re-organising DTI's Oil and Gas Projects and Supplies Office to bring together sponsorship of offshore upstream oil and gas activity and downstream refinery and petrochemical projects. A private sector secondee has been appointed as Chief Executive, with a board of business leaders chaired by Sir Alan Cockshaw.

TOURISM

4.22 Revenues from tourism amounted to £33 billion last year, 5 per cent of GDP. It was our fourth largest earner of foreign exchange. It provides jobs for 1.5 million people, 7 per cent of all jobs in the country. Employment in tourist related industries has increased by 25 per cent over the last ten years. Yet our world market share is falling. Our international tourism revenues have grown more slowly than most of our European competitors over the past decade, and new tourist destinations have emerged overseas.

Sponsorship activities

4.23 The Department of National Heritage, working with the British Tourist Authority and the English Tourist Board, has analysed the main challenges and opportunities facing the industry. The analysis confirmed that the fragmented nature of the industry had led to significant under-investment in marketing UK tourism overseas. It identified a need both to improve the flow of information to consumers and to reduce the difficulty of booking UK holidays.

4.24 Following close consultation with industry, the Department published in March a programme of action, "Tourism – Competing with the Best"[2]. This set out how the Government will work with industry to improve all aspects of performance. Measures proposed include:

- helping raise standards in hotels through benchmarking;

- a more relevant and better publicised hotel grading scheme;

- more effective overseas marketing;

- a promotional campaign for London in overseas markets; and

- making it easier to book domestic holidays.

4.25 Similar strategies have been published for Scotland, Wales and Northern Ireland. The aim is to enable the British tourist industry to compete with the world's best and win back lost market share.

DEREGULATION: TOURISM AND LEISURE

Deregulatory measures in support of tourism and leisure industries include:

- *removal of most controls on shop hours*

- *reducing controls on the minimum distance between motorway service areas*

- *easing restrictions on tourist road signs*

- *progressive liberalisation of European air services*

- *overhaul of food hygiene regulation and enforcement*

LONDON FASHION WEEK

Under the leadership of experienced management from the private sector, London Fashion Week is now established on the world fashion circuit as a serious contender with Paris, Milan and New York. The event this March was the most successful yet with visiting press and buyers up almost 20 per cent compared to the previous year.

As part of the sponsorship of the textiles and clothing industries, DTI has worked with the private sector to build up the impact of London Fashion Week. This event influences the perceptions of international opinion formers about the global competitiveness of the UK fashion industry and has wider implications for UK textiles and clothing prospects in overseas markets.

continues...

---

[2]*Tourism – Competing with the Best* [DNH] (1995)

LONDON FASHION WEEK *continued*

Between them, the British Fashion Council and DTI have:

◆ *arranged high profile Government receptions for those attending London Fashion Week*

◆ *brought together upcoming designers and established clothing companies. The companies can meet the designers' need for production in short runs and in turn benefit from the injection of new creative flair*

◆ *influenced big companies to pay small designer companies on time*

Jerry Hall models an Edina Ronay creation at last March's London Fashion Week which DTI helped sponsor.

INSURANCE

4.26 Insurance industry performance is improving. The profits of the five largest composite insurers rose to £1.9 billion in 1994, compared to a loss of £97 million in 1992. Over 800 authorised insurance companies operate in the UK, and the industry employs 370,000 people. Competitive pressures and greater use of IT are likely to lead to a reduction in the number of companies, and of those employed, in the insurance market. The UK domestic market was the fourth largest in the world in 1993. However, the major UK insurers are smaller than their European counterparts, with the largest UK company only the eighth largest in Europe. London remains a leading insurance centre, but faces increased competition as overseas markets are liberalised.

Sponsorship activities

4.27 DTI will publish this summer an analysis of the industry, prepared with the help of three industry secondees. As part of the follow-up, the Department is facilitating an insurance benchmarking initiative which will aim to identify and spread best practice, including IT development, throughout the industry.

4.28 Steps are being taken to improve the industry's international competitiveness:

◆ the 1995 Finance Act introduced changes in taxation of life insurance for overseas customers to provide UK life insurers with the same operating environment as European competitors; and

◆ insurance companies have been represented on Ministerial missions to seek access to insurance markets in Japan, India and South-East Asia. Notable progress has been made in Japan.

4.29 A Private Members Bill, supported by the Government, is before Parliament to allow insurers to create reserves in good years to offset losses in bad years ("Equalisation Reserves"). The Government is considering tax relief for reserves of this sort to put UK insurers on an equal footing with their European competitors. A joint Inland Revenue/DTI consultative document was issued in April.[3]

4.30 DTI has responded positively to the Financial Services Task Force's recommendations for deregulation. Draft regulations will be published this summer. The overall effect will be to require less, but more useful, information for regulatory purposes.

MULTIMEDIA

4.31 Multimedia involves the combination of the different media of voice, text, moving and still pictures. It is leading to the convergence of the telecommunications, IT, electronics, broadcasting and publishing industries, which together account for a European market of over £350 billion.

4.32 Multimedia offers a means of improving the efficiency of industrial, commercial and public service operations, changing the processes by which products and services are created and delivered, and increasing the responsiveness of the public and private sectors. It also enables the development of innovative products and services which will create new markets and opportunities.

SPONSORSHIP ACTIVITIES

4.33 The Government aims to foster a competitive environment in which a wide range of multimedia and other advanced services are delivered over world-class communication networks. Activities include:

◆ leadership. The Government set out its vision in "Creating the Superhighways of the Future: Developing Broadband Communications in the UK"[4], published last November;

◆ commercial environment. The Government recognises the need for a regulatory environment that encourages companies to invest in new network infrastructure and develop new services. The Government has established a Multimedia Industry Advisory Group which is considering standards, interoperability and the intellectual property rights of multimedia content;

◆ raising awareness. The Multimedia Industry Advisory Group is working to identify opportunities and raise awareness of the benefits of multimedia in areas

[3]*Equalisation Reserves for Insurance Companies' non-life Business* [DTT/Inland Revenue] (1995)

[4]*Creating the Superhighways of the Future: Developing Broadband Communications in the UK*
Cm 2734 [HMSO] (1994)

such as health and education. The UK is leading on two of the projects (Government On-line and Global Interoperability for Broadband Networks) announced at the G7 Conference on the Information Society in February. DTI is working with the IT and communications industries involved in the national Information Infrastructure Task Force; and

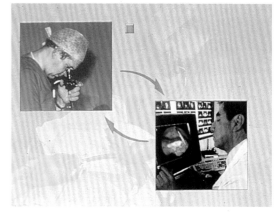

◆ Government as user. The Government will increase its use of the Internet's World Wide Web and will extend its use of video conferencing (for example see Chapter 12). The Department of Social Security is experimenting with multimedia kiosks to make information about state benefits more accessible to the public. The Department of Health is establishing an NHS-wide network capable of handling multimedia applications such as telemedicine.

Telemedicine enables doctors and specialists in different locations to share images and data about a patient's condition.

ROAD FREIGHT

4.34 Transport accounts for up to 15 per cent of business' total operating costs. It is a key factor in the competitiveness of manufacturing and retailing firms. In 1993, 63 per cent of freight moved by road. Over £40 billion is spent on road haulage each year, making the industry an important sector in its own right. Improved business practices, such as reduced running of empty lorries, increase the competitive advantage of an efficient distribution sector.

4.35 In the UK, road haulage is characterised by a handful of large world-class companies and a long tail of smaller operators. Last year there were over 400,000 vehicles specified on 125,000 operator licences, with half those licensed owning one lorry and a further third owning between two and five vehicles. Just 2 per cent of operators own 36 per cent of the fleet.

Sponsorship activities

4.36 The main thrust of Government action has been deregulation at home and liberalisation abroad. The Department of Transport plans to simplify goods vehicle operator licensing by the end of the year. The Department's proposals include replacing the current five-year licensing system with one of continuous licensing. This will benefit around 14,000 operators every year. Within the EU, the UK played a major part in negotiations which resulted in abolition of all restrictions on journeys between Member States, and pressed strongly for the agreement reached on progressive liberalisation of cabotage. By 1 July 1998, UK hauliers will be able without restriction to pick up and deliver goods within another Member State. Beyond the EU, the Department has succeeded in negotiating agreements with the newly independent nations of Central and Eastern Europe. The Department is currently working with the industry to help further develop the competitiveness of UK companies to enable them to take full advantage of new challenges and opportunities in UK and overseas markets.

CONSTRUCTION

4.37 The construction industry accounts for about 7 per cent of the UK economy (the building materials industry accounts for a further 3 per cent), with an annual output of about £50 billion produced by a workforce of 1.4 million. It is highly fragmented with 750,000 self-employed workers and about 200,000 firms, of which only about 12,000 employ more than seven people.

4.38 The industry has considerable strengths. It is large, diversified, adaptable, skilled in design and management and has a good science base.

4.39 The weaknesses of the industry largely stem from the cyclical nature of its activity. Work is erratic. Expenditure on training and accreditation schemes is lower than in other sectors and research suffers, particularly in a recession. Representative bodies tend to lose members in a recession and find it difficult to provide an effective service. The industry is also notable for the large number of disputes between parties on complex projects, and heavy expenditure on litigation.

Sponsorship activities

4.40 The Department of the Environment (DOE) has encouraged the industry to establish umbrella bodies, covering main contractors, specialist contractors, consultants and clients to streamline representations and improve communications between industry and Government. DOE staff have worked in industry for short periods, and secondees are working in the Department.

4.41 The industry is affected by a wide variety of Government policies. DOE has improved the information available to industry by publishing "Construction Monitor" and by regular meetings of the Construction Consultative Group. Improved statistics have been provided to aid industry decision makers and market forecasting is carried out with the industry.

4.42 The Department and the industry co-sponsored Sir Michael Latham's Report on procurement and contractual arrangements[5]. An Industry Board has been set up to implement the recommendations of the Report which are intended to reduce conflict and litigation, and lead to a 30 per cent reduction in costs.

4.43 A Construction Procurement Group has been set up between DOE and industry to help reduce the UK's trade deficit in construction products by increasing the number of companies which can offer competitive products and pricing. Six trade missions covering ten countries promoted the industry overseas during 1994.

[5]*Constructing the Team* [HMSO] (1994)

4.44 As part of the Construction Benchmarking Challenge the Department has provided financial assistance to four winning trade associations. They will carry out projects designed to enable construction companies to pool information and compare business processes so as to identify and achieve best practice.

4.45 A number of initiatives have been launched to expand research and innovation. These include the Whole Industry Research Strategy Group, which aims to guide the decisions of public and private investors in construction research, and the Construction Quality Forum, which seeks to improve quality across the industry by greater exchange of information.

AGRICULTURE AND FOOD

4.46 Over the last ten years, agriculture's share of GDP has fallen from 2 per cent to 1.4 per cent. This is due to declining real prices rather than a lower volume of output.

4.47 The UK is estimated to be 72 per cent self-sufficient in indigenous food and feed. Although the balance of trade deficit on food, feed and drink is just under £6 billion, this has been declining in real terms for several decades. The proportion of other UK exports needed to cover this adverse balance has fallen from about 20 per cent in 1970 to 5 per cent now.

4.48 In 1994 there were some 244,000 agricultural holdings, about a quarter of which produced some 80 per cent of total output. Average farm size is 66 hectares - over four times the EU average. And our farmers are among the most productive in Europe (Chart 4.2).

Sponsorship activities

4.49 While farming in the UK is known for technical excellence, marketing skills are not of comparable quality. Moreover, producers have shown reluctance to work together or with customers. Agricultural sponsorship activities include:

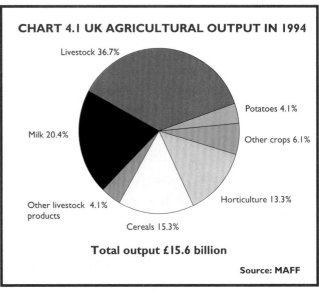

CHART 4.1 UK AGRICULTURAL OUTPUT IN 1994

Livestock 36.7%
Potatoes 4.1%
Other crops 6.1%
Milk 20.4%
Horticulture 13.3%
Other livestock products 4.1%
Cereals 15.3%

Total output £15.6 billion

Source: MAFF

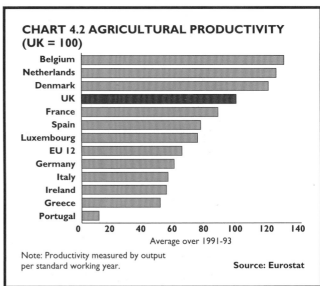

CHART 4.2 AGRICULTURAL PRODUCTIVITY (UK = 100)

Belgium
Netherlands
Denmark
UK
France
Spain
Luxembourg
EU 12
Germany
Italy
Ireland
Greece
Portugal

0 20 40 60 80 100 120 140
Average over 1991-93

Note: Productivity measured by output per standard working year.

Source: Eurostat

- encouraging the formation of stronger selling units. For example, two of the leading marketing groups for apples have merged;

- introducing a Marketing Development Scheme with an annual budget of £2.5 million; and

- helping strengthen the links between different parts of the food chain by encouraging food companies to provide non-executive directors to serve on the boards of farmer groups, and by helping retailers and producers to form longer-term relationships with UK suppliers.

4.50 Progress continues to be made on the supply side reforms referred to in the 1994 Competitiveness White Paper:

- the milk reforms, completed on 1 November 1994, introduced competition after 60 years of centralised planning under the Milk Marketing Schemes;

- the Potato Marketing Scheme will be operated in a less interventionist manner before its end in 1997; and

- the Agricultural Tenancies Act gives more freedom to landlords and tenants to negotiate tenancy agreements. This will encourage landowners to let more land, make it easier for new farmers to enter the industry and allow scope for them to diversify.

4.51 The Government continues to press for a favourable commercial environment for agriculture, with reform of the Common Agricultural Policy at the top of the agenda. Examples of this work include:

- resisting proposals which would have discriminated against Scotch whisky by removing compensation for higher priced EU grains;

- securing flexible arrangements for implementing EU commitments under the GATT, to ensure fair competition for UK traders and the UK food manufacturing industry;

- persuading the Commission to declare as illegal state aid to French pig farmers and Irish mushroom growers, and to require repayment;

- pressing for reductions in support prices and removal of supply controls; and

- pressing strongly for milk quotas to be transferable between producers in different states.

4.52 Ministerial initiatives on horticulture and catering have been aimed at encouraging wider understanding and take-up of market opportunities. The private sector Initiative on Food Marketing, set up at the Prime Minister's suggestion, is training farmers in marketing. Through a programme of overseas visits Ministers promote UK food and agriculture in countries where a Ministerial presence is especially likely to result in additional business.

BUSINESS REPRESENTATION

4.53 This Chapter has shown that the central role of sponsorship is to stimulate a debate within each industry about its international competitive position and to encourage each industry to take action to improve performance. Although many companies and industries already know where they stand against their competitors in the global marketplace, the evidence of a long tail of under-performing companies suggests that many do not. Trade associations and professional bodies have a vital leadership role in changing this situation.

4.54 Good trade associations and professional bodies are not only influential promoters of their sectors but are proactive in helping their members become internationally competitive. Two examples are the Society of Motor Manufacturers and Traders' (SMMT's) "Industry Forum" and the SBAC's "Competitiveness Challenge", both trade association initiatives supported by DTI to help member companies address the competitiveness challenges of the future.

4.55 Many DTI initiatives involve working in close partnership with trade associations. The success of these partnerships depends, in part, on the effectiveness and resources of the trade associations involved. In 1993 DTI ran a benchmarking challenge for trade associations. Twelve successful projects were given support aimed at benchmarking across a range of processes which are important to the competitiveness of the industries concerned. Chapter 12 of this White Paper announces an Export Challenge for trade associations to provide better support to companies exploiting export opportunities.

4.56 DTI initiatives encourage trade associations representing companies within the same sector to work more closely and effectively together. For example, the British Forging Industry Association and the British Industrial Fasteners Association have come together with DTI support to promote a major sectoral competitiveness project, Forging 2000.

4.57 Sponsorship encourages the development of more effective trade associations and professional bodies: it challenges and encourages member companies to set high standards for their representative organisations and to be critical if they fail to meet them. It also encourages the development of a well-resourced and effective trade association which can represent the interests of all companies within a particular sector. The more effective trade associations and professional bodies become, the more influence they will exert on Government and the greater the service they will render to their industries.

THE LOCAL PERSPECTIVE

5.1 The national policies set out in this White Paper need to be complemented by local efforts to ensure that they are effective and to help the local industries of every area of the UK become internationally competitive.

5.2 This chapter describes the three strands of the Government's approach to competitiveness at the local level:

◆ gaining a thorough understanding of the strengths and weaknesses of local economies, in order that national policy can take account of local needs;

◆ encouraging partnership between local interests – from the public, private and voluntary sectors – in order to extract the maximum value for the area from all available resources; and

◆ maximising the usefulness of the Government's services for companies through tailored local delivery by people best placed to understand the local business customer.

5.3 Many of the themes in this Chapter are also addressed in the recent Trade and Industry Select Committee Report on Regional Policy. The Government is considering the Report's recommendations and will respond to the Committee in due course.

Diversification and growth

5.4 The 1980s saw a transformation of local economies in the UK through a process of deep structural change which is continuing today.

5.5 Many local economies at the end of the 1970s were dependent on relatively few

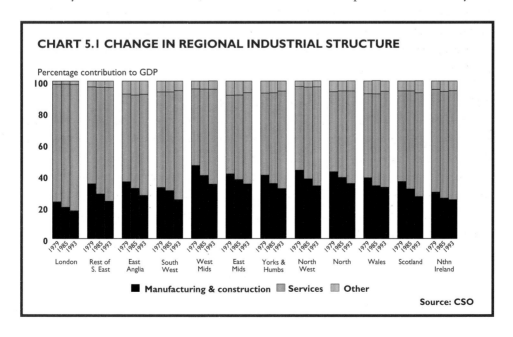

CHART 5.1 CHANGE IN REGIONAL INDUSTRIAL STRUCTURE

Percentage contribution to GDP

■ Manufacturing & construction   ▨ Services   ▨ Other

Source: CSO

heavy, traditional industries such as steel, coal and ship-building. As these and other manufacturing industries came under increasing pressure from world competition, they were forced to cut costs on a massive scale. As a result, local economies which had been dependent on these industries often suffered severe unemployment.

5.6 Despite this, the 1980s was a time of renewal. The decline of uncompetitive heavy industry was accompanied by a burst of fresh economic activity. The expansion of the small firms sector, described in Chapter 3, brought new vigour to many local economies. In addition, three trends have combined to transform local economies through diversification.

5.7 First, the fierce cost-cutting and down-sizing which had been forced on traditional manufacturing industries resulted in a turn-round in their competitive position. British Steel, for example, is now one of the most efficient steel producers in the world, taking only four man hours to produce one tonne of liquid steel, compared with 13 hours in 1979.

5.8 Second, new industries have grown in importance. The expansion of the service sector described in Chapter 3 has affected the structure of many local economies. In Yorkshire and Humberside, for example, financial services employment grew by nearly 60 per cent – by 70 per cent in Leeds alone – in the 1980s. In manufacturing, new technologies have had a significant effect. In Scotland, the electronics industry has become an international centre of excellence. Output has increased more than five-fold since 1979, with Scotland currently producing 11 per cent of Europe's semi-conductors, over 35 per cent of its personal computers, and over 50 per cent of its automated cash dispensers. The Scottish software industry, just emerging in the early 1980s, now employs over 4,000 people in 400 companies.

5.9 Third, in many regions inward investment has acted as a major stimulus to local economies (see Chapter 12).

5.10 The Government has played a crucial role in facilitating structural change. Government and

WALES

The Welsh economy has diversified over the last decade. Some 800 new plants have opened since 1980 and provide some 55,000 new employment opportunities. Manufacturing has moved towards the higher value-added end of the spectrum, with manufacturing output overall growing by 5.6 per cent over the last year.

Dependence on manufactured fuels and coal mining has been considerably diminished. There has been substantial growth in the output of sectors such as food and drink, consumer electronics and automotive components. Some 16,000 people are now employed by the 100 companies in the electronics and telecommunications industries. Around the recently privatised Cardiff airport, there are major aircraft industry and associated training developments.

Huge productivity gains, and investment of around £1.2 billion in the last ten years, have turned British Steel's Welsh plants into world-beaters. A further £22 million investment, announced recently at Llanwern, will increase that plant's hot rolling capacity by a third.

European funding has been – and continues to be – available to ease the often painful period of transition for individual areas. Since 1979:

◆ over £4 billion has been spent on grants to attract companies to areas of high unemployment. Regional Selective Assistance (RSA) has contributed to the growing influx of overseas investment. Regions with a high concentration of RSA–eligible areas are amongst those where the influence of foreign-owned companies has grown fastest;

◆ over £13 billion of European Structural Fund money has been spent in the UK, including through schemes targeting the particular problems of areas formerly dependent on industries such as ship-building, coal and defence; and

◆ about £13 billion has been spent on a wide range of programmes, now combined in England in the Single Regeneration Budget (SRB), to address the problems of deprived areas in the inner cities and elsewhere.

5.11 In addition, the Government has revolutionised the way its funds are spent, through emphasis on partnership between the public and private sectors. Starting with the Urban Development Corporations and other initiatives of the early 1980s, through to Scottish Urban Partnerships and the SRB today, its approach has been to

---

NORTHERN IRELAND

The Northern Ireland economy is strong in areas such as textiles and clothing, food, drink and tobacco, and has a significant aerospace sector. It provides a pleasant environment, and has a good supply of land for industrial development.

During the 1990s, the Northern Irish economy has performed well. Employment has increased by 5 per cent, manufacturing output by 12 per cent and output in textiles by 30 per cent.

The Government is building on this success. Investment in communications infrastructure has strengthened links with Britain and the rest of the world. Northern Ireland now has three civil airports, four efficient commercial ports and a modern, fibre-optic telecommunications system. The Belfast-Dublin rail link is also being upgraded to accommodate high-speed trains. A gas interconnector with Scotland is being built and there are plans for an electricity interconnector. There are policies to promote innovation, improve management and workforce skills, encourage enterprise and attract high quality inward investment.

Peaceful conditions now provide an opportunity for fuller realisation of the economy's potential, particularly in tourism and inward investment. The Prime Minister's Investment Forum in Belfast in December 1994 has already stimulated interest by overseas investors, and a White House conference for US industrialists hosted by President Clinton will take place at the end of May 1995.

use public money to lever in private sector funding and to encourage co-operation between local interests. The results have been impressive.

5.12 In the early 1980s, our unemployment rate was 2 per cent above the EU average, and employment levels varied significantly within the UK. In 1994, however, UK unemployment was 2 per cent below the EU average, and only Northern Ireland had an unemployment rate varying by more than 2 per cent from the UK average (see Chart 5.2).

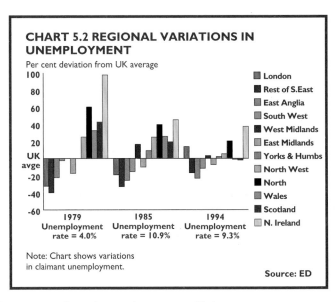

CHART 5.2 REGIONAL VARIATIONS IN UNEMPLOYMENT

Per cent deviation from UK average

Legend: London, Rest of S.East, East Anglia, South West, West Midlands, East Midlands, Yorks & Humbs, North West, North, Wales, Scotland, N. Ireland

1979 Unemployment rate = 4.0%
1985 Unemployment rate = 10.9%
1994 Unemployment rate = 9.3%

Note: Chart shows variations in claimant unemployment.

Source: ED

BUSINESS COMPETITIVENESS INDICATORS

DTI has worked with TECs to develop business competitiveness indicators, which Government Offices will be discussing with all TECs. The indicators are:

◆ *business formation and survival rates*

◆ *employment levels*

◆ *manufacturing output per employee*

◆ *average earnings*

◆ *GDP per head*

These indicators will not measure TEC performance. TECs operate in different local economies which cannot be improved by one local agent in isolation. But the indicators will give TECs a picture of how the local economy changes over time. They will be able to use the indicators to monitor economic performance and to ensure that local partners build on strengths and tackle weaknesses. Last year, for example, a study of manufacturing output[1] allowed Birmingham TEC to identify recent low investment by local industry as a problem, and to develop plans to address it.

5.13 This progress is welcome but not sufficient. The challenge for the 1990s is to build on the achievements and policies of the last decade, to ensure that each area of the UK maximises its competitive performance.

Understanding local performance

5.14 To achieve this, the starting point for each local economy must be a realistic, continually up-dated assessment of strengths and weaknesses.

5.15 Local partners are keen to develop measures of competitiveness to evaluate performance. Some Training and Enterprise Councils (TECs) are already involved in this. The indicators opposite represent best practice.

5.16 Local economic performance should not be seen in isolation. Comparisons between different parts of the country are not straightforward, since many factors which affect performance cannot be influenced at local level. Nonetheless, such comparisons – and comparisons with other countries too – can be valuable. Where indicators reveal, for example, higher than average levels of business failure, local partners need to determine why, and take appropriate action.

[1] *Manufacturing trends in Birmingham 1994-2005* [Birmingham Economic Information Centre] (1994)

Encouraging partnership

5.17 Individuals, firms and institutions each have a stake in improving the competitive position of their locality. The Government seeks to encourage these different interests to work together, so that available resources – from the private, voluntary and public sectors – can be brought to bear effectively.

5.18 Responsibility for much of what needs to be done lies with the private sector and with local authorities, although a wide range of other bodies has a role to play in different aspects of local competitiveness – the Government, TECs, Chambers of Commerce, voluntary organisations, agencies such as English Partnerships, the Scottish Enterprise Networks, the Welsh Development Agency and the Industrial Development Board and the Training and Employment Agency in Northern Ireland, and other local development organisations.

5.19 The Government's approach has been to use its funds to draw local authorities into partnership with the private sector, starting in the 1980s by linking urban grants to gearing from the private sector. The challenge approach, pioneered by City Challenge in the early 1990s, has been particularly powerful. By allocating funds to the bids which most effectively combine public and private sector resources, City Challenge has stimulated the development of existing partnerships and the formation of new ones. Local agencies have in some cases come together for the first time to prepare bids, establishing useful links even where bids did not win funding.

5.20 The approach has been a success. In the past, many areas were hampered by failure of local authorities and the private sector to work together. Now, both parties are committed to partnership.

- Increasingly, companies realise that their prosperity is linked to the prosperity of the locality in which they operate. Companies are working together to address competitiveness problems on a wide front. Initiatives range from supply-chain groups, spreading best practice from large companies to local suppliers, to wider strategic events such as "Industry 96", an initiative aiming to raise the profile of the West Midlands and improve public perceptions of industry and commerce; and

- Local authorities have become strategic "enablers", able and willing to work with the private sector and bring together other players as appropriate. They have a key role in ensuring effective provision of services, and as major local employers and regulators.

5.21 A notable example of business and local authorities working together is City Pride, an initiative currently being piloted in Birmingham, London and Manchester. Civic and business leaders have drawn up a prospectus describing a vision for their cities over the next 10-15 years and the practical steps needed to achieve that vision,

---

ENGLISH PARTNERSHIPS

English Partnerships was established in April 1994 as a new England-wide body to promote job creation, inward investment and environmental improvement through reclamation and development of vacant, derelict, under-used or contaminated land and buildings.

Through English Partnerships, the Government has brought together three formerly separate programmes – Derelict Land Grant, City Grant and English Estates - within a unified regime. English Partnerships operates as a strategic partner and investor in regeneration through a flexible mix of instruments (including grants, loan guarantees and joint ventures), tailored to the particular needs and opportunities of the project.

English Partnerships has an annual budget of some £250 million. It will maximise the impact of this by attracting EU and private sector funding for regeneration.

---

including public and private investment in infrastructure, training and regeneration.

5.22 Partnership has been helped by the creation of the Government Offices for the English Regions. These bring together the regional responsibilities of the Departments of Employment, Environment, Trade and Industry, and Transport. For the first time in England, they give a single focus at regional level for a wide range of policies affecting competitiveness. They give the Government a more strategic view of the problems faced by regions, and provide local partners with a single point of contact with the Government.

5.23 The Government Offices also have close links with the Home Office and the Department for Education. For example, they are working with the Department for Education to reinforce in the regions the full range of national policies for education, which are designed to raise standards in schools and colleges and improve the quality of the workforce (see Chapter 7).

5.24 The partnership approach is not limited to England. The Scottish and Welsh Offices and the Northern Ireland Department of Economic

Derelict flats on the Hulme housing estate in Manchester have been replaced by new housing as part of Hulme City Challenge. Hulme was one of the first successful City Challenge bids. From its start on 1 April 1992 to the end of 1994, £21 million of City Challenge money had attracted a further £36 million of other public money and £40 million of private sector investment.

Development have long provided the single focal point which Government Offices have recently brought to England. They coordinate efforts to enhance the competitiveness of the Scottish, Welsh and Northern Irish economies, working with local government, other local organisations and the private and voluntary sectors.

SCOTTISH URBAN PARTNERSHIPS

The four Urban Partnership Initiatives, set up in 1988 in parts of Dundee, Edinburgh, Glasgow and Paisley, demonstrate the benefits of partnership to urban regeneration. Each brings together, under Scottish Office leadership, the relevant local authorities and Local Enterprise Company, public agencies, the private sector and the local community. Their achievements include:

- *approximately 2,000 jobs and 1,350 training placements for local residents each year*

- *unemployment down by more than 40 per cent*

- *support for over 150 business start-ups*

- *7,000 homes refurbished and over 2,000 new homes built*

- *improved local education standards, community safety and quality of the local environment*

Reflecting the progress made, the Dundee Initiative will be wound up during 1995, with local arrangements to ensure sustained regeneration. A recent policy statement[2] proposed extending the approach to a wider range of disadvantaged areas, with resources allocated to initiatives which demonstrate the clearest commitment to partnership and to private sector involvement and finance.

Extending the challenge approach

5.25 Following the early success of City Challenge, the Government has extended the approach. The Single Regeneration Budget (SRB) for England, launched by the Government Offices last year:

- is a much bigger programme, with total resources of around £1.3 billion annually, and over £800 million available for bids over the next three years;

- aims to attract significant matching funding from the private sector and from European Structural Funds; and

- is available for projects anywhere in England that can demonstrate that they need support, are underpinned by a strong local partnership, and will enhance the quality of life and competitiveness of the area.

5.26 The first SRB Challenge Fund bidding round saw 201 successful bids, which stand to attract some £1.1 billion in SRB support over their projected lifetime of up

---

[2] *Programme for Partnership* [Scottish Office] (1995)

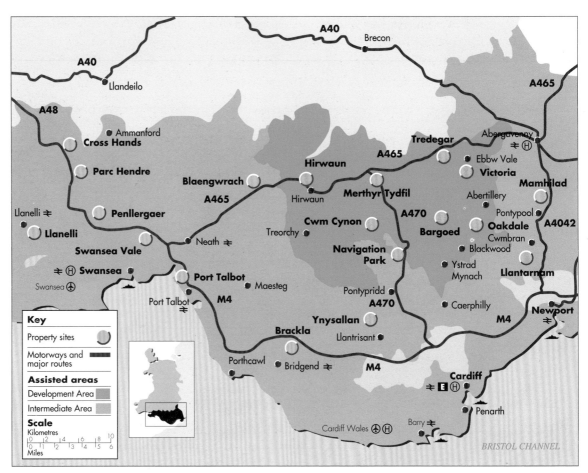

In Wales, with its strong tradition of joint working between the public and private sectors, the opportunities provided by the Private Finance Initiative have been harnessed to the cause of regenerating the South Wales Valleys. A portfolio of investment opportunities was published in December 1994, with details of 20 locations providing scope for private sector investment of up to £1 billion. The strategy for attracting private sector investment established in the Valleys will be extended to the rest of Wales during 1995.

to seven years. SRB support is expected to attract £2.9 billion in private investment and a further £1.8 billion in other public investment. On bidders' current estimates, the projects will support 60,000 new businesses, train 250,000 people and create or safeguard a further 250,000 jobs. Education and training initiatives have a major stake in the successful bids. The Government Offices will be encouraging future bids aimed at raising levels of educational achievement. The second bidding round was launched in April.

5.27 The challenge approach is being taken up in other ways:

◆ in November 1994, the Government announced the results of the first **Rural Challenge**: six partnerships won £1 million each to improve the competitiveness of less prosperous rural areas in England. A second bidding round is in progress.

Government supported schemes, in particular those operated by the Rural Development Commission, aim to encourage rural businesses to become more competitive and to enable the rural economy to diversify. The Rural White Paper to be published in the autumn will explore how best to ensure that rural areas make an increasing contribution to national competitiveness; and

◆ in February 1995, the Government launched **Regional Challenge**, setting aside around 12 per cent of European Structural Funds for the best ideas from local partnerships in most eligible areas.

The National Forest in the East Midlands is an example of a Government sponsored initiative to improve the quality of the local environment, enhancing its attractiveness as a business location.

Local delivery of Government services to business

5.28 In addition to its role in facilitating local action, the Government is responsible for delivering a range of services to business at local level.

5.29 The Government's approach over recent years has been to move service delivery nearer to the customer by asking local, private-sector bodies to define and provide the services needed to meet the Government's competitiveness objectives.

5.30 This approach was pioneered with the creation in England and Wales of the TECs in 1990. TECs have a key contribution to make to enhancing the performance of the local economy – both through their own activities to improve business competitiveness and develop workforce skills, and by taking a lead in co-ordinating local action. Over a thousand local business and community leaders are members of TEC Boards. In some areas, TECs and local Chambers of Commerce have merged and others are seeking to merge, with the aim of improving the quality of their services.

5.31 The Enterprise Networks play a similar role in Scotland.

SCOTLAND: THE ENTERPRISE NETWORKS

Scottish Enterprise and Highlands and Islands Enterprise were set up in 1991 to promote Scotland's industrial efficiency and international competitiveness. Both broke with the past in providing a single, integrated approach to competitiveness, with leadership by business people, and flexible local delivery. They provide the strategic framework for the activities of local enterprise companies (LECs) led by senior local business people. Each LEC adapts its services to the needs and opportunities of its area.

Scottish Enterprise has embarked on a major initiative to increase the rate of business start-ups in Scotland, after a study which showed that it was lower than the UK average. Its Business Birth Rate Strategy aims to help create an additional 25,000 businesses in Scotland by the year 2000.

In 1995-96 the Enterprise networks expect to:

◆ *assist over 15,500 businesses*

◆ *provide 38,000 square metres of commercial and industrial premises, and encourage a further £60 million of private sector property investment*

◆ *bring almost 700 hectares of derelict or contaminated land back into economic use*

◆ *train 37,000 young people, of whom a higher proportion will gain vocational qualifications than ever before*

◆ *provide training to help around 30,000 adults get back to work*

◆ *pilot a Small Business Loan Scheme and work with the London Stock Exchange on the Scottish launch of their Alternative Investment Market (see Chapter 13).*

5.32 In autumn 1993, the approach was widened in England to include all local business support services with the opening of the first Business Link. While TECs remain responsible for setting the strategic framework and defining business needs in their local area, the delivery of business support services – from DTI, TECs and, increasingly, other Departments – will now be through Business Link. Chambers of Commerce play an essential role in the partnerships behind Business Links.

5.33 The advent of Business Link amounts to a revolution in the delivery of support for business. For the first time, business will have a one stop, local source of help.

BUSINESS LINKS

The hundredth Business Link opened on 1 May 1995; by the end of the year, more than 200 will be open and Business Link services will be easily accessible to every business in England.

Business Links will:

- *provide a single point of access to a wide range of high quality business support services*

- *be open to all businesses, although they will concentrate particularly on SMEs with growth potential*

- *use leading-edge information technology, including electronic mail and video-conferencing, to bring local firms in contact with clients and suppliers across the country and ultimately across the globe*

- *be based on partnership between Government, TECs, local authorities, Chambers of Commerce and Enterprise Agencies*

- *be the normal delivery mechanism from April 1996 for all DTI's business services and, increasingly, those of other Government Departments*

The first port of call for most firms will be the Business Link Enquiry and Information Service. Every enquiry will get a speedy, accurate response, backed up by modern databases and technology. For more demanding enquiries, Business Link will agree exact requirements and a fair price before commencing work.

At the heart of the Business Link network will be a group of 600 Personal Business Advisers responsible for forging long-term relationships with business clients to help their development and growth. They will be supported by over 200 expert advisers – Export Development, Design and Innovation and Technology Counsellors – who will help businesses to develop their potential and to obtain specialist services locally, nationally and internationally.

The Government will fund Business Link for a three year pump-priming period. Beyond that period, it will continue to contribute funding to Business Link services. A rolling three-year programme will, subject to ongoing evaluation, ensure the financial stability of Business Link.

Within three years of opening, all Business Links will be independently assessed against rigorous accreditation criteria (ISO 9000 – for quality and consistency of service – and Investors in People). Only those which achieve and maintain the required standard will be allowed to stay within the Business Link network.

5.34 In Scotland, a network of Business Shops – run by local partnerships between LECs, local authorities and business support organisations – is being opened. Trained advisers provide information and direct enquiries to the business support services of local partners. Forty business shops will be open by the end of the year. A similar approach is being followed in Wales, through Business Connect Wales. In

Northern Ireland, the Local Enterprise Development Unit has offices throughout the region and there is an extensive network of local enterprise agencies.

5.35 The most recent development is the establishment in England of the Regional Supply Office network to promote local supply chains. Announced in the 1994 White Paper, these offices are now open. Staffed by people with business experience, they will:

- help purchasers find competitive suppliers;

- help suppliers exploit new market opportunities;

- encourage suppliers to use Business Link services; and

- aim for £260 million of contracts to be awarded by producers to suppliers introduced by the network in the first three years.

LONDON

London is one of the world's great cities – probably the greatest all-rounder – and accounts for a sixth of the UK's GDP. The success of London is vital to the competitiveness of the country as a whole, both because of its size and because it is the major contact point with the rest of the world. London is the most popular investment location in Europe because of its key strengths:

- *the world's largest centre for international finance, with more foreign banks (500) than anywhere; the largest foreign exchange market and the leading shipping market*

- *good and improving communications within London, with the rest of the UK and internationally*

- *a wide variety of skills; and world-class academic strength, including 12 universities and 10 colleges of higher education*

- *cultural facilities of international standing, including 20 major museums, 2 opera houses and 5 orchestras; theatre, opera and concert halls capable of seating 60,000 people every night*

- *internationally famous venues and events such as Wembley, Wimbledon and the London Marathon*

Developing partnership

Alongside success and prosperity, there are weaknesses which must be addressed if London is to retain the balance between economic growth, social cohesion and quality of life which makes it a great city. The Government's strategy is to create the conditions which will allow London to prosper. It will promote London vigorously,

Continues...

LONDON *continued*

invest in its long term future by careful targeting of regeneration resources, promote development of a wider manufacturing base, and encourage its diverse and vibrant service sector.

A crucial factor in the success of this strategy will be effective partnership. The Government's promotion of the challenge approach to economic development has helped to encourage local partnerships of high quality, such as in North West London.

Regeneration in North West London

The Park Royal Partnership submitted a successful SRB bid and was awarded £8.6 million over seven years. It aims to transform the Park Royal area by a series of measures to promote inward investment, sustain existing businesses and improve the environment. Part of the reason for the bid's success was the track record of an existing partnership including three local authorities, three TECs and strong private sector backing from West London Leadership. The 28 partners include 15 companies.

The Cabinet Sub-Committee on London co-ordinates Government policy in the capital. The Government is also working closely with a large number of organisations in the public, private and voluntary sectors, including:

- *London Pride Partnership, a grouping of a wide range of public and private sector organisations which published in January 1995 the London Pride Prospectus setting out their vision and proposals for the capital*

- *TECs, Chambers of Commerce, local authorities and other business support organisations which are joining forces to develop the Business Link network for London, expected to be phased in over the second half of 1995*

- *London First, English Partnerships, local authorities and others, to attract inward investment. The London First Centre was set up in April 1994 with funding from the Government, Westminster City Council, the Corporation of London and the London Docklands Development Corporation. It received over 160 investment enquiries in its first year. Ten investments have already taken place*

- *the Sports Council, local authorities and others to support and enhance London's international reputation for sporting venues of the highest calibre*

In addition to encouraging partnerships and facilitating the actions of others outside the public sector, the Government is contributing to the improvements of the infrastructure and regulatory framework of the London economy. Draft Strategic Guidance for London Planning Authorities was issued for consultation in March 1995. This sets out a framework for the development of London into the next century.

Continues…

LONDON *continued*

It gives a higher priority to the development of business, services and manufacturing.

Four other key issues will have a significant effect on London's economy:

Tourism

London is a tourist destination of worldwide appeal, making the London tourism industry a major contributor to the UK economy. Yet analysis reveals that the industry's growth rate is falling behind the worldwide average. The Department of National Heritage is providing additional resources to be matched by the private sector. This will help the London tourism market towards its full potential.

Education and training

Skills, particularly amongst young adults, are cause for concern. To address this, London TECs introduced in April 1995 a London-wide training credit scheme. Known as "Network", it allows young adults to choose between training options, including from September 1995 Modern Apprenticeships and Accelerated Modern Apprenticeships.

Manufacturing

The Government Office for London is working with manufacturers, TECs, local authorities and educational institutions to overcome obstacles to improving manufacturing, in which employment has dropped by over a quarter since 1989. A plan drawn up by the Government will be taken forward in partnership with manufacturers and local business organisations.

Transport

The key objective is to make the best possible use of the existing road network while the PFI is supplementing investment in public transport. Important PFI projects include:

- *Heathrow Express, a £300 million joint venture between BAA plc and British Railways Board*

- *Jubilee Line Extension, which includes £400 million of private sector funding. Construction is due for completion in 1998 when Westminster and the Channel Tunnel rail terminal at Waterloo will be linked with Docklands*

- *Docklands Light Railway, a joint venture PFI scheme to extend the DLR under the Thames from the Isle of Dogs to Greenwich and Lewisham. Construction is due to start in 1996 and the line to open in 1999*

LOOKING TO THE FUTURE

"I never think of the future. It comes soon enough." (Albert Einstein)

6.1 Today few people have the luxury of sharing Albert Einstein's sentiment.

6.2 The world is changing rapidly: markets turn global as information becomes a worldwide commodity and protectionism retreats in the face of deregulation and enlightened self-interest; new powerful economies emerge in the Far East and elsewhere; technology spawns new products and services.

6.3 Firms are drivers of change. They also have to respond rapidly to change or be pushed towards extinction. Their responses place increasing demands on management and the workforce, who need new flexibility and higher skills. Change has to be accommodated within the world's requirement for sustainable development and in the context of an ageing world population.

6.4 Despite its complexities and uncertainties, change presents opportunities. For many, however, these opportunities are difficult to evaluate or loom as a threat. But, whether we relish change or not, we have to assemble the information we need to reach sensible judgements about our futures. The better we do that, the less of a threat and more of an opportunity change becomes.

6.5 This Chapter is a contribution to that process. It looks at:

◆ the pace of change;

◆ the impact of the main drivers of change; and

◆ the implications for firms, citizens and Governments.

6.6 However, Government has no crystal ball. Even the most expert economic and social forecasts are fallible. Economic and social trends do not develop in a straight line, not least because they represent aggregations of individual decisions. The relationships between the different elements of change are also difficult to predict. Global political developments may have a considerable and unpredictable impact. Nonetheless, everyone needs to think through likely changes.

The pace of change

6.7 Technology and trade have traditionally been the main forces for change in the world economy.

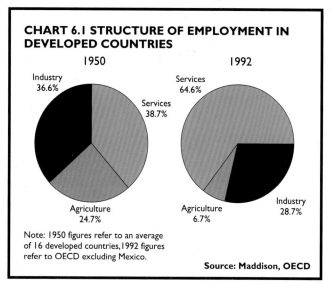

CHART 6.1 STRUCTURE OF EMPLOYMENT IN DEVELOPED COUNTRIES

1950

Industry 36.6%

Services 38.7%

Agriculture 24.7%

1992

Services 64.6%

Agriculture 6.7%

Industry 28.7%

Note: 1950 figures refer to an average of 16 developed countries, 1992 figures refer to OECD excluding Mexico.

Source: Maddison, OECD

6.8 In 1950, agriculture employed nearly a quarter of the population of the major economies. Today it employs less than 7 per cent. Over the same period, the service sector's share of employment has risen from just over one-third to two-thirds (Chart 6.1).

6.9 In recent years, new technologies, particularly information technologies, have intensified the pressure for change on industrial structures and have helped develop global markets.

◆ Many new technologies are now applied widely and quickly, even in sectors previously regarded as "low-tech". In developed economies, they can help such sectors to avoid decline. In the developing world, they can transform them into global competitors.

◆ New technologies can quickly create high-value markets around the world. Examples are films, publishing and the use of real-time information delivered by broad-band communication highways.

6.10 The pace of change is fastest in those developing nations which are open to world trade and encourage competition, both of which provide incentives for entrepreneurship and technological progress. It took Britain 60 years to double its real income per head after the start of the industrial revolution. The US took 50 years to do the same after industralisation got underway, Japan 35 years and South Korea around a decade. China has recently doubled its real income per head in less than ten years.

6.11 Successful developing countries grow faster than high-income countries because they start from a low base and because it is relatively easy and cheap to copy existing technology. Growth of the order of 10 per cent a year is unsustainable in the longer term. Nevertheless, if developed and developing countries grow at the rates currently forecast by the World Bank, the share of world output of today's industrialised countries could fall by 2020 to less than two-fifths (from just over a half now) and as many as nine of the largest 15 economies could be from today's less developed countries. China may already be the world's third largest economy in terms of total output, although still poor in terms of income per head.

Sustainable development

6.12 The Government is committed to economic growth. But that development must be sustainable[1], as the value of growth would be undermined if it was at the cost of an unacceptable depletion of resources or damage to the environment.

6.13 However, governments cannot take decisions alone. Economic development in the UK is affected by demands which others place on the world's resources and the environment. The economic aspirations of the developing world, where population is growing most rapidly, are a key factor.

[1] sustainable development is commonly defined as development which meets the needs of the present without compromising the ability of future generations to meet their needs.

6.14 In "Sustainable Development: the UK Strategy" the Government showed that policies for promoting sustainable development need, as far as possible, to work with the market[2]. But the market does not always reflect the full cost of using resources, particularly the environmental cost. Where the market cannot be relied upon to provide the best solutions, the Government must consider stepping in (see Chapter 15).

6.15 A commitment to sustainable development therefore has implications for business. For example, developed nations are likely to continue taking action to reduce pollution and waste. Less developed countries need help, advice and technologies to tackle emerging pollution problems. Firms need to anticipate such trends and to integrate environmental considerations into all aspects of strategy and management.

ENVIRONMENTAL IMPACTS: CFCs

"Inert" chlorofluorocarbons (CFCs) were adopted for a range of applications including refrigeration, firefighting and as solvents. They are safe in use, efficient and their production has placed limited demands on plentiful resources. But their release is a primary contributor to depletion of the ozone layer with significant implications for the environment and human health. In just eight years, use of this product has been virtually eliminated in developed countries.

6.16 Business use of transport cannot escape the pressures either. If current transport trends continue, the resulting traffic growth would have unacceptable consequences for both the environment and the economies of certain parts of the country. The Government needs to provide a framework in which people have access to goods, services and other people whilst reducing the need for transport and travel (see Chapter 14).

6.17 Since publication of its sustainable development strategy, the Government has been consulting on a waste strategy for England and Wales and has published "Air Quality: Meeting the Challenge". These papers set a framework for business[3].

6.18 The way firms respond to these pressures will be of increasing importance to their competitiveness.

◆ Firms which understand the impact of their business on the environment, including the impact of their products at every stage of their life cycle, will be best placed to seize the opportunities offered by new technologies, management techniques, procurement strategies and so on.

◆ Such far-sighted companies will secure competitive advantage by managing their impact on the environment and by minimising their use of resources.

◆ Market opportunities will emerge for products and processes that are less damaging to the environment.

---

[2] *Sustainable Development: the UK Strategy* Cm 2426 [HMSO] (1994)

[3] *Air Quality: Meeting the Challenge. The Government's Strategic Policies for Air Quality Management (Policy Paper)* [DOE, Welsh Office, Scottish Office, DOE (NI), DoT] (1995)

RENEWABLE ENERGY

The Government is stimulating the development of new and renewable energy sources by helping new firms and technologies to market, not least through the removal of barriers to entry.

One firm helped by Government action has developed a waste-to-energy plant in London. This £100 million project supplies enough electricity for 50,000 homes.

Another firm is developing a power-station fuelled from willow coppice plantations. Willow will be grown on set-aside land.

A third firm, helped by Government funding, has commissioned two commercial power stations fired by agricultural waste. It is a world leader in this technology. Success has generated export opportunities.

A medium-scale power station at Eye, Suffolk, fired by agricultural wastes. The plant is a world first and supplies the electricity it generates through the local utility to the National Grid.

6.19 Competitiveness also requires firms to be alert to the interests of their employees, consumers and suppliers, lenders and the wider public as well as managers and owners. In particular, firms can expect increasing interest in the link between environmental and financial performance. Firms which do not respond to market pressures to be efficient in their use of resources, or be responsible in the impact they have on the environment, will come under increasing pressure from the capital markets.

Population change

6.20 The world's population is changing rapidly.

- It will grow from over 5 billion in 1990 to nearly 8 billion in 2020. The increase will be mainly in Africa and Asia (Chart 6.2).

- At the same time the average age of populations is increasing, and not just in the West. Populations are ageing too in the developed Asian economies (Chart 6.3).

- The UK's population will age less rapidly than in some other economies, such as Japan and Germany.

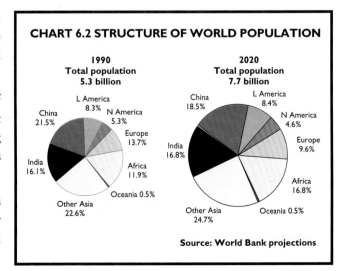

CHART 6.2 STRUCTURE OF WORLD POPULATION

1990
Total population
5.3 billion

China 21.5%
India 16.1%
Other Asia 22.6%
Oceania 0.5%
Africa 11.9%
Europe 13.7%
N America 5.3%
L America 8.3%

2020
Total population
7.7 billion

China 18.5%
India 16.8%
Other Asia 24.7%
Oceania 0.5%
Africa 16.8%
Europe 9.6%
N America 4.6%
L America 8.4%

Source: World Bank projections

6.21 These changes are of key importance to sustainable development. There will not just be more mouths in need of food: these extra people will place greater demands on all resources.

6.22 The ageing of the population has major implications too for economic and social development, although the ability of technological change to generate increased output with a smaller workforce must not be underestimated.

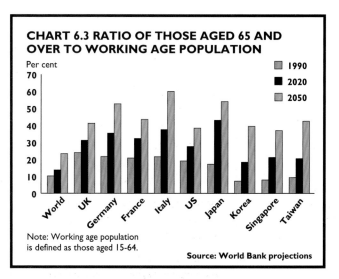

CHART 6.3 RATIO OF THOSE AGED 65 AND OVER TO WORKING AGE POPULATION

Per cent

■ 1990
■ 2020
■ 2050

World, UK, Germany, France, Italy, US, Japan, Korea, Singapore, Taiwan

Note: Working age population is defined as those aged 15-64.

Source: World Bank projections

FUNDING OLD AGE

In the West, governments play a key role in the provision of pensions. Ageing populations create pressure for higher expenditure on pensions, leading to higher taxes falling on fewer workers. And yet, in a world of global markets and capital flows, governments cannot increase taxes significantly without damaging national competitiveness. In these circumstances, individuals will not be able to look to the state to fund improvements in their living standards in old age.

Innovation

6.23 Innovation – the successful exploitation of new ideas – is a key factor in change. The accelerating pace of technology and the rapid evolution of global markets interact strongly to put pressure on firms to innovate. (Chapter 11 deals with innovation in detail.)

6.24 Knowledge and inventions are not in themselves drivers of change. It is their application that counts. New developments may remain unexploited for decades if they are not perceived to confer benefits, commercial or otherwise. Although the fax is thought of as a modern invention, its principles were patented in 1843 by Alexander Bain, a Scottish inventor, and first put into limited commercial use in 1860 in France. Full commercial use came over a century later.

6.25 The UK devotes substantial financial and intellectual resources to research and development, to acquire knowledge, know-how and skills for the future. If these assets are to be well used, industry, the academic community and Government need a full and shared understanding of emerging trends.

FUTURE MARKET OPPORTUNITIES

The Technology Foresight programme has developed a shared understanding of future market opportunities across a broad range of sectors over the next 20 years. Some are described below. (Follow-up to Technology Foresight is described in Chapter 11.)

Communications

Demand for multimedia and broadband services is generating rapid growth. Technology already exists to meet this demand. In the near future:

- *most commercial transactions other than the delivery of goods will take place over electronic networks*

- *interactive multimedia services will increasingly be used at home for entertainment, shopping and education*

Looking further ahead, the majority of these services will be available through hand-held, mobile equipment.

Construction

Demand for refurbishment and upgrading will increase in developed economies. Elsewhere, migration to cities and the need for new infrastructure will drive development. Construction will become technologically intensive and automated. Increased use of prefabrication will give major cost savings.

Financial services

The potential scope of capital markets has increased dramatically as a result of the fall of communism and the lowering of trade barriers. New technology will permit the rapid development of sophisticated financial services where only rudimentary capabilities exist today.

Health and life sciences

Competition is increasing, driven by rapid advances in science and technology. At the same time, ageing populations are creating new and expanding markets. Industry will need to build on genome research and molecular biology for new health care products and biotechnology applications.

IT and electronics

Access to, and analysis and exploitation of information will be crucial to competitiveness throughout industry and commerce. New information delivery services and major new 'infrastructure' businesses will provide growth in hardware, software and services. The countries with the best infrastructure will have an advantage.

Retailing and distribution

The expansion of remote and international retailing offer major opportunities for this industry. The effectiveness with which these are exploited will depend on the development of new technology (for example, the smart card) and on regulation which does not inhibit its use.

Energy

Increased demand from emerging economies and growing international concern for the environment will require the effective development of new energy sources and new products that use energy more efficiently.

The stock-exchange in Budapest, one of several to emerge in the post-communist democracies of Eastern Europe.

Globalisation

6.26 Investment now flows more readily across borders. Over the last decade, foreign direct investment has grown twice as fast as trade in goods. In the past, such investment took place between developed countries. More recently, investment has also flowed towards developing countries. This enables countries to specialise where they have a comparative advantage and, by enhancing competition, puts downward pressure on prices to the benefit of consumers worldwide. In addition, it helps open new markets. East Asia alone has 2 billion consumers with rapidly rising incomes.

6.27 Concern about the potential loss of manufacturing industry to developing countries fails to recognise the opportunities globalisation offers to open and competitive economies. The UK's task is to build a strong position from which to attack world markets. Our major competitors remain other G7 countries, not emerging Asian economies.

♦ Demand in the developing world, stimulated by Western investment, is creating new markets for our goods, even if most of the population remains poor. There is a rapidly growing middle class in India and China. The value of UK visible exports to the six "Asian tigers" grew by nearly 250 per cent over the last decade compared with 60 per cent to other non-EU countries.

♦ Labour costs are low in developing countries because productivity is low. Although competitive wages are always important, firms in developed economies do not have to match wages in such economies. They need to have higher labour productivity.

♦ Developed economies import no more from low-cost economies now than a decade ago. For the OECD as a whole, imports from developing economies currently account for around 4 per cent of GDP, compared with 5 per cent in the early 1980s. The proportion of UK imports of manufactures from countries with wages 25 per cent or more below UK rates is the same as 20 years ago.

♦ Although skill levels are rising rapidly in some developing countries, developed nations have a considerable lead. Nearly half the people in developing countries have no formal education and the average number of years of schooling of the adult population in the OECD is nearly three times higher than in developing countries.

♦ New technology, particularly information technology, is much further advanced in developed economies. It has the potential to secure an overall productivity advantage.

- Development of just-in-time production and pressure for customisation and early delivery of products reduce the benefit for manufacturers of transferring production to, or sourcing components from, overseas.

6.28 Trade blocs, particularly the EU and the North American Free Trade Agreement (NAFTA), influence the pace of globalisation. These blocs have generated contradictory pressures.

- At a regional level, they have helped reduce trade barriers. Worldwide, they have helped the negotiation of tariff reductions through co-ordination and narrowing of intra-regional differences.

- They have stimulated global investment from companies outside the bloc who wish to take advantage of a growing market within its boundaries. Our presence in the EU is a major factor attracting Far Eastern and North American investment to the UK.

- However, countries may join trade blocs for defensive reasons and, once members, may be reluctant to work to reduce trade barriers. The new World Trade Organisation (WTO) has a key role in overcoming this.

6.29 Globalisation increases wealth in both developed and developing countries. At the same time, it drives change in industrial structures. Low skilled jobs in sectors open to international trade face considerable competitive pressure. Firms and workers in these sectors need to:

- become more productive through investment in higher skills and through increased flexibility and efficiency; and

- move into new, typically higher value added, products and services.

6.30 Realistic alternatives do not exist.

- Protectionism would reduce gains from expanded world trade.

- Subsidies for jobs would increase taxes and decrease investment, which flows freely to where it can earn the greatest return.

Organisations and change

6.31 The pace of change in organisations is increasing. In many firms, management structures are becoming flatter, with a greater focus on customer needs and on team working, including partnership with other firms.

6.32 Firms are increasingly contracting out non-core functions. Networks of operations, involving strategic alliances, are coming together. Boundaries between firms at various stages of the supply chain may blur, without reaching the point of actual merger.

6.33 Information about customer needs is crucial to the successful development of products. Niche markets and customisation will require careful use of targeted marketing, and advertising will become more important.

COMPETITIVENESS IN INFORMATION SERVICES

The UK benefits from the widespread use of the English language and from a sophisticated communications infrastructure with a liberalised regulatory environment. Competition has led to the rapid growth of new services and networks, such as cellular radio. The UK is attracting investment from information supply industries and is becoming a test bed for advanced information and communication services. In turn this is encouraging user industries to locate in the UK to take advantage of the wide and growing range of commercial business information services and the advanced communications infrastructure already available and being developed.

A NETWORK APPROACH TO DISCOVERING NEW TECHNOLOGY

In Bristol, the TEC, further education college and business have formed the South Bristol Learning Network. The Network has trained 55 unemployed people in using information technology. Through workshops and roadshows, supported by ICL, the recruits have helped 1,500 people from small businesses, schools and Government to understand multimedia information and communication technology. The Network's approach has attracted interest from Europe and North America.

6.34 There are potential threats from increasing reliance on information systems. The reliability of systems becomes critical to a company's smooth running. Systems which are hard to monitor invite crime. More generally, the volume of information could become a hindrance, if firms cannot identify what is valuable.

6.35 Government will need to ensure that it is not left behind. The services it provides must be appropriate to a world of rapidly changing, highly-focused operations.

6.36 Higher education, too, will need to respond to global information flows and changing patterns of employment. The globalisation of companies' research efforts, and availability of information about research institutes' strengths, will enable those which are centres of excellence to attract interested students and companies from all over the world. The UK has a competitive advantage here. It has a large number of centres of excellence in proportion to its population and research costs are relatively low.

People, jobs and change

6.37 The need for firms to be more responsive to customer needs and to concentrate on their core business has significant implications for the workforce in the UK and other developed economies.

6.38 Change in organisations and industrial structures is already reshaping the labour market and the way we work (see Chapter 8).

6.39 Change of this nature has major implications for the Government, firms and individuals.

- A highly skilled workforce depends on high educational standards. The UK is now closing the gap on its major competitors.

- The take up of Investors in People demonstrates that more companies are recognising the strategic importance of developing people. But research indicates that employees of small firms, older workers, women, people working part-time, and people working at lower skill levels undertake less training. The self-employed can also miss out.

- Individuals will need to take increasing responsibility for their own adaptability and re-skilling throughout their working lives. Government and business will need to encourage and support individuals investing in their own development. Over the past decade, large employers have already set up Employee Development Programmes to encourage learning which goes beyond immediate job-related training. Such programmes are voluntary and allow the employee choice in course content and how training is provided.

- More frequent changes in employment also have implications for pensions. These need to be flexible but secure.

TELEWORKING

Teleworking, using telecommunications to work away from the office, has developed rapidly, particularly in journalism, consultancy and computer programming.

Teleworking is not just about being at the end of a telephone. Employees can work through "real-time" access to their firms' computer networks, regardless of their distance from the "office".

The benefits include:

- *less time spent travelling to work*

- *greater personal control over working hours and considerable scope to work out of normal hours*

- *accommodation cost savings for employers*

- *improved retention and recruitment of staff*

- *opportunities for remote areas to attract employment*

Highlands and Islands Enterprise has promoted the use of new telecommunications networks. As a result, 200 jobs have been created for teleworkers. One company based in Argyll employs around 15 teleworkers in editing and abstracting medical articles. Six tele-centres have been established in the Shetland Islands. Parking tickets for some London boroughs are issued from Elgin in the North of Scotland.

These opportunities will be enhanced by Government plans to promote further competition for radio-based telecommunications in remote areas.[4]

The Employment Department has published "A Manager's Guide to Teleworking", to provide practical advice to managers who are considering the introduction of telework.[5]

---

[4] *Radio Fixed Access – Increasing the Choice, A Consultative Document* [DTI] (May 1995)

[5] *A Manager's Guide to Teleworking* [ED] (1995)

Government in a shrinking world

6.40 Much of the analysis in this Chapter has dealt with the economics of change. However, the forces for change are not confined to the world of economics. They are enmeshed with the world of ideas and of political institutions. However compelling the pressure for economic development, the pace of change depends on the community's willingness to accept it. The openness of nations to new ideas and the flexibility of their political institutions has a significant influence on whether they ride on the wave of economic development or are submerged by it.

6.41 Perhaps the greatest test of these institutions is their ability to take decisions in an international context. Gradually during the course of this century we have addressed more issues in partnership with other nations. Over the next decade pressures will build for international cooperation in new areas. For example, the globalisation of markets in services will generate demand for new international standards.

6.42 The collapse of communism in Eastern Europe, the former Soviet Union and elsewhere has meant that principles long accepted in the West have wider currency. The scope for international collaboration is enhanced. But we have to collaborate with more countries with different interests. At the same time, the speed with which ideas secure a place in international debate has accelerated as communications have improved.

6.43 Against this background, the challenges facing governments include how to:

- reconcile the need for decisions and progress on global issues whilst representing the interests of constituents;

- facilitate the involvement of citizens in international debate without undermining effective international negotiation and decision taking; and

- negotiate, implement and enforce international decisions without creating undue international bureaucracy.

6.44 These challenges are surmountable. Success depends on our ability to exploit the democratic strengths of our institutions, while reconciling change with legitimate special interests. At the same time we must foster recognition within those institutions of the need to adapt, within the limits set by their democratic principles. The retention of control over the implementation of new policies by institutions close to those being regulated will reinforce public acceptance of the need for change.

7.1 To compete internationally the UK needs a highly motivated and well qualified workforce. We need young people who are well prepared for work, employers who see the importance of developing the skills of their employees, and people in the labour force who take their development seriously. The Government's role is to help create the necessary conditions for this to happen.

7.2 The 1994 Competitiveness White Paper asked people to join in creating a world class workforce. Employers and providers widely welcomed the programme of action it set out. This chapter reports what we have achieved and what more needs to be done.

The international picture

7.3 The UK must set a world pace in education and training. To do that, we need to know where we stand against the best of our international competitors.

7.4 It is a mixed picture.

- At first degree level, we are an EU leader in graduate output (Chart 7.1).

- The participation rates of our young people in education and training at 16 are now – at long last – challenging those of our main competitors, although we do less well at 17 (Chart 7.2).

- The most recent comparisons of mathematical and scientific attainment of pupils aged 9 and 13 suggest that, overall, pupils in England achieve at around the average of the Western European and North American countries which participated in the survey (Chart 7.3).

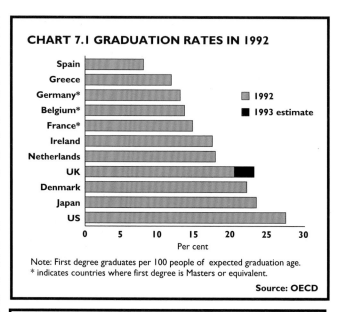

CHART 7.1 GRADUATION RATES IN 1992

Note: First degree graduates per 100 people of expected graduation age.
* indicates countries where first degree is Masters or equivalent.

Source: OECD

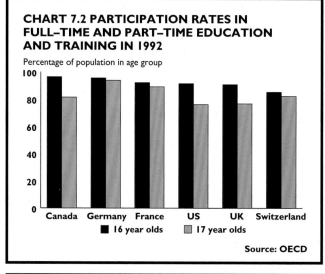

CHART 7.2 PARTICIPATION RATES IN FULL–TIME AND PART–TIME EDUCATION AND TRAINING IN 1992

Percentage of population in age group

■ 16 year olds   ■ 17 year olds

Source: OECD

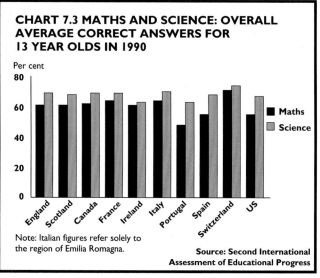

CHART 7.3 MATHS AND SCIENCE: OVERALL AVERAGE CORRECT ANSWERS FOR 13 YEAR OLDS IN 1990

Per cent

■ Maths   ■ Science

Note: Italian figures refer solely to the region of Emilia Romagna.

Source: Second International Assessment of Educational Progress

♦ Our major policy developments, the Investors In People standard, NVQs and SVQs, GNVQs and GSVQs and Modern Apprenticeships, attract worldwide interest.

7.5 The Government will continue to monitor progress against our competitors by:

♦ participating in the Third International Mathematics and Science Study, currently nearing completion, which will compare standards achieved by 9 and 13 year olds in England and Scotland with those of our main international competitors;

♦ seeking agreement through the OECD on further cost-effective international comparisons of pupils' achievements;

♦ participating in the International Adult Literacy Survey; and

♦ examining other ways to benchmark ourselves against our strongest competitors.

The challenge ahead: the National Targets

7.6 We know already that we need to aim higher. Since their launch, the National Targets for Education and Training, endorsed by the Government, have provided a demanding set of goals. Employers, schools and colleges, Training and Enterprise Councils (TECs), individual learners and the Government all have a role to play in working towards them. We have made real progress, (Charts 7.4 and 7.5), but the rest of the world is not standing still.

7.7 In the 1994 White Paper, the Government asked the National Advisory Council for Education and Training Targets (NACETT) to consider the case for raising the Targets to match our competitors' achievements. After wide-ranging consultation and review, NACETT has recommended an updated set of Targets for the year 2000. The Government endorses the new Targets as the focus for its education and training efforts and hopes that employers, teachers and the wider community will also do so. New targets have already been set in Scotland.

THE NEW NATIONAL TARGETS FOR EDUCATION AND TRAINING

"DEVELOPING SKILLS FOR A SUCCESSFUL FUTURE"

Aim

To improve the UK's international competitiveness by raising standards and attainment levels in education and training to world class levels through ensuring that:

1. *all employers invest in employee development to achieve business success*

2. *all individuals have access to education and training opportunities, leading to recognised qualifications, which meet their needs and aspirations*

3. *all education and training develops self-reliance, flexibility and breadth, in particular through fostering competence in core skills*

Targets for 2000

Foundation Learning

1. *By age 19, 85 per cent of young people to achieve five GCSEs at grade C or above, an Intermediate GNVQ or an NVQ level 2*

2. *75 per cent of young people to achieve level 2 competence in communication, numeracy and IT by age 19; and 35 per cent to achieve level 3 competence in these core skills by age 21*

3. *By age 21, 60 per cent of young people to achieve two GCE A levels, an Advanced GNVQ or NVQ level 3*

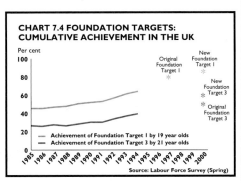

CHART 7.4 FOUNDATION TARGETS: CUMULATIVE ACHIEVEMENT IN THE UK

— Achievement of Foundation Target 1 by 19 year olds
— Achievement of Foundation Target 3 by 21 year olds

Source: Labour Force Survey (Spring)

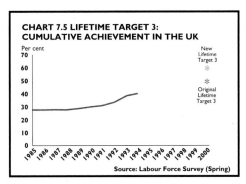

CHART 7.5 LIFETIME TARGET 3: CUMULATIVE ACHIEVEMENT IN THE UK

Source: Labour Force Survey (Spring)

Lifetime Learning

1. *60 per cent of the workforce to be qualified to NVQ level 3, Advanced GNVQ or two GCE A level standard*

2. *30 per cent of the workforce to have a vocational, professional, management or academic qualification at NVQ level 4 or above*

3. *70 per cent of all organisations employing 200 or more employees, and 35 per cent of those employing 50 or more, to be recognised as Investors in People*

7.8 The new Targets are more precise and more challenging than their predecessors and for the first time cover higher level skills and the core skills (communication, numeracy and IT) which employers have consistently identified as the foundation for effective transition to work. These core skills will be developed throughout life. Through learning methods which encourage initiative and autonomy young people can develop their core skills within the National Curriculum and through the qualifications available to them at 16 and beyond. They can improve their core skills and make them more transferable through a range of opportunities to apply these skills in work related settings, for example through managed work experience and vocational options such as GNVQs and Modern Apprenticeships.

7.9 The Government will work closely with NACETT to:

◆ promote the new Targets;

◆ encourage TECs with their local partners to set local targets underpinning the national ones;

◆ work with those Industry Training Organisations (ITOs) who are developing sector specific targets;

◆ encourage schools, colleges and universities to set their own targets underpinning the national ones; and

◆ ensure that its education and training strategy effectively supports the National Targets.

Today's workforce: improving the stock

THE GOVERNMENT'S TRAINING STRATEGY

The Government's training strategy aims to increase individual and national prosperity by stimulating enterprise and developing excellence in skills. This will be achieved by:

◆ *employers, the self-employed, and individual people in the workforce investing effectively in the skills needed for business creation and growth, and for individual success*

◆ *people who are out of work or at a disadvantage in the labour market acquiring and maintaining relevant skills and obtaining appropriate support to enable them to compete better for employment or self employment and to contribute more effectively to the economy*

◆ *encouraging and enabling young people to gain the skills and enterprising attitudes needed for entry to the workforce and to prepare them to realise their full potential throughout working life, and in particular to progress to NVQ3 and beyond, if they are able*

◆ *making the market for vocational education and training work better so that it responds to the changing needs of employers and individuals quickly and cost effectively*

7.10 We are witnessing the beginning of the culture change we need.

- TECs and Investors in People UK have done much to improve employers' attitudes to training and make the Investors standard a key tool for managing people to achieve business goals. Over 15,200 organisations covering 19 per cent of the employed workforce are now committed to the Investors standard (Charts 7.6 and 7.7).

- Between 1987 and 1994, the number of economically active people of working age with a qualification rose by over 3.9 million to 81 per cent; and those with a qualification at, or above, GCE A level or equivalent rose by 2.7 million to 47 per cent. Over 750,000 people have now gained an NVQ.

- Within the growing total of vocational learning, the proportion funded by individuals has risen from nine per cent in 1986 to 17 per cent in 1993.

7.11 These improvements, though welcome, are from a comparatively modest base. Too few individuals recognise the need to invest their time and money in developing occupational skills. In an economy where firms are increasingly competing on the basis of the skills of their workforce, individuals who do not keep up to date will lose employability and opportunities for advancement. The Government's analysis suggests that employers will need to increase their training performance further if the new lifetime learning Targets are to be achieved.

7.12 Small firms face particular problems in tackling their skill needs. Their size and the immediate pressures of running a business can make training appear disproportionately costly. Smaller companies lead the way in job creation but they often overlook training as a key investment in longer term growth. The Government

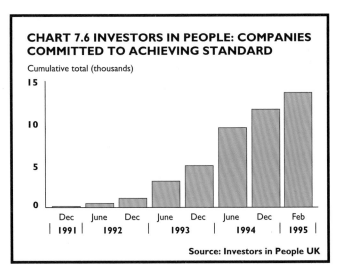

CHART 7.6 INVESTORS IN PEOPLE: COMPANIES COMMITTED TO ACHIEVING STANDARD

Cumulative total (thousands)

Source: Investors in People UK

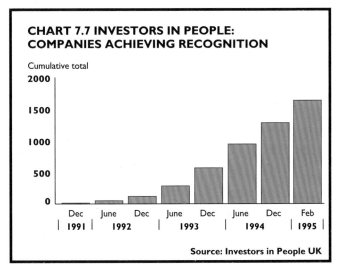

CHART 7.7 INVESTORS IN PEOPLE: COMPANIES ACHIEVING RECOGNITION

Cumulative total

Source: Investors in People UK

pays particular attention to the needs of small firms in all its training initiatives, and recognises the importance of Business Links integrating training advice with the other services they offer.

7.13 Skills for Small Businesses, launched by all TECs in April 1995, enables firms to develop and implement training plans which meet business needs and help their workforces to gain NVQs. This builds on Small Firms Training Loans, launched in June 1994. The Government wishes to help more small companies see training as an important investment in their future and to help publicise ways of overcoming the obstacles they face. Much can be achieved by groups of companies working together to share the costs of training.

7.14 The Government will therefore hold a Small Firms Training Challenge with a prize fund of £5m. The idea of a challenge has been used in other areas to bring forward innovative ideas which can show best practice in action. This Challenge, to be run jointly by the Employment Department and the Department of Trade and Industry, will allow the best ideas for coordinated training initiatives put forward by groups of ten or more companies to be put into practice. Over a thousand companies will benefit directly from this fund by taking part in projects, and the ideas developed can be copied by many more. A prospectus giving further details and inviting bids will be available later this year.

7.15 The challenge approach also has a role to play in taking forward the National Targets. The Government will work with NACETT to support a complementary Sector Targets Challenge for ITOs and other representative bodies later this year. This will provide support to pilot the development of sector targets within the framework of the updated National Targets.

7.16 The Government's objective is that the UK should develop the best qualified workforce in Europe. The Government will examine the UK's performance at the level of basic qualifications for employment and compare it with those of our leading competitors. The Government will similarly work with ITOs and NACETT to benchmark companies' training effort and output for the workforce in work. That will enable us to see clearly where the comparisons suggest that UK may be lagging, in order to help the Government to evaluate the effectiveness of its programmes and encourage companies to focus their efforts. The Government will report the outcome of this work in its next national survey of competitiveness.

Lifetime learning

7.17 The Government supports a wide range of measures to encourage and help people take responsibility for improving their skills. These include:

- working with others to raise awareness, for example through the "Free Your Potential" qualifications campaign and support for the proposed 1996 European Year of Lifelong Learning;

- sponsoring work to agree a national standard for basic skills; extending the remit of the Basic Skills Agency; and encouraging employers to tackle shortfalls in employees' basic skills. The Basic Skills Agency has produced a new work programme to reflect its new remit. The Government will participate in the International Adult Literacy Survey, which is to be managed by the OPCS;

- funding work to strengthen NVQs and SVQs. A survey of the top 100 NVQs and SVQs will be carried out this year and all NVQs and SVQs will be reviewed by March 1998. The National Council for Vocational Qualifications (NCVQ) will consider how the knowledge and understanding included in NVQs and SVQs might be separately certified in a form of NVQ Part One, and the desirability of doing this. Help is being given to the open learning industry to make learning materials relevant to NVQs and user friendly;

- encouraging the provision of vocational information, advice and guidance services to adults, and enabling TECs in England to spend up to £20 million (subject to their matching contributions) on these services over two years from April 1995. Similar action is in hand in Wales;

- helping adults with the costs of learning. People buying their own training leading to NVQs and SVQs already get tax relief. From September 1995, the Government will pilot a scheme in one region to allow borrowers who have completed training funded by a Career Development Loan (CDL) to delay the start of their repayments by up to 18 months in certain circumstances. The Government will also seek ways of increasing the use of CDLs in further and higher education for students not eligible for mandatory awards;

- offering support to around 30 TECs and up to five ITOs to develop and implement local and sectoral strategies for lifetime learning;

- training unemployed people through Training for Work (TfW) and maintaining at 1994-95 levels the number of places for people with disabilities, those needing literacy or numeracy training, those for whom English is a second language, and those under 25 unemployed for over two years; and

- maintaining the number of unemployed people allowed to study part time while on benefit, provided that they remain available for work and continue to seek it actively.

7.18 However, the Government recognises that further impetus is needed, particularly to encourage individuals. It therefore intends to publish a consultation document on individual responsibility for lifelong vocational learning, seeking views on a wide range of issues.

Employer commitment to training

7.19 The volume of employer training held up well during the recession and has continued to do so (Chart 7.8). The Labour Force Survey found that over 15 per cent of employees had received training during the four weeks prior to the survey in both 1990 and 1994.

7.20 TECs and Local Enterprise Companies (LECs) are helping employers to diagnose training needs and invest to meet them. Over 1,000 local business and community leaders are directors of TECs. They are having a considerable impact. In 1993-94, there was a near 50 per cent improvement over the previous year in the numbers ending TfW courses with a job or qualification. TfW and Youth Training (YT) unit costs for these outputs fell by 40 per cent and 17 per cent respectively. Surveys show that 85 per cent of employers using TEC services are satisfied. TECs have also led in forming Business Links. The TEC Licensing Framework announced in May 1994 emphasised the Government's confidence in them. It provides a stable business relationship for those that demonstrate high performance and capability. By April 1995, 22 TECs had been licensed.

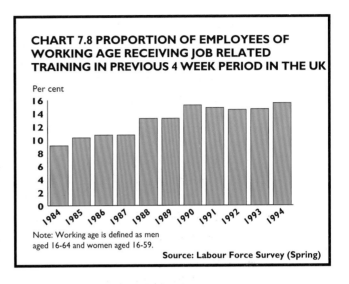

CHART 7.8 PROPORTION OF EMPLOYEES OF WORKING AGE RECEIVING JOB RELATED TRAINING IN PREVIOUS 4 WEEK PERIOD IN THE UK

Per cent

Note: Working age is defined as men aged 16-64 and women aged 16-59.

Source: Labour Force Survey (Spring)

PROFITS FROM TRAINING

Humberside TEC is developing a multimedia CD ROM package designed to show companies the effect of training on their profitability and to encourage further investment in training.

COMPANIES GAIN COMPETITIVE ADVANTAGE FROM INVESTING IN TRAINING.........

HP Bulmer plc installed a canning line and matched the investment in plant with investment in people. A comprehensive training programme was agreed which included training staff to NVQ standards. The company found NVQs to be extremely helpful in enabling their staff to adjust to modern technology. The line efficiency target of 70 per cent was achieved.

Birds Eye Walls, Gloucestershire, is recognised as an Investor in People. The company found that an NVQ programme brought widespread improvement enabling it to become world class. Three years ago exports were minimal: in 1994 they represented 23 per cent of sales.

> **.....OVER 30 PER CENT OF ORGANISATIONS WINNING NATIONAL TRAINING AWARDS IN 1994 WERE RECOGNISED AS INVESTORS IN PEOPLE. THEY TOO HAVE REAPED SIGNIFICANT BENEFITS.**
>
> *The three year training plan of C-Mac Microcircuits raised the sights of this manufacturing company and its employees. Morale improved and absenteeism fell from 6.4 per cent to 3 per cent. The commitment to staff training and development allowed the company to fill 36 out of 46 jobs by internal promotion. A loss of £240,000 in 1989 turned into a profit of £610,000 in 1993.*
>
> *An employee-led training programme in the Peugeot dealership Appleyard of Chesterfield produced a learning culture and resulted in a widespread increase in multi-skilling. This flexibility led to the firm winning Peugeot's first "Xpress Fit" centre in Europe. Overall 1993 sales were a third above targets.*
>
> *By training arable workers in building skills JSR Farms Ltd solved the problem of seasonal labour fluctuations while investing cost effectively in new farm units. Building projects have saved the company over £50,000 against the contractor's quoted price.*

7.21 ITOs are already playing a major role at sectoral level, for example: developing Modern and accelerated Modern Apprenticeships in partnership with TECs, helping to implement NVQs and SVQs and promoting Investors in People. Some have already started to develop sectoral targets to help underpin the National Targets.

The workforce of tomorrow: improving the flow

7.22 Much has changed in education and training. Fifteen years ago, most young people abandoned formal learning at the first opportunity, many with no qualifications. Only 14 per cent gained two GCE A levels. Only one in eight gained a place in higher education. In 1994:

- eighty nine per cent of 16 year olds and 78 per cent of 17 year olds in the UK participated in full-time education and training (Chart 7.9);

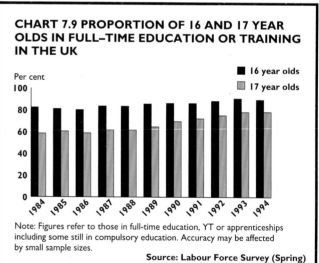

CHART 7.9 PROPORTION OF 16 AND 17 YEAR OLDS IN FULL–TIME EDUCATION OR TRAINING IN THE UK

Per cent

■ 16 year olds
▨ 17 year olds

Note: Figures refer to those in full-time education, YT or apprenticeships including some still in compulsory education. Accuracy may be affected by small sample sizes.

Source: Labour Force Survey (Spring)

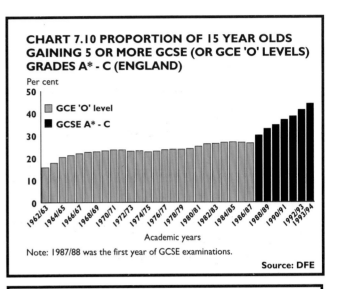

CHART 7.10 PROPORTION OF 15 YEAR OLDS GAINING 5 OR MORE GCSE (OR GCE 'O' LEVELS) GRADES A* - C (ENGLAND)

Per cent

GCE 'O' level
GCSE A* - C

Academic years

Note: 1987/88 was the first year of GCSE examinations.

Source: DFE

◆ a record 43 per cent of young people in England gained five or more good GCSEs (Chart 7.10);

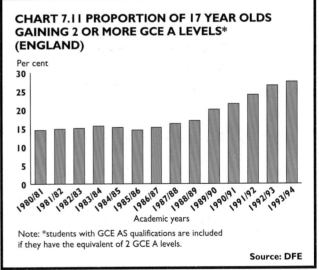

CHART 7.11 PROPORTION OF 17 YEAR OLDS GAINING 2 OR MORE GCE A LEVELS* (ENGLAND)

Per cent

Academic years

Note: *students with GCE AS qualifications are included if they have the equivalent of 2 GCE A levels.

Source: DFE

◆ twenty eight per cent gained two or more GCE A levels (Chart 7.11);

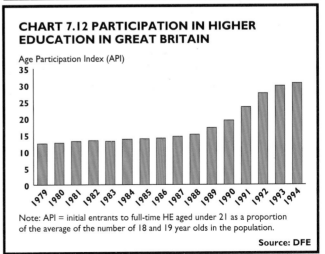

CHART 7.12 PARTICIPATION IN HIGHER EDUCATION IN GREAT BRITAIN

Age Participation Index (API)

Note: API = initial entrants to full-time HE aged under 21 as a proportion of the average of the number of 18 and 19 year olds in the population.

Source: DFE

◆ almost one in three young people went on to higher education (Chart 7.12); and

◆ seventy eight per cent of young people completing YT went into jobs, further education or training. Seventy one per cent gained a qualification or credit towards one.

7.23 There is much to celebrate here, but there is more to do if the the new Targets are to be met. We must increase choice and raise standards to:

♦ eliminate weaknesses and low expectations wherever they occur;

♦ increase opportunities for young people to undertake high quality training, particularly at the key NVQ and SVQ level 3, as technicians, craft workers, or junior managers; and

♦ make provision more responsive to the needs of young people, parents and employers.

Increasing choice

7.24 The Government is committed to providing, over time, a pre-school place for all four year olds whose parents wish to take it up. The new programme, details of which will be announced soon, will provide good quality new places, respond to parental wishes and be cost-effective.

7.25 The extended specialist schools programme will support schools wishing to develop their strengths as Technology Colleges or Language Colleges. This will further enhance the choice of education on offer by local authority schools, grant-maintained schools, City Technology Colleges and independent schools through the Assisted Places Scheme.

7.26 The new Part One GNVQ, to be piloted from September, offers an attractive and practical option for 14 year olds of all abilities. The pilot will be evaluated to ensure that these qualifications are of high quality, manageable for teachers and rewarding for pupils, and provide clear routes to further education and work based training opportunities beyond sixteen.

7.27 School sixth forms, the thriving new Further Education sector, youth training and industry's introduction of Modern Apprenticeships for 16-19 year olds provide choice beyond 16. Young people can now study and combine a wide range of different qualifications. GCE A level and AS examinations remain a valued and substantial element in that choice whilst Advanced GNVQs and NVQs at level 3 now provide a vocational route to high quality qualifications. This is very good progress. We must, however, ensure that we can build on these firm foundations so as to encourage relevance, progression, coherence and breadth in education and training post sixteen. We must ensure that both general and vocational

> **CASE STUDY ON MODERN APPRENTICESHIPS**
>
> *ICL has been an active participant in the prototype Modern Apprenticeships in Information Technology. Its Local Government (UK) Division took on its first nine apprentices in 1994 to work on development and support for software applications in local authorities. ICL sees this as a very worthwhile opportunity to bring young school leavers into the company. It reports that the apprentices are already showing promise and starting to make their mark.*

CASE STUDIES ON GNVQs

*After ill-health had plagued her secondary school education, **Michelle Brennan** entered post-16 education with trepidation. She enrolled at Kingshurst CTC on an advanced Business GNVQ course, and soon found her confidence growing: "I enjoyed two excellent work experience placements and participated in many new activities. I hope that other potential students learn from my experience." A job with British Gas followed Michelle's GNVQ, and she now intends to study for a business degree at university.*

*Instead of staying on to retake her GCSEs, **Leleith Spence** opted for an Intermediate GNVQ in Business at Clarendon College. The GNVQ showed her the extent of her potential, and she has now progressed to the Advanced GNVQ. The breadth of the GNVQ has also led Leleith to a keen interest in law, and when she has completed her advanced level course she plans to study law at university.*

qualifications are delivered cost effectively and take steps to reduce wastage without compromising standards.

7.28 Decisions on how the qualifications framework might evolve in the longer term have to be based on hard evidence. To help inform their deliberations, the Secretaries of State for Education, Employment and for Wales have commissioned Sir Ron Dearing to undertake a review of 16-19 qualifications. The review was announced on 10 April 1995 and will take about one year, with an initial report in July this year. Sir Ron will be working very closely with Michael Heron, the Chairman of the NCVQ, and will be talking to organisations representing the education and training world, including higher education, and to employers. He will also be looking at how other countries prepare their young people for work and higher education.

7.29 Over 160,000 students started GNVQs in 1994. The UK is well on course to meet the target of 25 per cent of 16 year olds starting GNVQs in 1996. The first students to gain Advanced GNVQs are settling into their university courses.

7.30 By April 1995, every TEC in England had introduced Youth Credits for access to YT and Modern Apprenticeships. With Government funding, over 50 industry sectors are developing Modern Apprenticeship frameworks covering over 150 occupations with NVQ3 qualifications. Around 1,400 young people are already on prototype Modern Apprenticeships. Modern and accelerated Modern Apprenticeships will start throughout England in the Autumn of 1995. The Government will fund a small number of TECs to investigate how training opportunities can be designed and delivered to best meet the needs of all young people, including those who do not currently enter work, further education or training.

Modern Apprentice working in a television studio.

7.31 More choice inevitably means a greater need for timely and objective careers education and guidance. The piloted training for new Careers Advisers and careers teachers has been widely welcomed. Current work is aimed at ensuring that the Careers Service, schools and colleges forge an effective partnership. Arrangements are now in place to deliver by 1997-98 the enhanced levels of guidance at ages 13, 15, and 17 announced in the 1994 White Paper. Young people aged 13 are already benefitting from improvements to careers advice.

♦ Rapid progress is being made in improving the management of the Careers Service. Early evaluation indicates significant benefits from introducing modern business practice. Forty three Careers Services in England already operate under contract and all will do so by April 1996.

♦ The Government has published "Better Choices", setting out the underlying principles for good careers education and guidance. It will publish a follow-up document with examples of good practice this summer, together with new curriculum guidelines for careers education in schools.

♦ The Government will encourage higher education institutions to make available information about the employment of new graduates, by subject, including if practicable details of average starting salaries. This will help potential higher education students to make better informed decisions.

7.32 In the White Paper the Government also announced that it would consult on the practical implications of learning credits for all 16-19 year olds. Learning credits would provide young people with the means to purchase education and training courses direct from providers. They would help to motivate young people to acquire marketable skills and qualifications. They would encourage education and training providers to be more responsive.

7.33 The Government then employed consultants (Coopers and Lybrand) to prepare a feasibility study. It also organised a conference, with the CBI, to which many representative bodies were invited. The views expressed at the conference assisted the consultancy work, which is now complete. The Government remains attracted to the principle of learning credits. It has today published the consultants' report and would welcome views before deciding how best to develop the idea further.

7.34 The report also suggested some measures, not involving a fully fledged learning credits system, which might help the Government achieve its education and training policy objectives. These measures were intended, for example, to increase the price competition between providers and remove the structural rigidities that make it difficult for new providers to become established. They could be expected to improve decision taking by young people and to remove financial distortions which prevent fair competition between providers.

7.35 The Government has decided to implement many of these measures in England (the Secretaries of State for Scotland, Wales and Northern Ireland will consider what parallel measures are needed in those countries, having regard to the distinctive arrangements for the education and training of young people there).

7.36 To ensure that pupils and students are able to make better informed decisions, it will:

- legislate at an early opportunity (following consultation) to improve careers education and guidance in maintained schools and colleges, in particular by:

    - securing the provision of careers education in maintained schools;

    - making schools and colleges responsible for working with the careers services and providing facilities for them; and

    - ensuring that young people receive information on both work based and further education options;

- work with the School Curriculum and Assessment Authority to develop guidance on coaching, case studies and project work, to improve pupils' negotiating and decision making skills; and

- develop and publish data on achievement and career routes from schools, colleges and work based learning options, to provide pupils with more informed choices at age 16.

George Abbott Comprehensive School pupils in a chemistry lesson.

7.37 To improve the relevance to labour markets of provision for 16-19 year olds, it will:

- improve the links between the various bodies responsible for quality assurance (OFSTED, the Further Education Inspectorate and the Employment Department's Quality Assurance operation);

- require schools to demonstrate their awareness of the needs of labour markets and higher education through school development plans;

- strengthen the OFSTED Framework of Inspection to ensure that inspectors seek evidence that schools have provided good careers education and impartial guidance; and

- develop closer team working on careers education inspections, between the three inspectorates responsible, once the current round of OFSTED primary school inspections is largely complete.

7.38 To facilitate competition between providers to encourage them to be more responsive to the demands of young people it will:

- investigate whether there is a case for encouraging a more consistent approach to funding methodologies across the sectors (for example, Local Management of Schools schemes might incorporate some of the output-related funding criteria underpinning funding by TECs and the Further Education Funding Council) and to funding levels for similar qualifications in different sectors;

◆ legislate to remove the requirement that potential new further education providers must gain the sponsorship of an existing college before being able to receive FEFC funding;

◆ consider relaxing the detailed central government controls over the opening and closing of sixth forms;

◆ consider further the case for introducing capital charging for schools and further education sector colleges, to put them on the same financial basis; and

◆ legislate to remove borrowing restrictions on grant maintained schools, thus placing them on the same basis as further education sector colleges.

Higher achievement and higher standards.

7.39 Young people, parents and employers are entitled to expect that education and training should not fail them. Quality assurance must be systematic and rigorous.

◆ The most recent report from Her Majesty's Chief Inspector of Schools shows that there are many successful schools, but that some schools underachieve and underestimate the potential of their pupils.

◆ The first Chief Inspector's report on behalf of the Further Education Funding Council for England (FEFC) found that over 90 per cent of provision inspected achieved three or better on a five point scale. But there is more to do, for example, in reducing student drop-out. The FEFC will address this.

◆ The Higher Education Funding Council for England (HEFCE) has published 425 quality assessments of universities and colleges, judging 72 per cent satisfactory, 27 per cent excellent and only 1 per cent unsatisfactory.

◆ The first round of quality audits of the systems that TECs use to manage providers of YT indicate that they are effective and have driven up standards.

7.40 Qualification standards must be maintained. In addition to strengthening NVQs and SVQs:

◆ the Government has agreed steps to reinforce the consistency of GCSE grading and further refined the mandatory Code of Practice for GCSE;

◆ the new Code of Practice for GCE A level and AS examinations is well on the way to full implementation; and

◆ the Government's six-point action plan to enhance rigour and consistency in GNVQs and provide support and guidance for teachers is under way. An additional £29 million was announced in the 1994 Budget for further work over the three years 1995-96 to 1998-99. There will be a further £14 million to support vocational education in schools in 1995-96 with particular emphasis on training for teachers.

7.41 Sir Ron Dearing in undertaking his review of the 16-19 qualifications framework, will, first and foremost, have regard to the Government's key priorities of ensuring that the rigour and standards of GCE A levels are maintained and the need for the current programmes of development and improvement of GNVQs and NVQs to be vigorously pursued.

7.42 The streamlined National Curriculum emphasises high standards, particularly in English and mathematics, while giving greater discretion to schools. The national assessment and testing arrangements will show how pupils measure up to those standards. In 1994:

- roughly three-quarters of seven year olds and two thirds of 14 year olds reached or surpassed the standards set in English, mathematics and science; and

- the proportion of girls passing science and maths at GCSE had risen to the same level as for boys.

7.43 However, a core of young people still leave with no qualifications and a track record of disruption and truancy. The Government is putting forward a comprehensive programme to identify and promote a range of measures to enhance the effectiveness of schools. Several failing schools are to close. In others, standards are noticeably improving.

CASE STUDY ON IMPACT OF THE POLICY ON FAILING SCHOOLS

Brookside Special School in Derbyshire was designated a failing school in November 1993. A plan to improve it was introduced by Derbyshire LEA. The head teacher was replaced and the school's Governing Body restructured to help improve decision-making. Uncertainty over the school's long term role was resolved, raising morale and creating a sense of purpose amongst staff. In March 1995 HMI inspected the school: its report confirmed significant improvement and recommended that the school no longer required special measures.

IMPACT OF PERFORMANCE TABLES

Spurred on by low GCSE results in the 1992 tables, the Nicholas School in Essex developed strategies for improvement, including mentoring for GCSE students and supervised after school study sessions. The proportion of pupils achieving five or more GCSEs at Grade A*-C increased from 4 per cent in 1993 to 18 per cent in 1994.

Rhyn Park School in Shropshire has also shown a significant all-round improvement. Strategies to support achievements have included improving attendance, raising literacy and recognising successes at all levels, supported by business-sponsored awards. Staying-on rates have improved, and pupils achieving five or more GCSEs at grade A*-C have risen from 32 per cent to 59 per cent over the last three years.

7.44 The school and college performance tables published in November 1994 contain more information than ever before. They are a continuing challenge to identify good practice and develop strategies for raising achievement. The Government attaches importance to the development of measures of the progress pupils and students make over time – "value added". DFE has recently published a briefing paper on "value added" in education[1].

---

[1]*Value Added in Education – A briefing paper from DFE* [Department for Education] (1995)

7.45 Twenty per cent of young people are likely to have special needs at some time during their school years. The 1994 Code of Practice on the identification and assessment of special educational needs, designed to ensure that schools match provision to the needs of children, has been welcomed. The Government is supporting implementation with targeted funding. In further and higher education and training the Government is committed to addressing the needs of students with learning difficulties and disabilities. The Funding Councils, local education authorities, TECs and learning institutions have complementary parts to play.

7.46 Effective teaching and management are crucial in modern learning institutions. Three hundred and twenty six schools, colleges and training providers are now recognised Investors in People with a further 1,954 commitments. In England the Government:

- established the Teacher Training Agency in September 1994 to raise standards of teaching and improve quality and efficiency of all routes into teaching;

- introduced the HEADLAMP scheme this year to help head teachers develop their leadership and management skills;

- established the Further Education Development Agency to support continuing improvement in the managerial and teaching skills of further education staff; and

- welcomed the HEFCE's £3 million pilot to transfer best practice in teaching from university departments rated as excellent.

7.47 The Government has increased the supply of highly qualified people to meet the country's needs. Graduate output this year is set to reach some 200,000, double the level in 1979. Around a third qualify in science, engineering and medicine. Our universities and colleges also produce some 80,000 holders of vocational diplomas and a similar number of post-graduates each year. Recent estimates suggest that just over half of today's young people will take up a place in higher education at some stage in their life. As already announced, the Government is reviewing higher education.

Swansea students studying for BEng in materials engineering.

7.48 Respected worldwide, the UK education system is also a significant export earner. Universities attracted 116,000 EU and other overseas students in 1994, making the UK the fourth most popular destination in the world for students studying abroad. They also generated £54 million from overseas research contracts outside the EU in 1993, on top of £76 million from EU sources.

ENHANCING EDUCATION AND TRAINING THROUGH TECHNOLOGY

IT now contributes to the delivery of all National Curriculum subjects as well as being a core competence in its own right. IT is included in the new National Target for core skills.

Primary schools in Wales can opt into a scheme to provide them with portable computers or multimedia suites.

The industry-led "Schools On Line" initiative connecting about 50 schools to the Internet was launched with Government support in March 1995. The pilot will enable schools to gain experience using networks and assess the educational benefits.

Members of the Cable Communication Association now plan to connect any school passed by cable to their network free of charge.

For many years BT has been working on distance learning applications in collaboration with schools and HE in the UK. Four thousand schools use BT's on line database service, Campus 2000, which will be enhanced later this year and will provide access to the Internet.

SuperJANET offers the higher education and research communities a leading edge broadband information highway, facilitating distance learning, collaborative research and remote access to special expertise and information. It is currently one of the largest high perfomance networks in the world.

The Government issued a consultation paper[2] in April 1995 seeking views from industry and education on the value of the Information Superhighway in education and inviting innovative projects to explore educational potential.

The Government is monitoring the Superhighway's potential to deliver and disseminate information about vocational education and training opportunities.

From September 1995 Modern and Accelerated Modern Apprenticeships will be publicised on the Internet.

Developments in multimedia and information highways will improve access to training and enable people to control the time and pace at which they learn.

Education and business

7.49 Schools and colleges must work closely with employers to improve standards and ensure that young people are prepared effectively for the world of work. The Government is taking action to raise the level and further improve the quality of the links between business and education.

◆ A new framework of objectives for education business links is in place.

◆ Guides for schools and employers on organising work experience for pupils, and for employers on effective school-business links were published in 1995. Funding is available to allow all pupils in their last year of compulsory education to have at least a week's work experience.

[2]*Superhighways for Education* [HMSO] (1995)

CASE STUDIES ON CO-OPERATION BETWEEN BUSINESS AND SCHOOLS

MINI-PACK SAMPLE SOLUTIONS AND THE TOYNBEE SCHOOL, CHANDLERS FORD, SOUTHAMPTON

Following a placement, a technology teacher from the school supported the company in a "design and make" activity during the school enterprise week. After visits to the company and briefing by its staff, Year 9 pupils formed companies to market a product using blister packs. They used market analysis to identify suitable products in the UK and France. Foreign language students from the local Sixth Form College acted as consultants. The company commented very favourably on the quality of the work.

TYLMANS OF LEEK AND BIDDULPH MOOR SCHOOL, STAFFORDSHIRE

Twenty Year 4 pupils worked with Tylmans of Leek, a two-man company making furniture to order. The pupils designed children's bedroom furniture as part of a technology project, and gained a new perspective on their English, mathematics and science work. The project generated new ideas which were used by the company.

◆ Last year over 30,000 teachers went on placement with employers. Over 180,000 young people, 10,000 employers and 800 schools are participating in compacts which offer pupils employment-related incentives such as training, in return for achieving defined standards. At the same time the lessons of the Technical and Vocational Education Initiative (TVEI) are being widely disseminated and action is in hand to embed its key themes in the work of all schools.

CASE STUDY ON EFFECTIVE COLLEGE/TEC CO-OPERATION

West London TEC has set up a coordinating group for all its local colleges to produce a joint Competitiveness Fund bid to support the skills needed to use the information superhighway. The bid is supported by British Telecom and other high technology companies in the area.

CASE STUDY ON CO-OPERATION BETWEEN INDUSTRY AND HE

Universities in the Manchester area have collaborated to form CONTACT (the Consortium for Advanced Continuing Education and Training). This partnership serves as a single access point for employers seeking continuing education and training from HE.

Manchester Metropolitan University's Retail and Marketing Department has teamed up with Building Adhesives Ltd, a leading UK tile adhesives manufacturer and supplier, to develop a marketing and trading strategy.

◆ The Government is working to ensure that the FEFC receives and acts on timely and useful guidance on labour market needs.

◆ Links between business and colleges are being strengthened by the involvement of TECs and the development of the FE Competitiveness Fund.

◆ Universities and HE colleges have done much to establish closer links with industry. Many universities and HE colleges now play a significant part in the economic development of their regions.

7.50 Throughout the UK there is a common understanding of the contribution which effective education and training can and must make to competitiveness. But structures and points of emphasis vary. Wales, Scotland and Northern Ireland each have particular work in hand.

WALES

The Secretary of State for Wales has published "People and Prosperity"[3] which sets out the action that will be taken to achieve the National Targets for Education and Training in ways which deliver the skills important to the Welsh economy.

Education in Wales will help people develop initiative, understand industry and recognise the opportunities offered by setting up in business. All schools and further and higher education institutions will in addition set themselves targets contributing towards the National Targets.

The Welsh Office is placing particular emphasis on developing the skills needed to support Wales' expanding manufacturing industries. Nearly 500 people began Modern Apprenticeships in manufacturing in Wales in 1994-95.

The recently published "A Bright Future"[4] complements this by defining the key challenges for improving standards of attainment in Welsh schools. It sets out a programme to help performance, in particular by:

◆ *encouraging higher expectations amongst schools, parents and pupils*

◆ *better leadership and support for teachers*

◆ *broadening the range of qualifications to include vocational qualifications for school age children*

◆ *ensuring that schools and employers work together to help pupils make progress*

◆ *spending money wisely*

"A Bright Future" consults on a target to raise current levels of GCSE results in Wales in the key disciplines of literacy, numeracy and scientific understanding. The final target will be published in the Autumn of 1995.

---

[3]*People and Prosperity: An agenda for action in Wales* [Welsh Office] (1995)
[4]*A Bright Future: Getting the best from every pupil at school in Wales* [Welsh Office] (1995)

SCOTLAND

Training for the future

Following responses to the consultation paper "Training for the Future"[5], the Secretary of State for Scotland has announced plans to spend £25.5 million over the next three years on:

- *the introduction of Modern Apprenticeships and Accelerated Modern Apprenticeships within Skillseekers youth credits*

- *new support for the training of key workers in firms of under 50 employees as trainers and assessors*

- *enhanced support for the promotion and delivery of Investors in People*

- *a new fund to pay for equipment necessary for training to meet skill needs*

- *support for a project in Fife which will pilot an extension of training credits by including full-time further education for 16-18 year olds on the Skillseekers programme.*

Scottish targets for competitiveness

Reflecting Scotland's own achievements and needs, the Advisory Scottish Council for Education and Training Targets launched new targets for Scotland last year. By the year 2000:

- *85 per cent of young people will attain SVQ level 2*

- *75 per cent of young people will attain SVQ level 3*

- *60 per cent of the workforce will attain at least SVQ level 3*

- *50 per cent of organisations will be recognised as, or committed to, Investors in People*

There are further targets for lifetime learning and for the development of self-reliance, flexibility and breadth of knowledge.

The targets now feature in the business plans of all LECs, who have brought together training and business development to meet local needs. Some have set higher targets.

Strengthening careers education and guidance for young people

By the summer of 1995, Scotland will have new careers service companies committed to deliver high quality careers information and guidance. The companies jointly set up by education authorities and LECs will help young people make the best education, training and job choices. Careers guidance and education are to benefit from an expected £8.5 million boost over the coming three years. Careers Offices will spend more time with S4-S6 pupils, and there will be extra training for careers officers and teachers of careers education. An important aim is that young people take informed responsibility for developing their career plans and see the value of education and training beyond school.

Continues...

[5]*Training for the Future* [Scottish Office] (1994)

SCOTLAND *continued*

Better teaching and learning

In schools, the reforms of the curriculum for 5-14 year olds are now well advanced. Plans are also well advanced to introduce major changes in post-16 education to enable more young people to gain qualifications, to ensure equality of esteem between vocational and academic qualifications and to give greater prominence to the attainment of core skills.

In January 1995, the first annual figures on attendance and absence were published. These complement information already published annually on examination results, school leaver destinations and school costs.

"Framework for Action"[6] was launched in March 1995 buiding on record levels of pupils work experience and encouraging further developments of the work-related curriculum.

HIGHER EDUCATION

Over 38 per cent of young Scots entered courses of higher education in 1993/94. The participation rate has more than doubled since 1979.

The partnership between Scottish HEIs and business is growing steadily. Income for research from industry as well as public sector customers and charities grew by around 40 per cent over the past three years.

Scottish higher education is an important wealth-generating industry. For example, the Esmee Fairbairn Research Centre of Heriot-Watt University won the Queen's Award for Export Achievement in 1994 for its innovative MBA programme by distance learning. Within four years of its launch in 1990 the programme was being followed in over 100 countries.

[6]*Education Industry Links in Scotland 5 - 18: A framework for action* [Scottish Consultative Council on the Curriculum] (1995)

NORTHERN IRELAND

The streamlined Northern Ireland Curriculum for 4-16 year olds, supported by the system of assessment, places renewed emphasis on raising standards, especially in basic subjects, whilst providing time for other subjects such as pilots of GNVQ Part One in 1995-96.

The Raising Schools Standards Initiative, focused on some 30 post-primary and 60 primary schools, will raise the educational attainments and qualification levels of pupils with the greatest educational need. It is designed to enhance both the motivation and employability of pupils.

The Northern Ireland Business Education Partnership aims to increase the involvement of pupils with work.

The University Marketing Initiative will support the universities in marketing services more widely to industry, and particularly to SMEs. It will further strengthen the universities' role in regenerating local economies.

A new Jobskills training programme was introduced in April 1995, for young people and adults. All participants will receive pre-entry careers advice and guidance from Adult Guidance centres. The new programme focuses on the delivery of NVQs and is intended to increase the level of successful training.

The Northern Ireland Modern Apprenticeship initiative will be introduced in 1995. A set of framework apprenticeship standards is being established in agreement with sectoral bodies.

The improvement of skills and the competitiveness of business is promoted through the Company and Sectoral Development Programmes, which encourage production of structural training plans and the measurement of improved business performance. Investors in People is increasingly recognised in Northern Ireland companies as the standard in human resource development.

EMPLOYMENT

8.1 The Government's employment and labour market policies aim to support economic growth by promoting a competitive, efficient and flexible labour market. Flexible labour markets benefit individuals, business and the whole economy. They are a key component of a competitive economy. Industry endorsed that message in its responses to the 1994 Competitiveness White Paper.

8.2 Unemployment is a major problem for industrialised countries, particularly in Europe. The inflexibility of European labour markets was identified as a principal cause of unemployment in the OECD's Jobs Study[1]. In the US, almost 40 million jobs were created between 1970 and 1992. In the EU, which had similar economic growth, employment increased by fewer than 6 million, with the great majority of those jobs in the public sector (Chart 8.1).

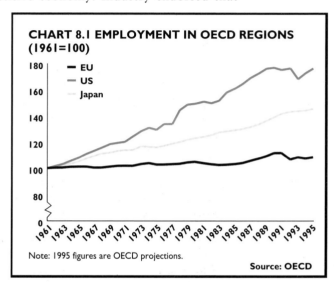

CHART 8.1 EMPLOYMENT IN OECD REGIONS (1961=100)

Note: 1995 figures are OECD projections.

Source: OECD

CHARACTERISTICS OF EFFICIENT AND FLEXIBLE LABOUR MARKETS

An efficient and flexible labour market is one in which:

♦ *employment and labour productivity are maximised by efficient matching of supply and demand. It is vital that higher real wages are earned by productivity improvements and do not act as a brake on investment or reduce job opportunities for unemployed people*

♦ *people have the opportunity to make a full economic contribution, free from discrimination and workplace demarcation*

♦ *unemployed people are helped and encouraged to compete effectively for jobs*

♦ *the benefits system provides people with incentives to work*

♦ *working practices and patterns are not unduly constrained by regulation*

♦ *individuals can acquire skills, without restrictive practices preventing their use*

♦ *wages reflect local labour market conditions and reward good performance*

♦ *enterprises benefit from good industrial relations and flexible pay arrangements*

♦ *employment protection legislation provides people with necessary protection, without discouraging recruitment*

8.3 EU Heads of Government at the Brussels and subsequent European Councils recognised that Member States needed to tackle inflexible labour markets and the

[1]*OECD Jobs Study [OECD] (1994)*

other structural problems which have led to persistently high levels of unemployment in recent years.

The UK Labour Market

Structure

8.4 Charts 8.2 to 8.4 describe the main features of the UK labour market.

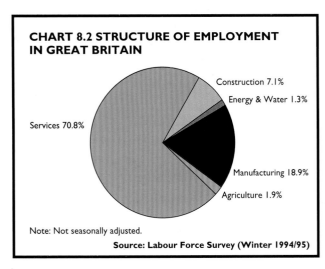

CHART 8.2 STRUCTURE OF EMPLOYMENT IN GREAT BRITAIN

Construction 7.1%

Energy & Water 1.3%

Services 70.8%

Manufacturing 18.9%

Agriculture 1.9%

Note: Not seasonally adjusted.

Source: Labour Force Survey (Winter 1994/95)

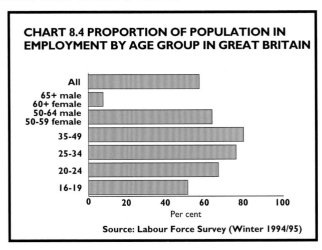

CHART 8.4 PROPORTION OF POPULATION IN EMPLOYMENT BY AGE GROUP IN GREAT BRITAIN

All

65+ male
60+ female
50-64 male
50-59 female

35-49

25-34

20-24

16-19

0　　20　　40　　60　　80　　100

Per cent

Source: Labour Force Survey (Winter 1994/95)

CHART 8.3 ADULT EMPLOYMENT AND UNEMPLOYMENT IN GREAT BRITAIN

Self employed
3.3m

Unemployed
2.4m

Employees
22.1m

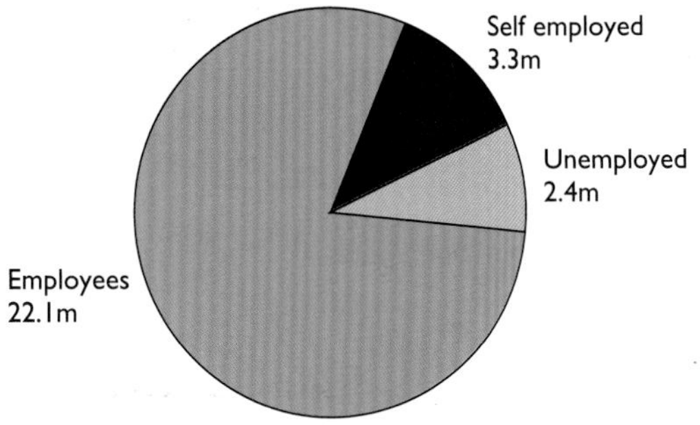

Note: "Employees" includes employees in employment (21.7m), those on government employment and training schemes (0.3m) and unpaid family workers (0.1m).

Source: Labour Force Survey (Winter 1994/95)

8.5 The labour market is dynamic. Each year there are about 7 million job changes. Most people who become unemployed leave unemployment quickly – two out of three within six months.

CHANGES IN THE STRUCTURE OF EMPLOYMENT

As a proportion of total employment, employment in manufacturing has fallen and employment in services has grown, as it has in other countries (Chart 8.5).

Employment in manufacturing peaked in 1966. In 1971, 36 per cent of employees worked in manufacturing. Now 20 per cent do so. As much as 30 per cent of this decline may have been due to contracting out (see Chapter 3).

Banking, finance and business services employed 1.3 million people in 1971. Now these services employ 2.8 million.

Over the same period, the number of employees in health-related services has risen by two-thirds, more than 600,000.

In the last economic cycle (1979-1990), UK self-employment rose by 1.5 million to 3.5 million. The number of businesses increased by 1.1 million, changing the balance between employment in small and large firms.

Continues...

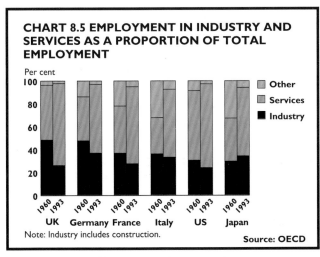

CHART 8.5 EMPLOYMENT IN INDUSTRY AND SERVICES AS A PROPORTION OF TOTAL EMPLOYMENT

Note: Industry includes construction.

Source: OECD

CHANGES IN THE STRUCTURE OF EMPLOYMENT *continued*

Part-time employment has been rising for many years. There were 6.7 million part-time jobs in December 1994, an increase of 1.9 million since March 1983.

There has been growth in the employment of women over many years. There are now 18 per cent more women in full-time employment than in 1984, and 17 per cent more women in part-time employment.

Recent performance

8.6 Since 1979, the Government has pursued a wide-ranging strategy to improve the operation of the labour market. That strategy continues and the latter part of this Chapter shows how the Government is pursuing further essential reforms. The UK labour market is already performing better.

Employment and unemployment

8.7 Employment began to grow, and unemployment to fall, at earlier stages in the current recovery than in previous economic cycles, suggesting that the labour market is now more responsive to changes in output.

- Employment grew by over 1.5 million in the last economic cycle, the best performance during an economic cycle since 1960. Growth in the private sector was as strong as in the public sector. Employment is high by comparison with other countries. The UK employment rate is one of the highest in the EU, and rose during the last economic cycle (Charts 8.6 and 8.7). Employment is also recovering well in the current cycle and rose by almost 300,000 in the year to the winter of 1994-1995.

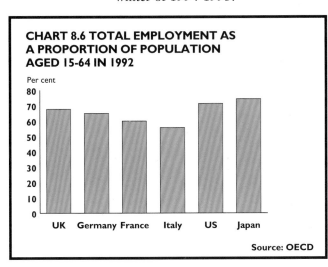

CHART 8.6 TOTAL EMPLOYMENT AS A PROPORTION OF POPULATION AGED 15-64 IN 1992

Source: OECD

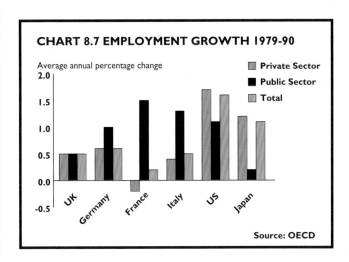

CHART 8.7 EMPLOYMENT GROWTH 1979-90

Source: OECD

- Claimant unemployment has fallen by over 600,000 since labour market recovery began, and UK unemployment now stands more than two percentage points below the EU average. For the first time since the 1960s, the most recent peak in unemployment was below the peak in the previous economic cycle. The most recent peak in long term unemployment was almost 290,000 below the peak in the previous cycle and long term unemployment remains substantially lower now than at a similar stage in the last cycle. Some other EU countries have continued to experience successively higher cyclical peaks in unemployment (Chart 8.8).

Industrial relations, wages and costs

8.8 The dramatic improvement in the UK's industrial relations continues.

- 1994 saw the lowest levels of industrial action in over 100 years of strike statistics. The UK strike rate has been well below the EU average in every year since 1986, and in recent years has been below that in the US (Chart 8.9).

- The loss of 0.26 million working days in 1994 is under 1 per cent of the 1979 figure and well below the 1980s average of 7.2 million days lost per year.

8.9 UK hourly labour costs for production workers in manufacturing have been below those in other G7 countries for many years. Our low non-wage labour costs are a major factor in this (Chart 8.10).

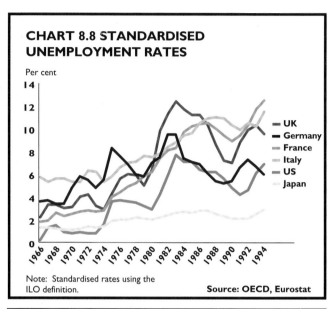

CHART 8.8 STANDARDISED UNEMPLOYMENT RATES

Per cent

Legend: UK, Germany, France, Italy, US, Japan

Note: Standardised rates using the ILO definition.

Source: OECD, Eurostat

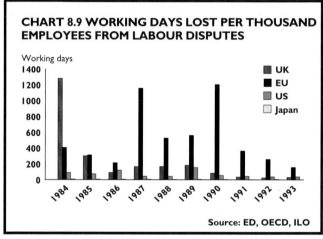

CHART 8.9 WORKING DAYS LOST PER THOUSAND EMPLOYEES FROM LABOUR DISPUTES

Working days

Legend: UK, EU, US, Japan

Source: ED, OECD, ILO

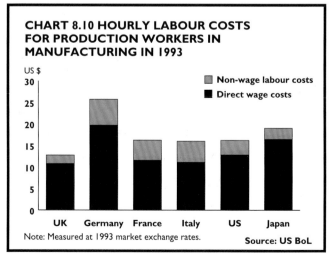

CHART 8.10 HOURLY LABOUR COSTS FOR PRODUCTION WORKERS IN MANUFACTURING IN 1993

US $

Legend: Non-wage labour costs, Direct wage costs

UK   Germany   France   Italy   US   Japan

Note: Measured at 1993 market exchange rates.

Source: US BoL

8.10 Fewer than half of all employees now have their pay determined by collective bargaining. Three-quarters of employers with more than 25 employees now use performance-related pay.

DEREGULATION: HEALTH AND SAFETY

Since the 1994 White Paper

♦ *A programme is in hand to reduce the rulebook by 40 per cent following a review*

♦ *Ninety-seven per cent of the recommendations of Lord Sainsbury's task force have been accepted (see Chapter 15)*

For the future

♦ *A major initiative to simplify guidance and reduce paperwork is planned*

♦ *Implementation of six key EU directives on health and safety – the "Six Pack" – is to be evaluated*

♦ *Legislative regimes for onshore and offshore pipelines will be rationalised*

♦ *A discussion document on health and safety for small firms and the self-employed will be published*

Flexibility

8.11 A range of micro-economic indicators suggests that the UK labour market has become more flexible since the end of the 1970s.

♦ The UK has fewer constraints on the freedom of employers and employees to agree working hours than almost any other EU country (Chart 8.11).

♦ A considerable and growing number of people have new kinds of flexible working patterns. Nearly 2 million employees work under an annual hours system. Many businesses use teleworking – 6 per cent now use it extensively. Nearly 250,000 employees share jobs.

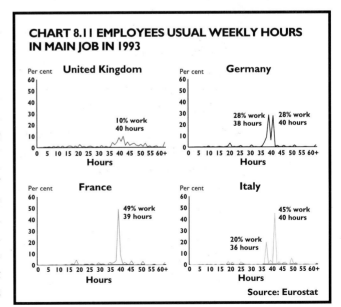

CHART 8.11 EMPLOYEES USUAL WEEKLY HOURS IN MAIN JOB IN 1993

Source: Eurostat

8.12 Manufacturing firms took steps during the 1980s to increase their ability to assign employees to a range of tasks and so cope more easily with variations in demand, mainly by removing barriers such as rigid job demarcations. The 1990 Workplace Industrial Relations Survey found that managers in more than two-thirds of workplaces felt there were no constraints on their ability to organise work.

8.13 Skill differentials widened in the 1980s, providing the incentives for individuals and employers to invest in education and training. Regional and industrial wages have also become more responsive to labour market conditions.

8.14 The 1994 White Paper noted the need for action on pensions to aid mobility of labour. The Pensions Bill, introduced in December 1994, includes measures to speed up the "transfer payments" made when people move their pension rights from one scheme to another, and to give early leavers greater certainty about the level of transfer payments they can expect.

8.15 Following deregulation in the housing market in the 1980s, a long period of decline in the private rented sector has been reversed. Over 2 million households in England now rent privately, an increase of nearly 350,000 in five years. The Government will continue to encourage investment in the private sector, promote the development of affordable rented homes and support schemes which make it easier for tenants in social housing to move.

Further improving the performance of the UK labour market

8.16 The Government will continue to pursue reforms to improve labour market performance further. Priorities are:

◆ an improved benefit system through the introduction of the Jobseeker's Allowance;

◆ stronger active labour market policies;

◆ better incentives to work;

◆ greater real wage flexibility;

◆ increased equality of opportunity for individuals; and

◆ improvement in the quality of the workforce (see Chapter 7).

An improved benefit system

8.17 The benefit system must offer strong encouragement to unemployed people to make efforts to find work. The Jobseekers Bill, introduced in December 1994, aims to do this and to help people get back to work.

JOBSEEKER'S ALLOWANCE: AIMS AND PRINCIPAL FEATURES

Aims

The introduction of JSA:

- *improves the operation of the labour market by helping people in their search for work, while ensuring that they understand and fulfil the conditions for receipt of benefit*

- *secures better value for money for the taxpayer by streamlined administration, closer targeting on those who need financial support and a regime which more effectively helps people back into work*

- *improves services to unemployed people by a simpler, clearer, more consistent benefit structure and by better service delivery*

Features

The Government's proposals for JSA bring forward a range of positive measures to help people back to work.

The Jobseeker's Agreement

- *All unemployed people will sign an individually-tailored Agreement as a basic condition for receipt of benefit. This will help the jobseeker and the Employment Service to identify together the appropriate steps to get the jobseeker back to work and will provide the basis for further guidance and reviews of the jobseeker's efforts. The Agreement will provide information about the expert advice and services available at Jobcentres*

Eligibility tests attuned to labour market conditions

- *Unemployed people are currently required to satisfy the test of "actively seeking work". This will be broadened so as to encourage unemployed people to explore other ways of making their job search more effective (for example, preparing CVs)*

Incentives

- *JSA will be part of a more unified system of in-work and out-of-work benefits designed to minimise the effects of the "unemployment trap" and to reduce the disincentives for unemployed people and their partners to find work*

- *The Back to Work Bonus will encourage unemployed people to make a real effort to keep in touch with the labour market by working part-time as a step towards full-time employment. The Bonus will mean that claimants with legitimate part-time earnings will be able to build up entitlement to a cash lump sum of up to £1,000 which they would receive when they got a job which took them off JSA or Income Support*

Stronger active labour market policies

8.18 The most effective way of raising the living standards and prospects of unemployed people is to help them to return to work. Active labour market policies increase the ability of unemployed people to find jobs. Some unemployed people –

especially those who are unemployed for a long period – need help to remain active in the labour market and to get a job.

8.19 Through its national network of almost 1,200 Jobcentres, the Employment Service provides help for people who are looking for work, particularly those at a disadvantage in the labour market. Since 1990 it has:

A customer being interviewed at Perry Bar Jobcentre.

♦ increased the numbers of unemployed people helped into jobs – to almost 1.9 million in 1994-95;

♦ doubled the number of disabled people for whom jobs have been found by Employment Service Advisers, to over 70,000 in 1994-95; and

♦ more than doubled the numbers of long term unemployed people placed into jobs each year, to over 550,000 in 1994-95.

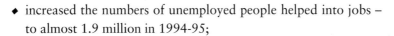

EMPLOYMENT SERVICE IN THE INNER CITIES

The Employment Service has Inner City Officers with in-depth knowledge of their local communities. They provide specialist help for groups such as lone parents, homeless people, people with literacy and numeracy difficulties, and ex-offenders.

The Employment Service has an extensive Jobcentre network in inner city areas and in 1994-95 placed over 520,000 inner city residents into jobs. Examples include:

♦ *outreach activities such as establishing Jobshops on housing estates to help unemployed people look for work. In London, the Angel Town Jobshop provides extra facilities, with local employers involved in mock interviews*

♦ *projects targeted on people with literacy and numeracy problems. One project in Nottingham gave advice to over 350 unemployed people in six months, three quarters of whom were also offered additional help to enhance their employment prospects*

♦ *projects to help unemployed women to overcome barriers to returning to work. In Hull, a Women's Centre in Bransholme provided confidence-building, advice, guidance and work placements. In the first year the project's support helped almost 100 women to enter full time education or find work*

8.20 The 1994 Budget included a range of measures to strengthen the effectiveness of active labour market policies and programmes in helping unemployed people to get back to work.

Better incentives to work

8.21 For a number of years the Government has been addressing the need to strengthen incentives to work through improvements to the social security system. The 1994 Budget also included a number of measures to increase incentives to work.

1994 BUDGET : HELP FOR UNEMPLOYED PEOPLE AND WORK INCENTIVES

The package of measures announced in the November 1994 Budget included:

Training for work

The main training programme for long-term unemployed people will focus more sharply on getting people into work.

Measures to keep unemployed people in touch with the labour market

- *The 1-2-1 and Workwise pilots will be extended nationally to provide each year help with job search for up to 130,000 18-24 year olds who have been unemployed for one year or more*

- *Community Action will be extended to provide each year work experience and help with job search for some 40,000 people unemployed for a year or more*

Measures to encourage employers to recruit unemployed people

- *Employer national insurance contributions (NICs) have been cut by 0.6 per cent for all employees earning less than £205 per week*

- *From April 1996, an employer NICs holiday will mean that employers recruiting someone unemployed for at least two years will get full NIC rebate for that person for up to a year. On average employers will save £375 per recruit*

- *There will be more Work Trials – 150,000 over the next three years – enabling employers to take on people who have been unemployed for 6 months or more for a three week "free trial"*

- *New Workstart pilots will provide financial incentives to employers to recruit up to 5,000 of the very long term unemployed from April 1995*

Measures to ease the transition from unemployment to work

- *Action to speed up the payment of housing benefit and council tax benefit will be taken, including providing a four-week guarantee of housing help for certain groups of unemployed people taking jobs. 440,000 people will benefit*

- *Jobfinder's Grant has been extended nationally and will this year help about 25,000 people who have been unemployed for two years or more to meet the initial expenses of taking a job*

- *Action to speed up the payment of Family Credit will mean that almost all new claims will be dealt with in five days*

continues...

1994 BUDGET : HELP FOR UNEMPLOYED PEOPLE AND WORK INCENTIVES
continued

Measures to help people who want full time work

◆ *From July 1995, there will be more support for Family Credit claimants working full-time. Those entitled who take a job working at least 30 hours per week will receive an additional £10 per week. 350,000 families on low incomes will be helped*

◆ *New Jobmatch pilots will help people unemployed for two years or more to take a part-time job as the first step towards full time wages. There will be 3,000 opportunities per year*

New ways of helping people without children

◆ *From October 1996, there will be a new pilot of in-work benefit for people without children who take low paid work. 20,000 people will be included in the pilot*

Greater real wage flexibility

8.22 Everyone wants to see the proportion of highly paid, highly productive and highly skilled individuals in the workforce increase. To achieve that, pay must be responsive to the market and the performance of companies and individuals. While wages are becoming more sensitive to economic circumstances, further progress is required in both the public and private sectors.

8.23 Later this year, the Government will publish a guide for employers, drawn up in conjunction with industry, which offers a range of successful examples of pay flexibility. The Government will also continue to introduce greater flexibility in public sector pay through local pay determination and performance pay.

8.24 No business can sustain a situation in which employees are paid more than the value they add through their work. That is why the Government continues to oppose the imposition of a national minimum wage. A minimum wage can lead to job losses. The more that highly paid workers are able to restore their previous wage differentials, the greater the job loss. The TUC proposal to set a minimum wage of half male median earnings would lead to a loss of 750,000 jobs if higher paid workers were to achieve a 50 per cent restoration of pay differentials.

Increased equality of opportunity

8.25 The 1994 White Paper made clear the priority the Government attaches to tackling discrimination and creating more opportunities for people with disabilities. In January 1995, the Government introduced the Disability Discrimination Bill. The Bill includes provision for a statutory right of non-discrimination against disabled people in employment to replace the ineffective quota scheme. That right will be supported by a Code of Practice and guidance. Several other initiatives demonstrate the Government's commitment to equal opportunities.

EQUAL OPPORTUNITIES INITIATIVES

♦ *In April 1995, the Government launched An Equal Opportunities Guide for Small Employers[2]. The guide gives straightforward examples of good practice*

♦ *"Positive Action", published in June 1994[3], contains revised guidance for employers interested in providing encouragement and training for members of racial groups under-represented in particular kinds of work*

♦ *Since its launch in June 1994, the Access to Work programme has helped over 7,000 disabled people to overcome barriers to work. Over 1,200 employers have now adopted the disability symbol and its five commitments to good practice in the employment of disabled people*

♦ *The Out-of-School Childcare Grant helped provide over 19,000 additional childcare places in 1994-95*

♦ *The Fair Play for Women initiative, launched in April 1994, aims to help women realise their full potential. New, broadly-based partnerships in each English Region have now begun to implement locally-based plans. In Wales, Chwarae Teg has been promoting action to further the role of women in the workforce since 1992. Scottish Enterprise is developing proposals for a Fair Play initiative as well as supporting Training 2000*

♦ *The Government has published two booklets[4,5] about the employment of older workers: "Getting On" illustrates the benefits some employers have achieved by removing age barriers; "Too Old...Who Says?" provides advice and information for older workers about job seeking*

♦ *In Northern Ireland, the Fair Employment Commission, following consultation with small businesses, established a Small Business Unit to help employers fulfil their legal obligations*

[2]*Equal Opportunities Guide for Small Employers.* [Employment Department] (June 1994)
[3]*Positive Action.* [Employment Department] (June 1994)
[4]*Getting On.* [Employment Department] (March 1994)
[5]*Too Old ...Who Says?* [Employment Department] (January 1994)

MANAGEMENT

9.1 Whatever advantages organisations have in terms of resources and the environment in which they operate, their success depends on how well they are managed at all levels.

9.2 Management has changed substantially in the last 20 years. More people at all levels have management responsibilities. Driven by competitors and the expectations of customers and investors, the private sector - including the former nationalised industries - has changed faster than the public sector. It is in the private sector, where market pressures are more intense and results easier to quantify, that the most impressive examples of excellence in management are found.

9.3 The Government has limited ability to influence the quality of management in the private sector, and particularly within individual firms. The freedoms which enable companies to compete are incompatible with Government interference. Companies must decide to what extent they look outside for pointers on improving their performance.

9.4 This chapter is therefore not a vehicle for the Government to tell the private sector how to manage. Instead it:

- identifies the characteristics of good management by drawing on and describing best private sector practice;

- considers how well UK management overall matches those characteristics, compared with management overseas; and

- reviews how firms, individuals and professional bodies are addressing shortcomings, and how the Government can help, by contributing to the spread of best practice and setting a framework for standards and qualifications in management. (Its role in working with the private sector to provide guidance on corporate governance within a statutory framework is covered in Chapters 13 and 15.)

So what are the characteristics of the best?

9.5 In 1994 DTI and the CBI explored what role – if any – they have in spreading more widely the standards of the best. Effective practice is best learned from the best-run organisations. So they asked leaders of over 100 of the UK's most successful companies what makes a winning organisation. The conclusions of this study were published in the "Winning" report[1].

9.6 The leaders who took part emphasised that successful companies unlock the potential of their people. This is confirmed by evidence collected by the Royal Society of Arts in its continuing enquiry, "Tomorrow's Company"[2]. For people at all levels to understand, own and contribute to business objectives, they need:

---

[1]*Competitiveness – How the best UK Companies are Winning.* [CBI/DTI] (1994)
[2]*Tomorrow's Company – preliminary report.* [RSA] (1994) Final report to be published shortly.

- high quality training;

- effective teamworking;

- successful delegation of responsibility and accountability;

- clear communication of company performance to all employees; and

- simplified internal systems and rapid access to information, particularly on customers and finances.

9.7 They also stressed that competitiveness requires continuous change to improve performance across a range of factors. They stressed that companies need leaders who:

- are visionary, enthusiastic champions of change;

- create cultures which encourage change and recognise opportunity;

- work in partnership with customers and suppliers;

- use demanding but realistic targets; and

- lead by example and manage risk effectively.

9.8 The "Winning" report also shows how successful firms improve their performance and drive improvements in the supply chain by continually introducing new, customised products and services which exceed customer expectations. This requires them to:

- seek and assess customers' views on their products and services, and anticipate future needs;

- understand the market and how to beat competitors;

- focus on quality in all activities, including customer service;

- improve their products and services, in particular through automation and reduced costs; and

- be forward-looking in the development of products, by exploiting new technology or legislation and reducing time to market.

9.9 The "Winning" report's findings are valid for all sectors and all sizes of firm. The TEC National Council and TECs spread across England and Wales have studied 537 manufacturing companies in 15 sectors. This work confirms the conclusions of the "Winning" report and will be published later this year.

9.10 Coopers & Lybrand surveyed Middle Market companies in the UK[3], and found that 5 per cent of the firms they studied had doubled their turnover and employees during the last three years. These "Hypergrowth" firms were distinguished in several ways. They pioneered new markets at home and abroad, had a higher proportion

[3]*The Middle Market Survey* [Coopers and Lybrand] (May 1994) *Hypergrowth Companies* [Coopers and Lybrand] (April 1995)

than average of graduates as senior managers, placed a higher priority on training, education and team development, and had managers who made more time for strategic issues. They also developed and launched new products or services more frequently, and had reduced their product development lead times by about a third compared with other firms in the survey.

And how does the UK match up?

9.11 Some UK companies are world-class in size and in quality of their product or service. In terms of profitability 16 of the top 25 companies in Europe are UK-based. In world terms:

◆ Shell is the largest private sector oil company and BP the third largest, both for production and reserves;

◆ ICI is the second largest paint manufacturer;

◆ Rolls Royce is one of the big three aero engine manufacturers and has the widest range of civil engines. Over 50,000 of its engines are in service with over 300 airline customers in more than 100 countries;

◆ British Airways is the largest international passenger airline, and was the second most profitable in 1993;

◆ British Steel is the fourth biggest steel producer;

◆ Holiday Inn Worldwide is the largest single-brand hotel company with over 1950 hotels in over 50 countries;

◆ Glaxo Wellcome is the largest pharmaceutical company, and SmithKline Beecham the fifth largest;

◆ Coats Viyella is the leader in industrial sewing thread;

◆ three of the four largest spirits companies are Guinness, Grand Metropolitan and Allied Domecq; and

◆ Reuters is the leading supplier of information and transactional services to the world's financial community and of information services to the media.

9.12 Many others are world-class, too – including medium and smaller companies which often export most of their output to customers overseas. The UK now benefits from being host to some of the world's best managed overseas companies, such as Honda, Nissan, Toyota, Samsung, 3M, Ford, ABB and Siemens. There are many other companies which are sharing their expertise with UK firms.

9.13 Despite these examples of excellence, commentators frequently point to deficiencies in the rest. It is difficult to make international comparisons of overall management performance. Nevertheless, IBM Consulting and London Business

School[4] jointly conducted a detailed assessment of company best practice in over 600 manufacturing companies, almost all in the UK, Germany and the Netherlands. This established a benchmark for a world-class company in best management practice. It concluded that:

♦ UK companies can compete successfully. The UK has a similar proportion to Germany of world class firms in manufacturing and more than the Netherlands;

♦ however, the UK has a significantly higher proportion of companies which lag badly in key respects (Chart 9.1).

9.14 The study showed that the relative strengths and weaknesses of the firms investigated reflect differing business priorities.

♦ In the UK, managers more often put customer service as their top priority. Consequently, their strengths lie in good relationships with suppliers, in effective management of systems, and in product reliability. However, they are more likely to pay too little attention to the achievements of their competitors, to equipment layout and to automation.

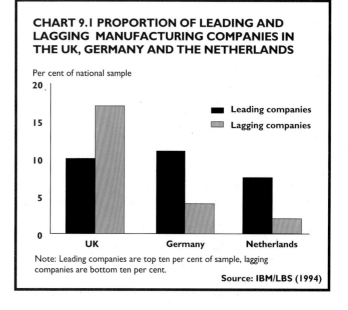

CHART 9.1 PROPORTION OF LEADING AND LAGGING MANUFACTURING COMPANIES IN THE UK, GERMANY AND THE NETHERLANDS

Per cent of national sample

■ Leading companies
▨ Lagging companies

Note: Leading companies are top ten per cent of sample, lagging companies are bottom ten per cent.

Source: IBM/LBS (1994)

♦ In Germany, the top priority is to reduce manufacturing costs. German firms are strong in benchmarking themselves against competitors, in, for example, automation, equipment layout and employee involvement. They are often weaker where the UK is strong.

9.15 There are no prescriptive solutions. Incomparably the most important factor is the willingness and enthusiasm of individual managements to find out about the quality and performance of companies which lead the world in their field, to work out how to get and stay ahead, and to face up to the pains as well as the gains of doing so.

[4]*Made in Europe: A Four Nations Best Practice Study* [IBM and LBS] (November 1994)

Management performance can be improved....

9.16 In partnership with companies and other organisations, the Government is working to provide business – and especially smaller firms – with more opportunities to improve management performance.

... by spreading best practice....

9.17 The Government is helping small and medium sized firms to capitalise on strengths. Help with technology is discussed in Chapter 12 and help with exports in Chapter 11. A key strand in the Government's strategy is the Business Link network, described in Chapter 5.

- The Government will make available £100 million over four years from 1995-96 to support bids from Business Link partnerships and regional consortia to deliver locally-designed business development programmes, such as encouraging world-class manufacturing, stimulating business networking, helping start-ups with growth potential, improving access to finance, and providing export assistance.

- Specialist Business Counsellors on Export, Design, and Innovation and Technology may be needed beyond the three years for which Government funding is currently agreed. DTI will review their performance so as to maximise future effectiveness. Subject to this review, it will extend funding to help meet the continuing costs of their services.

- The Government will continue to support the training of key staff within Training and Enterprise Councils (TECs) to enable them to provide effective advice on management development.

9.18 Since 1989, DTI's Managing in the 90s programme has promoted best practice in smaller firms through over 3,300 events attracting more than 100,000 participants. In 1994, over 800 events, including Roadshows and visits to exemplar firms, were held throughout the UK. The programme has been revised to take account of the "Winning" report and other findings, and will be relaunched this summer. Business Links will be the main delivery route in England. Key goals of the new programme are to:

**COMPANY TURNAROUND:
A REAL-LIFE EXAMPLE**

European Gas Turbines Ltd, East Midlands, employs 2000 people, and manufactures industrial gas turbines.

The Gains

- *Sales increased 60 per cent in five years*
- *Return on capital doubled*
- *Quality measurably improved*
- *On-time delivery improved from 60 per cent to over 95 per cent*

The Pains

- *Overhauling every aspect of company performance*
- *People were frustrated, cynical and resistant to change*
- *Perfection has not been achieved. Results are patchy*
- *Not everyone likes team-working*

The Approach

- *Strategy driven from the top*
- *Organised the company into manageable chunks*
- *Introduced team-working, with responsibilities passed to shop floor*
- *Forced each individual to ask "Who is my customer?"*
- *Introduced targets for everything*
- *Many forms of training*
- *Continually seeking out best practice*

Source: The "Winning" report

◆ highlight best business practice;

◆ help managers evaluate their firm's strengths and weaknesses, and set targets for profitable change;

◆ promote best practice networks to exchange ideas and know-how among firms; and

◆ involve a wider range of firms. The target is an increase of 25 per cent per year in the number of companies participating in inter-company visits (5000 for 1995-96). The target for the Managing in the 90s programme as a whole is the involvement of more than 200,000 people over the next three years.

Delegates at one of over 800 workshops and seminars on management held during 1994-95.

9.19 Working with the CBI and others, DTI is introducing a national benchmarking service to be operated on PCs through business support organisations including Business Links, Government Offices, the CBI and trade associations. The pilot scheme begins in the autumn of 1995, and from 1996 firms will be able to obtain performance comparisons against national and sectoral benchmarks.

9.20 Spreading best practice is not just a task for the Government. Representative organisations and firms are heavily involved.

9.21 The engineering community has responded positively to the 1994 Competitiveness White Paper. The Engineering Council has already announced higher standards for educating, training and developing engineers and technicians. The Council itself is to be reformed in January 1996, to provide a unified structure for the profession. In addition, Action for Engineering is increasing the influence and involvement of professional engineers and technicians for the benefit of British industry, by:

◆ highlighting achievements within engineering;

◆ stimulating the flow of high-quality men and women into engineering;

◆ making better use of engineers for wealth creation;

◆ encouraging employers to train many more technicians and supervisors to raise the quality of the engineering workforce as a whole to world-class standards;

◆ facilitating the continuing development of engineers and technicians; and

◆ improving the appreciation of engineering amongst company directors, financial institutions and opinion formers.

Action for Engineering is committed to promoting best practice in these areas through national and regional networks. It aims to publish guides in early 1996 to facilitate a revolution in engineering skills.

9.22 Team-working, which has a particularly important role in promoting best practice, is increasing rapidly in all sectors of business.

- Over 70,000 firms are now members of 500 Business Clubs, where companies make contacts, share information and learn from each other. Business Links are helping such clubs to develop. The DoE and DTI are supporting a pilot group of 11 business and environmental clubs to help small firms with environmental issues.

- Sectoral initiatives have also been started by trade associations and Industrial Training Organisations (ITOs), again in partnership with Government.

SECTORAL INITIATIVES

"Creating the World Class Business: Success through People" is the Engineering Employers Federation's programme of seminars and workshops which aims to help manufacturing businesses manage people more effectively. It is part of the CBI's National Manufacturing Council Competitiveness Forum.

The Federation of Electronic Industries (FEI) and six leading players in the telecoms industry have launched Telecoms 2000 with DTI support. Over 100 smaller companies have attended seminars showing ways to achieve continuous improvement. The FEI followed this up with the Electronics Industry Forum, which aims to help the electronics and telecoms industries improve their competitive position by, for instance, improving their Time to Market performance.

The Market Research Association and the Fine Art Trade Guild are putting together Good Practice Guides for their trades.

The Clothing and Allied Products Industrial Training Board and the Marine and Engineering Training Association have integrated the management standards (see below) into qualifications for their sectors.

- Interdisciplinary working is growing. For example, the Chartered Institute of Marketing and the Design Council are promoting the importance of innovation and incorporating marketing and design into product development and other areas.

- Professional and trade organisations are recognising the need to improve services to members by capitalising on working together. An example is the creation of the Marketing Council in the summer of 1995.

MARKETING AND THE MARKETING COUNCIL

Marketing is central to competitiveness.....

Anticipating customer need, creating new markets, exploiting new technologies and leading change in customer behaviour are key marketing capabilities. Marketing is crucial to innovation, product development, the development of brands and the exploitation of intellectual property.

...whether by winning markets...

Glaxo was not the first into the market with one particular medicine, but its international marketing gave it global leadership. This success rested on local alliances with the sales forces of other major pharmaceutical companies and precisely-targeted clinical data.

....creating markets...

Marks and Spencer has transformed the market in chilled foods by its example in successfully introducing new products. Marks and Spencer concentrated on customer satisfaction at the beginning of this innovation process, and delivered quality through partnership with suppliers.

...or transforming marketing standards...

Faced with global competition, British Airways focused its business processes on customer satisfaction and set out to transform company practices, learning and culture. The result has been a major increase in customer satisfaction, numbers of passengers flown, awards for quality and excellence, and greatly enhanced profitability.

....and the Marketing Council is spreading best practice.

The Marketing Council has been set up to:

- *benchmark UK marketing performance across all industry sectors*

- *identify and analyse world-class marketing, and spread best practice*

- *develop world-class standards in marketing education and training, and integrate marketing into business studies*

- *form an occupational training organisation to promote NVQs in sales, marketing, customer service, supply chain management and international trade*

Reports, roadshows and training courses on benchmarking and marketing best practice will be available. In particular, smaller firms will have access to training through Business Links.

The Government supports this initiative, and the work which the Chartered Institute of Marketing and others are doing to research and promote best practice in all aspects of marketing, including advertising, market research sales, direct marketing and design.

**BUSINESS
LINK**

◆ Business services - including advertising, market research, public relations and management consultancy - can enable firms to gain and maintain competitive advantage. DTI is supporting initiatives to encourage more widespread and effective use of such services by producing good practice guides and raising awareness through Business Links.

ADVERTISING

World-class companies regard advertising as central to their business development strategies.

The UK advertising industry is recognised as first-class. It is a major winner of international awards.

DTI is supporting initiatives to encourage companies of all sizes and in all sectors to use advertising effectively by:

◆ *publishing a Best Practice guide in summer 1995*

◆ *holding regional seminars*

◆ *supporting a pilot Business Link event in the West Midlands on advertising and other marketing communication services in the autumn of 1995*

The UK enjoys a successful regime of self-regulation in advertising. The Government:

◆ *recognises the need for a legislative and regulatory environment that minimises restrictions on freedom to advertise*

◆ *is encouraging other EU states to adopt this approach*

◆ *is working with industry on a response this summer to the EU Green Paper on Commercial Communication*

....and developing standards and qualifications for management ....

9.23 The Government helps to define and set standards for management practice, products and quality of service, and oversees the accreditation of bodies which certify that those standards have been reached.

9.24 The Government has been working with other organisations to promote the leadership skills identified in the "Winning" report.

◆ On behalf of the Employment Department (ED), the Management Charter Initiative (MCI) published, in February 1995, standards for senior managers which specifically include leadership. They will be marketed through MCI members and used by many training providers and professional bodies in development programmes.

◆ Company Directors have a strategic role which goes beyond the requirements of good management. The Institute of Directors (IoD), with support from ED, developed standards of good practice for Boards of Directors which they launched in March. ED will encourage IoD to adapt those standards for public sector boards such as those within the National Health Service.

... with linked development and training opportunities,...

9.25 Studies show that success depends on the development of all levels and types of management. The Government can help with this.

- The Investors in People standard is the key tool to help firms assess and manage their employees' development to meet business objectives. The Government continues to place a high priority on promoting Investors in People (see Chapter 7).

- ED is promoting the wider adoption of competence-based qualifications in business schools, with the aim that 50 per cent will offer them within two years. It is encouraging business schools to develop qualifications based on the management standards. Over a third of business schools already offer these and a mapping exercise will be carried out in 1996 to monitor progress. It is also promoting the development of a Masters Degree based on the senior management standards.

- Government will ask MCI to:

  - generate learning materials to support Business Link activities;

  - develop standards for management consultants; and

  - explore competence-based approaches to the continuing professional development of managers.

- The Government will continue to encourage institutions of higher education to develop courses which meet industry's needs.

- Encouraged by DTI, 15 universities and business schools[5] now provide modular post-graduate courses on the management of technology. These will help managers keep up-to-date without disrupting their careers.

- The Government will encourage all TECs to develop strategies for improving the skills of management in local companies.

> ### MANAGEMENT NVQs AND SVQs
>
> - *Vocational qualifications in management are now available for supervisors, first line and middle managers*
>
> - *About 900 centres now offer NVQs or SVQs in management*
>
> - *Over 10,000 managers and supervisors have already obtained NVQs or SVQs and a further 35,000 are working towards them*
>
> - *Qualifications will be revised to meet more closely the needs of companies of all sizes, and to allow managers more flexibility*

[5] Brunel University, Keele University, The Open University, UMIST, University of Brighton, University of Humberside, University of Paisley, University of Sussex, Henley Management College, Liverpool John Moores University, Queens University of Belfast, University of Bradford, University of Glasgow, University of Lancaster, University of Warwick.

... and standards for environmental management....

9.26 Firms can gain competitive advantage through:

♦ planning for increases in costs of environmentally damaging products and processes;

♦ taking environmental action which is financially beneficial or cost-neutral. Waste minimisation and energy efficiency are two areas where improved environmental practice can bring direct economic benefits to a business;

♦ effective management of environmental risk;

♦ exploiting new market opportunities for environmental technologies, services and products (see also Chapter 15). The global market for these is large - and growing;

♦ effective compliance with environmental regulation; and

♦ meeting the changing expectations of customers, employees, investors and other stakeholders concerning the environmental impact of products and processes.

THE ENVIRONMENT

Waste minimisation

Project Catalyst, the largest waste minimisation project in the UK, was based in the Mersey basin and funded jointly by DTI, the BOC Foundation for the Environment and participating companies. It identified potential savings totalling £8.9 million per year.

The Aire and Calder project between companies from various sectors in Yorkshire identified 671 opportunities for savings amounting to £3.3 million per year. The CBI and BOC Foundation will follow up the project by holding a series of waste minimisation roadshows around the country this summer.

9.27 Environmental management is growing in importance in the UK. See also Chapter 6.

♦ The UK introduced the first industry standard in the world for environmental management systems (BS 7750), and two out of three UK companies now have a formal environmental policy.

♦ The EU Eco-Management and Audit Scheme (EMAS) was launched in April 1995. The UK took the lead in developing this for Europe.

♦ In February 1995, DOE launched a scheme to help small firms introduce energy and environmental management systems (SCEEMAS).

♦ In June 1994, DOE and DTI jointly launched the Environmental Technology Best Practice Programme. Over five years it aims to generate projects which, when replicated, will by 2010 achieve annual net cost savings of £160 million to UK industry as well as environmental benefits.

♦ The Government is working with external partners to develop standards and NVQ/SVQ units for both energy and environmental management.

....and quality management.

9.28 The Government continues to promote quality. Research shows that companies which have successfully introduced quality management systems report significant benefits, including fewer complaints, efficiency gains (fewer rejects and a reduction in wastage), new customers, and valuable marketing advantages[6].

Teamworking on the shop floor at Land Rover. Rover group was one of the winners of the 1994 UK quality award.

◆ The National Accreditation Council for Certification Bodies, and the Certification Bodies themselves, have made certification to the quality management system standard (ISO 9000, formerly BS 5750) more accessible for smaller firms.

◆ DTI is working to ensure that the merger of the National Measurement Accreditation Service and the National Accreditation Council for Certification Bodies enhances the benefits of accredited certification under ISO 9000.

◆ DTI and the British Standards Institution are planning the next revision of ISO 9000, to ensure that the concept of continuous improvement is reflected.

◆ In 1994, the business-led UK Quality Award was launched. It recognises outstanding performance in quality management.

◆ The first three winners of the European Quality Award have all been UK-based companies.

◆ MCI has developed and will promote competence standards for quality management based on best practice in all sectors.

◆ Standards and NVQs and SVQs have been developed, with ED backing, for small business support and information services, and for owner-managers in business planning. Similar qualifications for business implementation and development are being developed and will be available in the summer. These should give confidence to investors while providing a sound basis for training and development in smaller firms.

◆ Through Business Links, DTI will promote a more coherent approach to quality by encouraging industry to use a combination of ISO 9000, benchmarking, Investors in People, Quality Awards and quality-related NVQs and SVQs to improve business performance.

BUSINESS **LINK**

[6]*Quality Consultancy Scheme Clients 1988 – 1990* [PERA-Salford] (1992)

BS 5750 Implementation and Value Added [Vanguard Consulting] (1993)

BS 5750 A Business Perspective [London Chamber of Commerce] (1994)

Small Businesses and BS 5750 [Small Business Research Trust] (1994)

The challenge for the future

9.29 The best UK management is amongst the best in the world. It sets a high standard for others to reach, whether in managing people, assets or risk. It recognises above all the need for innovation in management and for continuous improvement. The Government is helping others in business to learn from the best – and, equally importantly, learning from them itself. Today's management challenges are stretching – and there will be more of them tomorrow.

MANAGEMENT IN THE PUBLIC SECTOR

Public sector reform...

10.1 The scale, complexity and pace of activity in the late twentieth century have increased the problem of managing on a very large scale and simultaneously exposed management's performance to an increasingly well informed and critical audience. In the public sector, the need for public accountability makes the task harder.

10.2 As the 1994 Competitiveness White Paper made clear, competitiveness is not just an issue for the private sector. A well managed public sector will minimise the burden on UK companies and allow lower taxes and better services. Under the Citizen's Charter programme, the Government is emphasising the need for real commitment to continuous improvements in standards of service throughout the public sector. There is considerable scope for further improvement.

10.3 Governments across the world of all political persuasions are going back to fundamental principles, to ensure they provide only those functions which are both necessary and best carried out in the public sector. The UK has been at the forefront of the drive to limit the role of the state, while recognising the need to raise standards of essential services. Since 1979, the number of public sector employees has fallen from 7.4 million to 5.3 million (Chart 10.1). The Civil Service has reduced from 730,000 to 530,000.

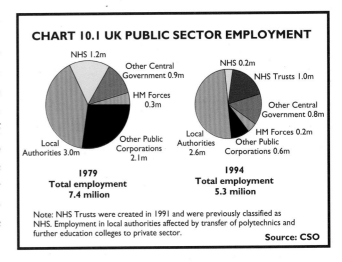

CHART 10.1 UK PUBLIC SECTOR EMPLOYMENT

NHS 1.2m
Other Central Government 0.9m
HM Forces 0.3m
Local Authorities 3.0m
Other Public Corporations 2.1m

1979
Total employment
7.4 milion

NHS 0.2m
NHS Trusts 1.0m
Other Central Government 0.8m
HM Forces 0.2m
Local Authorities 2.6m
Other Public Corporations 0.6m

1994
Total employment
5.3 milion

Note: NHS Trusts were created in 1991 and were previously classified as NHS. Employment in local authorities affected by transfer of polytechnics and further education colleges to private sector.
Source: CSO

...involving the market...

10.4 The Government examines regularly the functions it carries out and the services it delivers, applying "prior options" tests. Reviews are normally undertaken every five years. The timing and terms of reviews are made public to encourage organisations to bid.

◆ Where a job no longer needs doing, the function is abolished.

◆ If a service need not be the responsibility of the Government, it is privatised.

◆ Where a service cannot be provided by the private sector alone, its expertise and resources will be involved as far as practicable in partnership with the public sector, for example through the Private Finance Initiative. This will bring benefits to taxpayers and consumers.

◆ If the Government needs to retain responsibility for a service, it may not need to

AEA Technology are specialists in decommissioning all kinds of nuclear facilities, such as this remote dismantling of a hot cell, and also in the processing, packaging, transport and disposal of radioactive wastes.

carry out day-to-day operations. Services are opened up to competition to establish which method of delivery ensures best value for money.

♦ In some cases, the nature of the job means that it is best supplied direct by the Government. Under the Next Steps Programme, executive agencies are established, with wide financial and management scope, including the recruitment of private sector expertise.

♦ The Government is also committed to continuous improvements in efficiency and quality in core Civil Service functions which cannot be commercialised.

...through privatisation...

10.5 The reforms implemented in the UK public sector, including the Citizen's Charter, have been widely adopted throughout the world. The most significant of these changes, and the most copied, has been the transformation of the formerly nationalised industries into free-standing companies. Some of these are now world-class. Since 1979, the Government has put 48 major businesses into the private sector. This will continue. For example, a Bill to enable privatisation of AEA Technology, which has around 4,000 employees and is the commercial arm of the UK Atomic Energy Authority, was introduced on 1 March 1995.

10.6 The focus now is on extending the benefits of privatisation to Government services.

10.7 Where privatisation is not practicable, the Government will, where possible, introduce private sector management to organisations likely to benefit. An example is the National Physical Laboratory, which, subject to negotiation, will be managed by a private sector contractor.

PRIVATISATION IN GOVERNMENT

5,500 central Government staff have transferred through privatisation to the private sector in the last three years. For the future, the Government has announced its intention to privatise all or part of ten services:

Central Government

♦ *Natural Resources Institute (ODA), Transport Research Laboratory (DoT), National Engineering Laboratory (DTI), Laboratory of the Government Chemist (DTI), National Measurement Accreditation Service (DTI), NHS Estates Agency (DH), ADAS (MAFF/Welsh Office)*

Other public bodies

♦ *Crown Agents (ODA), Electrical Equipment Certification Service (ED), Scottish Homes Building Division*

...competition...

10.8 The outsourcing of services has become commonplace in the private sector which has the flexibility to buy from a range of different producers, offering a variety of options. The same is true for Government, which is allowing the private sector to bid against in-house service providers. This puts work where it can be done most effectively and improves the performance of the public sector.

10.9 In-house activities (for example, printing, catering and IT) are obviously limited in potential by the demands of the parent organisation. They have no incentive or opportunity to expand. Career prospects for specialised staff are limited. When such services enter the private sector, they are free to expand, offer wider opportunities to staff, create new jobs and so enrich the economy.

10.10 The Competing for Quality Programme has so far exposed 11 per cent of central Government's running costs to competition. External contractors have won about half of contracts in competition with in-house providers and over £1 billion worth of work in total. Between April 1992 and September 1994:

◆ activities costing £2 billion and covering more than 54,000 civil service posts were reviewed. 80 per cent of reviews involved a competitive tender;

◆ the number of Civil Service posts was reduced by over 26,000;

◆ annual savings of over £410 million were achieved - an average of 20 per cent; and

◆ quality improvements were specified in a third of reviews, and quality maintained in the rest.

10.11 Departments are examining services worth a further £860 million in the year to September 1995. Programmes from non-departmental public bodies, amounting to £250 million, bring the total to over £1 billion.

10.12 The Deregulation and Contracting Out Act 1994 makes possible the increased use of private sector contractors in delivering a wide range of statutory services, allowing further competition.

...and in partnership with the private sector.

10.13 There is no absolute frontier between the public and private sectors. Through partnership, the drive to raise standards and improve value for money in public services can be fully realised.

10.14 Partnership gives Government access to private sector expertise and best practice. Examples of partnership activities include:

◆ staff interchange with industry and commerce. This is continuing at all levels and enables skills transfer between the sectors. In 1994 there were 366 Civil Service secondments to the private sector, 315 private sector secondees to the Civil Service (almost half in DTI) and more than 60 short-term attachments at senior levels under the annual Whitehall and Industry Group programme;

◆ in a project with the private sector, the Central Statistical Office (CSO) is producing reports on individual sectors of industry to meet business needs. The CSO plans to expand the range of statistics available on services. With DTI it is setting up a Business Statistics Users Group. The CSO is encouraging data sharing, and promoting best practice among data collectors; and

◆ a contract for a strategic partnership between DTI's Internal Audit section and Ernst and Young. The aim is to improve the performance and reduce the cost of the Internal Audit service, drawing on the private sector's significant investment in automated audit methodologies and techniques and also its pool of specialists.

10.15 The Private Finance Initiative (PFI) harnesses skills and finance from the private sector in the delivery and management of services in partnership.

PRIVATE FINANCE INITIATIVE

The Government is on course to let contracts under the PFI, leading to around £5 billion of capital investment in 1995. As well as these projects, which include the Channel Tunnel Rail Link, a number of other proposals are under consideration in the following areas:

◆ *some £5 billion worth of **transport** projects identified. Chapters 5 and 14 have further examples*

◆ *some £1.2 billion worth of **Information Technology** projects identified including a replacement for the ageing National Insurance Recording System. Contract negotiations were completed in April and the system is due to be introduced in 1997-8*

◆ *six **health** projects worth £300 million for the design, build, finance and operation of District General Hospitals (or large extensions) have been advertised in the Official Journal. In Scotland there is a similar project for the proposed new Edinburgh Royal Infirmary worth some £140 million*

◆ *final tenders received to finance privately the design, construction and management of two new **prisons** at Bridgend and Fazakerley*

◆ *the **Treasury building** is to be refurbished using private finance. The project is worth up to £200 million*

10.16 The initiative was originally tightly focussed on transport projects. Progress is now being made on a much broader front, for example, in health, information technology, and property. The Chancellor of the Exchequer announced to the CBI in November 1994 that in future the Treasury would not approve any capital projects unless private finance options had been explored.

10.17 The Government is now extending this initiative. New rules to encourage partnerships between local authorities and the private sector came into effect in April. These rules, together with proposals to allow grant maintained schools to borrow, will help promote PFI in schools. The NHS Executive recently distributed guidance on how to take forward PFI projects in the health service.

Developing a customer focus in the public sector.....

10.18 Where services continue to be provided by the public sector, they must be responsive to customer needs, combining standards with value for money in line with the principles of the Citizen's Charter. To achieve these objectives public sector managers need:

- clear lines of responsibility;

- to measure and set targets for outputs as well as inputs;

- to make available information on performance;

- to delegate effectively, with freedom to manage within agreed objectives; and

- to identify and adopt best practice.

10.19 Over the past 15 years, public services have been transformed through these disciplines. In particular, the creation of Executive Agencies has radically reformed the work of the majority of civil servants.

10.20 Two-thirds of the Civil Service now work in a total of 108 Executive Agencies. A further 65 agencies are in the pipeline. Three quarters of civil servants will then be working in Next Steps organisations.

10.21 Agency targets have become more demanding year-on-year. Agencies nevertheless met 80 per cent of their key targets in 1993-94, compared to 77 per cent in 1992-93 and 76 per cent in 1991-92[1].

> ## IMPROVED EFFICIENCY AND SERVICES IN AGENCIES
>
> - *The Patent Office has reduced staff numbers by one quarter (300 people), allowing fees to remain steady for the last three years - a reduction of 5.3 per cent in real terms*
>
> - *The Passport Agency has reduced the maximum time for processing straightforward passport applications from 95 working days in 1989 to 16 working days in 1994. In 1993-4 the unit cost of passport services was reduced by 4.3 per cent in real terms*
>
> - *HM Land Registry computerised 8.8 million titles in 1993-94 compared with 6.3 million in 1992-93. The Registry achieved a reduction of almost 3 per cent in unit costs in real terms in 1993-94*
>
> - *The Driving Standards Agency halved average waiting time for car driving tests from 13 weeks in 1988 to under 6 weeks in 1994*

10.22 In 1995, the Next Steps Review will for the first time include trends, reporting on agencies' performance against their targets over three financial years. This will further demonstrate that targets are getting tougher, while standards and value for money are improving.

[1]*Next Steps Review 1994.* Cm 2750 [HMSO] (1994)

...through greater openness and accountability...

10.23 The Citizen's Charter programme brings together accountability, measurement and continuous improvement. Its key principles are published standards, openness and information, choice and consultation, courtesy and helpfulness, redress when things go wrong, and value for money.

10.24 For example, the Jobseeker's Charter has led to significant improvements:

- in 98 per cent of Employment Service offices, clients are seen within 10 minutes on average;

- in 99 per cent of offices, phone calls are answered within 30 seconds on average;

- jobs on display are kept up-to-date; and

- letters are answered within 5 working days.

10.25 The Charter sets a national framework of standards. But individual local services are increasingly developing their own standards of service to meet the needs of users.

10.26 Some of the very best local performers have been awarded Charter Marks. Launched in 1992, Charter Mark Awards recognise schools and colleges, hospitals, benefits agencies, local authorities and other organisations which deliver high quality services.

Public Service Minister, David Hunt, with Frank Bruno and the children of Swaffield Primary School, South London, launching the 1995 Charter Mark Scheme. For the first time service users can nominate organisations for a Charter Mark.

- Highlands and Islands Enterprise (H&IE) is the first agency in the TEC and LEC network to achieve the Charter Mark. To ensure that customers can reach its services, H&IE takes services out to village halls and local hotels, and provides one-stop counselling centres.

- Caerphilly and Heads of the Valleys Employment Service helps place some 13,000 people in jobs every year. The service pioneered "Customer Consultant Groups" where customers and staff meet to discuss the service. This innovation has been taken up nationally by the Employment Service.

- The Northumbria Ambulance Service NHS Trust is the first ambulance service to be awarded BS 5750; first to achieve the Investors in People standard; and first to win a Charter Mark. Surplus income generated from management consultancy has been invested in new vehicles and equipment, further improving the service.

10.27 In 1995, new Charter Mark Awards will be made for the best customer and staff suggestions successfully implemented. Customers of public services can also nominate organisations for an Award.

...and also seeking continuous improvement in core functions.

10.28 Of all the spheres of public sector activity, core functions have been least reformed. However, a start has been made and some major initiatives are under way.

- From the Spring of 1995, Departments have been developing three-year Efficiency Plans to show what efficiency savings are expected. These plans build on the techniques developed under the Competing for Quality Programme and include benchmarking, privatisation, contracting out and market testing. Departments and agencies will be encouraged to adopt best practice from both private and public sectors.

- Efficiency Scrutinies have been a major tool for improving efficiency in Government since 1979. The 1994 White Paper announced a scrutiny of management planning and control systems. That scrutiny has now been

---

DEREGULATION: FORMS AND SURVEYS

The Government is taking measures to reduce the burden of surveys and to strengthen survey control through:

- *a programme to cut out duplication of data collected from business and keep down the number of random sample surveys sent to the same firm*

- *best practice guides on administrative and survey forms, which will be published by the summer of 1995. These will, amongst other things, stress the importance of:*

  - *taking a critical look at need*

  - *keeping down the number of questions*

  - *simplifying guidance notes*

  - *using tick boxes*

  - *piloting new forms with business*

- *more electronic collection of financial and statistical information*

- *consideration of more business representation in the CSO's advisory structures*

completed and its report published[2]. It makes 56 recommendations to bring the management planning systems in all Departments up to the best standards found in the private and public sectors. The Government has welcomed the report and Ministers will be taking forward its recommendations.

♦ In 1992 the Government launched a series of Fundamental Expenditure Reviews covering Government Departments of State. These consider long-term trends in spending, how services could be delivered more effectively and economically, and whether there are further areas from which the state should withdraw altogether. The aim is to complete the programme during the course of this Parliament. Completed reviews have led to policy reforms and efficiency savings. For example, measures so far agreed on social security will result in annual savings of over £4 billion by the year 2000.

IMPROVEMENTS IN THE MANAGEMENT OF THE NATIONAL HEALTH SERVICE

The NHS is one of the largest organisations in the world, with a budget of £87.5 million every day. Thanks to the universal health care provided by the NHS, British companies are not obliged to meet the health care costs of their employees through insurance schemes. The NHS is one of the most cost-effective health care systems in the world. It is also the second biggest element of UK public expenditure. It is vital to our competitiveness and the health of the nation that the NHS is effectively managed.

The introduction of general management in 1984, followed by the health service reforms in 1990, has transformed the management of the NHS. In combination these changes have brought:

♦ *clarity of objectives and systematic measurement of performance against these objectives*

♦ *focus on quality of service for patients*

♦ *emphasis on value for money*

They have delivered impressive gains for patients:

♦ *record increases in the number of patients treated – 118 patients treated today for every 100 in 1990/91*

♦ *substantial reductions in waiting times - the average wait for non-urgent treatment has fallen from over eight months in 1990 to less than five months today*

♦ *there have been gains in efficiency, amounting to 17 per cent over ten years – equivalent to an extra £2.8 billion spent on patient care*

10.29 Where tasks still need to be paid for by the taxpayer and carried out by the Government, the people delivering the services must be in the right structures, have

[2]*Resource Management Systems: An Efficiency Unit Scrutiny.* [Efficiency Unit Scrutiny] (May 1995)

the right skills and the right attitudes. Last July, a White Paper, "Continuity and Change" was published[3] as a basis for consultation on the future of the Civil Service.

10.30 In January, the Government published[4] a further White Paper, "Taking Forward Continuity and Change", which incorporated the response to consultation and to the recommendations of the report by the Treasury and Civil Service Committee on the role of the Civil Service. The key proposals are:

◆ a new Senior Civil Service - a cohesive group of professional advisers and managers to lead the Service, maintain core values and secure improvements in performance;

◆ further delegation to Departments and Agencies, including the delegation of pay and grading from April 1996; and

◆ the introduction of a Civil Service Code summarising the values expected of civil servants.

10.31 Investors in People is increasingly recognised as establishing a standard for successful organisations. By April 1995, 16 central Government organisations, or parts of organisations, representing 10 per cent of Civil Service staff had achieved the Investors in People standard, and a further 41 had made a formal commitment to do so.

Improved local government performance matters too

10.32 With over 40 per cent of the public sector employed by local authorities, its management performance is also of key importance to national competitiveness. The Government has, therefore, set a framework within which local authorities must test and publicise their performance. Compulsory competitive tendering (CCT) requires local authorities to seek bids from the private sector before awarding work to in-house teams. For blue collar work already subject to CCT, savings of 7 per cent have been achieved[5], equivalent to £115 million[6]. Significantly higher savings have been achieved in some services, for example, in refuse collection. CCT is now being extended to white collar services.

10.33 By December 1994, under the Charter programme, all local authorities had for the first time published information about their performance in key services. In March 1995, the Audit Commission published a national comparison of these performance indicators. For the first time each authority's performance has been compared with others. There is a wide dispersion in performance. It is for business, council taxpayers and elected members of authorities and their officials to use this information to improve quality and value for money.

[3]*The Civil Service: Continuity and Change.* Cm 2627 [HMSO] (1994)

[4]*The Civil Service: Taking Forward Continuity and Change.* Cm 2748 [HMSO] (1995)

[5]H Davis and K Welsh *Competition and Service: The Impact of The Local Government Act 1988.* [HMSO] (1993).

[6]based on the total value of current contracts for each service area identified in the LGMBs CCT Information Service Report for June 1994

10.34 Savings made through improved management performance need not affect front line services. The Audit Commission's reports[7,8], "Paying the Piper", and, "Calling the Tune", published in January 1995, set out techniques through which many local authorities have achieved savings of 5 to 10 per cent of pay bill without harm to services. The Commission concluded that "If all councils saved 5 per cent of their pay bill, national savings of more than £500 million would be available".

10.35 Efficient and effective local government is essential if unnecessary burdens are not to be imposed on local businesses and if the services provided to business are to be responsive to their needs. The Government also considers that local government faces unnecessary bureaucratic requirements which impair its performance. Therefore, on 6 March, DOE and the Welsh Office[9] published a consultation document "Deregulating Local Government - the First Steps". This contains specific proposals for removing unnecessary burdens from local government. Decisions on implementation will be taken as soon as practicable in the light of comments received.

10.36 The way in which local authorities carry out enforcement activity can also place unnecessary burdens on business. Last year DOE and DTI jointly published for consultation a report[10] on ways of minimising such burdens. The local authority associations intend to produce a good practice guide on enforcement this summer. A package of other measures will be announced shortly.

Government in the supply chain

10.37 As the country's largest purchaser, the Government strives for continuous improvement in public procurement (see Chapter 13 on prompt payment). Its aims are value for money and improving the competitiveness of suppliers. A strategy for improving performance is being published concurrently in the White Paper[11], "Setting New Standards". It includes:

- continuing emphasis on competition and co-operation between purchasers and suppliers;

- taking account of the whole cycle of acquisition and use, and whole-life costs and benefits;

- a commitment to enhanced training and skill development;

- cross-functional teams to improve procurement; and

- a statement of good practice on relationships with suppliers.

10.38 All Departments are preparing action plans to implement "Setting New Standards". Work will include reviews of procurement processes and relations with

[7]*Paying the Piper: People and Pay Management in Local Government.* [Audit Commission] (1995)
[8]*Calling the Tune: Performance Management in Local Government.* [Audit Commission] (1995)
[9]*Deregulating Local Government - the First Steps* [DOE/Welsh Office] (March 1995)
[10]*Local Government Enforcement - Report of the Inter-Departmental Review Team.* [DOE/DTI] (September 1994)
[11]*Setting New Standards.* Cm 2840 [HMSO] (1995)

suppliers. There will be greater emphasis on collaboration between Departments. Improvements resulting from these developments will be published in Departmental Reports.

10.39 Some Departments are working in a trial of a service sponsored by the Chartered Institute of Purchasing and Supply to benchmark their procurement against outside organisations. The results will be available later this year.

10.40 In late 1994, the Government undertook a survey of suppliers' views of its procurement performance. Most respondents were satisfied with the professional standards of procurement, their opportunities to compete, the information they received about requirements, and relations with purchasers. However, some had concerns about:

- Government purchasers not getting to know the business of suppliers;
- lack of opportunities to offer innovative solutions;
- over-complicated procedures;
- lack of information about evaluation criteria; and
- requests for unnecessary information.

Departments are dealing with these weaknesses.

10.41 Government has also reviewed its procurement from SMEs. Follow up work will establish best practice in publications for SMEs and help small firms gain access to Government contracts.

10.42 In line with Departments' environmental strategies, purchasing procedures may include specifications which encourage suppliers to provide environmentally-friendly products. DOE, for example, has published guidance which combines the aims of quality standards and reducing environmental impact.

10.43 EU legislation has a major impact on public procurement. The Commission is starting a review of purchasing directives in 1996. The Government will consult widely beforehand. It will seek simpler procedures consistent with competitiveness and value for money.

More remains to be done

10.44 Value for money and high quality services are at the heart of the Citizen's Charter and the Government's programme of reforms. An efficient and effective public sector enhances the quality of life and competitiveness. The Government is committed to a process of continuous improvement in standards of service.

INNOVATION

11.1 Innovation is often confused with research and development (R&D) or science and technology (S&T). Whilst these are important aspects of innovation, innovation itself involves attitudes and practices stretching over a much wider range of activities.

Innovation is essential for competitiveness....

11.2 Innovation is the successful exploitation of new ideas. Often this will require enhanced knowledge or technology – but not always. Successful innovation is essential in every sector and in all aspects of business – finance, marketing, operations, design, human resources, research and development. It depends above all on good management and the full involvement of the workforce. Innovation depends on people's ability to embrace new thinking. It is stimulated by education, training and experience.

....but UK performance is mixed.

11.3 Innovation is difficult to measure in any comprehensive sense. Some indicators, however, can be separated out for analysis, and comparisons drawn between the performance of UK companies and their principal competitors.

11.4 UK business's R&D spend has increased over the past decade. It recovered strongly after the last recession (Chart 11.1). However, R&D spend has increased much faster in other countries. Some economies are starting from a very low level of expenditure, and increasing at a faster rate to catch up. In terms of spending relative to GDP, the UK's international position is middling (Chart 11.2). However, the effectiveness of the spend matters as much as the quantity. The Government's contribution to business enterprise expenditure on defence R&D has fallen, mainly because of declining defence R&D. A significant proportion of business enterprise expenditure on R&D (BERD) funded by Government in the UK, France and the US relates to defence (Chart 11.3).

INNOVATION
IDEAS FROM THE WORKFORCE

TOYOTA

Toyota in Derbyshire regularly receives suggestions from its workforce for improving performance.

- *The paint supply to robot paint sprayers used to be turned off as each car was finished, and then flushed out to clean the system for the next colour*

Toyota reduced cost and minimised waste by turning off the paint supply fractionally before the end of the paint cycle, leaving less paint to be flushed out.

- *Paper waste which used to be sent to landfill is now separated for recycling, and sold by the company, thus turning a cost into a revenue*

UNIPART

The Unipart Group, a foremost supplier to the motor industry, encourages all its employees to form quality circles – known as "Our Contribution Counts" circles.

- *Since 1991, 550 circles have saved the Group £5 million*

- *One circle implemented a programme of dealer visits which generated a closer understanding of customer needs and fewer mistakes in packing*

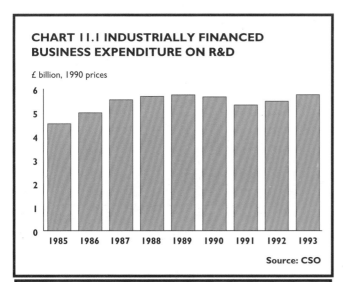

CHART 11.1 INDUSTRIALLY FINANCED BUSINESS EXPENDITURE ON R&D

£ billion, 1990 prices

Source: CSO

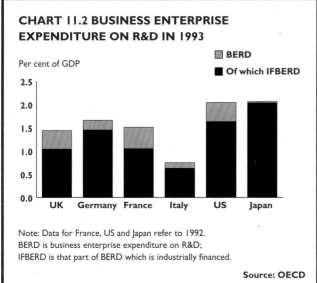

CHART 11.2 BUSINESS ENTERPRISE EXPENDITURE ON R&D IN 1993

Per cent of GDP

■ BERD
■ Of which IFBERD

Note: Data for France, US and Japan refer to 1992.
BERD is business enterprise expenditure on R&D;
IFBERD is that part of BERD which is industrially financed.

Source: OECD

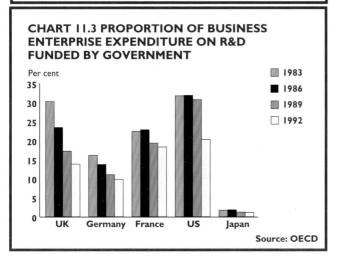

CHART 11.3 PROPORTION OF BUSINESS ENTERPRISE EXPENDITURE ON R&D FUNDED BY GOVERNMENT

Per cent

■ 1983
■ 1986
■ 1989
□ 1992

Source: OECD

11.5 The UK has the second largest number of Nobel Prizewinners for science after the US – more than Germany and Japan, despite their larger populations.

11.6 These data only show part of the picture. As the senior managers interviewed for the "Winning" report[1] highlighted, truly innovative companies are those which generate a culture in which people welcome change, continuous improvement and managed risk-taking, translate values into action and listen to their customers. Earlier findings[2], however, suggest that overall only one in ten UK companies is truly innovative.

11.7 While the UK has a proud scientific record and can display some evidence of high-quality innovative activity, there is ground to make up in commercial exploitation. There are huge opportunities ahead for the UK, if we focus on clear targets and move fast.

So Government is responding ....

11.8 Government policies on innovation are designed to encourage innovation in its widest sense and help UK firms to exploit it most effectively. Business takes the lead, but its ability to do so is affected by the climate in which it operates. The Government can help by:

◆ raising awareness of the importance of innovation;

◆ spreading best practice within firms;

◆ facilitating co-operation between organisations at home and overseas;

◆ establishing a framework of incentives for collaboration between academics, research facilities and companies;

[1]*Competitiveness – How the Best UK Companies are Winning* [CBI and DTI] (1994)
[2]*Innovation – the Best Practice – the report* [CBI Technology Group and DTI Innovation Unit] (1993)

SUCCESSFUL INNOVATION IN LARGE AND SMALL UK COMPANIES

One large organisation with an international reputation for successful innovation turned its research section into a company.

◆ *It is now more effective in turning ideas into profitable processes and products*

◆ *In 1994 it generated over 90 per cent of research funding from outside sources, much of it from licensing technology*

A small company focused on improving partnerships with the world's leading electronics companies. It has:

◆ *developed a world-class technology which forms the basis of the latest generation of handheld Personal Digital Assistants, incorporating handwriting recognition*

◆ *shortened production time for these high-performance products*

◆ *grown substantially. In 1991 it had 13 employees, sales of £1 million and one partner. Now its sales are £7 million (profit £3 million before tax), it employs over 100 people in the UK, US and Japan, and has seven partners*

◆ securing access for UK companies to the widest possible range of world technologies and know-how;

◆ ensuring that the Government's activities in science and technology contribute to national competitiveness;

◆ encouraging a supply of people with the right skills; and

◆ ensuring that regulation in the UK and in the EU does not inhibit innovation, and that the legislative framework is permissive rather than restrictive (Chapter 15).

11.9 Organisations representing business share the Government's concern that every company should give priority to innovation. Their view in response to the 1994 Competitiveness White Paper was that the Government should increase efforts to enable, stimulate and foster innovation. The Government has developed its activities in conformity with these views.

.... by encouraging partnership ....

11.10 For the nation, partnership can help make the most of our strengths: the knowledge and talent in our universities and research establishments, and the management and marketing skills of our businesses. The exchange of technological know-how and best practice between firms raises the general level of performance and prosperity. Such collaboration is contributing substantially to economic development in many parts of the UK.

The Innovation North West Forum in session.

INNOVATION ACTIVITIES ACROSS THE UK

Business Networking has developed in all UK regions (for instance Innovation North West, and both North East Technology Support and the Business Exchange Network in the North East). In the South West a regional networking project is promoting co-operation and collaboration among small firms, allowing them to achieve more collectively than each could individually.

In Yorkshire and Humberside, Univentures International brings together middle managers with skills in engineering, marketing, finance or general management. It helps them shape new enterprises. Since October 1994 it has set up eight hi-tech companies in telecommunications and bioscience. In addition, an annual competition called Headstart helps graduates with business ideas to set up businesses in the region.

In the West Midlands, innovation will be a major theme of Industry 96, involving inward investment promotion and outward trade missions, as well as conferences and exhibitions highlighting local industrial, scientific and educational strengths.

In the North West, the five major universities of Manchester, with the local TEC and six major local companies, have pooled training resources in advanced manufacturing for the benefit of all local industry.

In Scotland, Scottish Enterprise and the Royal Society of Edinburgh are studying ways of converting research into wealth-creating products and services.

In Wales, 1995 has been designated the "Year of Innovation". Seminars and exhibitions targeted at business sectors will raise awareness of the importance of technology and innovation to the success of the Principality.

In Northern Ireland, investment in R&D facilities by Du Pont and Seagate (the result of projects collectively valued at £38 million) is strengthening the province's innovation and technology infrastructure.

.... helping to improve the climate for innovation ....

11.11 Government is working with others to create an improved climate for innovation. Examples include:

◆ the business-led Myners Group, which reported in February 1995 on the relationships between institutional investors, trustees and industry[3] (Chapter 13);

◆ the Innovation Lecture (presented this year by Peter Williams, Chief Executive of Oxford Instruments) and the R&D Scoreboard, which help raise the profile of innovation. The Scoreboard reported a 9 per cent increase in R&D spend by UK-based companies. The Government is developing a more comprehensive Innovation Index for introduction during 1996 to promote further analysis and debate about innovation in firms;

◆ education, which makes a powerful long-term contribution to encouraging an

---

[3]*Developing a Winning Partnership – How companies and institutional investors are working together.* [Report by the Myners Group] (February 1995)

innovative culture. Students who experience innovation in business at first hand, as part of their school or university career, more readily acquire the skills associated with wealth creation (see also Chapter 7). The Enterprise in Higher Education Initiative helped universities and colleges adapt courses to develop more entrepreneurial graduates. Educational Business partnerships foster high-quality links between schools and business. The Government is also introducing ten regional innovation prizes for products of Young Enterprise companies set up to give young people practical business experience, and launching a "Making Sense of Science" programme, with industrial sponsors, to promote better primary school science teaching and increase links with industry; and

◆ the Office of Public Service and Science's promotion of public understanding of science and technology through activities such as National Science, Engineering and Technology Week, which this year involved more than 3,000 events across the country.

11.12 In addition, the Government has an important role in providing technical infrastructure, such as the UK's internationally-harmonised National Measurement System.

.... and developing know-how for the future. Technology Foresight points the way.

11.13 Technology Foresight, announced in the 1993 White Paper on Science, Engineering and Technology[4], has reported[5] in parallel with this White Paper. Panels of experts have identified promising market opportunities within fifteen sectors across the economy in the next 10-20 years, and the technologies and skills we need to exploit them[6]. This programme is the most comprehensive in the world, building on experience in the US, Japan and Germany.

11.14 The Government will disseminate Foresight findings widely. It will co-ordinate a national programme of workshops and conferences to spread awareness and encourage business – especially small firms – to join in. The Government will:

◆ retain the broad structure of the sector panels to continue disseminating the findings;

◆ secure the services of senior business people to support the panels' work with industry;

◆ encourage Trade Associations, Research and Technology Organisations (RTOs), professional bodies, the CBI and existing regional networks to spread Foresight findings and promote follow-up;

◆ follow up a recent consultation exercise in Scotland on public understanding of Science and Technology; and

◆ use Business Links and Chambers of Commerce to extend awareness of Foresight, especially to small firms.

[4]*Realising our Potential: a Strategy for Science, Engineering and Technology. Cm 2250* [HMSO] (1993)
[5]*Progress through Partnership: Report from the Steering Group of the Technology Foresight Programme 1995* [HMSO] (1995)
[6]*Progress through Partnership 1–15: Reports from the Technology Foresight panels* [HMSO] (March and April 1995)

KEY ASPECTS OF TECHNOLOGY FORESIGHT

Technology Foresight involves people from industry, the academic community and Government working in partnership. Over 10,000 have participated so far. Continuing work will bring more people into the programme.

Important cross-sectoral priorities include:

- *getting right the relationships between people, science and technology and new business processes*
- *harnessing future communication and computing power effectively in response to market signals*
- *maximising opportunities for new organisms, processes and products arising from modern biotechnology*
- *exploiting new materials and processing technologies for manufactured goods*
- *getting greater precision, control and security into the management of production by deploying information-processing and sensor technologies*

Foresight will:

- *ensure that scientific excellence is sustained*
- *increase collaboration between industry and academic institutions in areas of economic importance by building on the science and business networks generated in the initial exercise*
- *influence Government priorities in science, engineering and technology programmes and regulation and training responsibilities*
- *help direct future priorities where support from academic institutions would be most helpful*
- *help industry develop more informed business and investment strategies*

11.15 The Foresight reports identify many opportunities for the public and private sectors to work together on R&D projects with commercial potential. The Government intends to:

- develop, with business and science, new LINK programmes in areas of promise identified by Foresight. OPSS and DTI have jointly committed an extra £6 million this year to support them, with additional funding for later years; and
- launch a competitive Foresight Challenge, under which business

---

LINK

LINK promotes effective partnership between industry and science in support of wealth creation and improved quality of life.

Since the launch of LINK in 1986, over 570 individual projects worth over £300 million have been initiated, involving more than 800 companies and 130 science institutions. Many of these projects have led to new marketable products, processes and services.

By March 1995, there were 40 LINK programmes, 19 open to new project proposals and 21 having closed. Around 230 projects had been completed.

LINK was re-launched in March 1995, with improvements to enable participants to start joint projects more quickly.

and academic interests will be invited to make proposals, in consortia, for collaborative R&D initiatives in areas identified by the Foresight report as having high economic promise. The Government will provide an additional £40 million over the next three years, on the basis of industry providing at least matching funding to ensure a sharp market focus. The Challenge will be based on existing mechanisms for collaboration, in particular the successful LINK mechanism.

11.16 One of the key messages emerging from the Technology Foresight Programme is that rapid development in information and communication technologies will create many new opportunities for improved performance. Suppliers are developing new kinds of services such as tele-shopping, tele-banking and distance learning. Users are finding opportunities for productivity increases and improved responsiveness to customer needs.

11.17 DTI plans to launch a major Information Society initiative in the autumn to encourage business to develop products and services for the Information Society, and to demonstrate to users the practical benefits of multimedia and advanced technologies. The initiative will combine within a single coherent package existing as well as new support programmes, and aims to:

◆ raise awareness of the opportunities;

◆ encourage technology transfer within and between supplier sectors (for example IT, telecommunications, broadcasting and publishing);

◆ promote the development of competitive sources of key underpinning technologies; and

◆ spread best practice in the use of information highways and multimedia services.

Industry and user groups will be invited to compete for support for innovative Information Society projects in targeted areas.

TOWARDS THE INFORMATION SOCIETY

BRITISH INTERACTIVE MULTIMEDIA ASSOCIATION AWARDS:

UK BASED WINNERS IN 1994

The Chemistry Set is an interactive library and encyclopaedia of chemical experiments and information, for students from the age of ten to much more advanced levels. Produced by New Media and the University of Nottingham, it includes video sequences of over 350 experiments, 3-D full-motion interactive molecular structures, photographs of elements, databases and text files.

AT&T Global Information Solutions produced for Galleria 21 (UK) Ltd the Galleria 21 Electronic Catalogue, which provides 24-hour access to a wide range of goods from about 20 up-market suppliers. It is available in all 4 terminals at Heathrow Airport. Goods can be ordered in 6 languages, shipped to over 30 countries and paid for by credit card.

Cytovision was produced by The Open Learning Unit, Liverpool John Moores University. It provides improved quality assurance and standardisation of the British National Cervical Cancer Screening Programme. It contains a database of resource materials in various media forms, and teaching material.

We also need to spread best practice....

11.18 Promoting best practice in innovation is a feature of DTI's Managing in the 90s Programme, and of other recently launched programmes, including the electronics sector's "Time to Market Association", the Environmental Technology Best Practice Programme and the Energy Design Advice Scheme, and "Biotechnology means Business".

11.19 The Design Council has been relaunched, with Government funding, as an effective and powerful national advocate of design, providing advice to Government, industry and education.

DESIGN AND COMPETITIVENESS

The effective use of design is fundamental to the creation of innovative products, processes and services. Good design can significantly add value to products, lead to growth in sales and enable both the exploitation of new markets and the consolidation of existing ones.

The benefits of good design can be seen in:

◆ *processes improved by gradual innovation*

◆ *redesign of existing products in response to user needs, new markets and competitor products*

◆ *development of new products by anticipating new market opportunities*

The challenge is to integrate design into business processes. Many individuals at all levels in firms take decisions which have an impact on design. Effective management of the decision-making process is vital to business success.

Some companies already use cross-functional teams of designers, engineers and commercial staff to respond more rapidly to demands for new and improved products.

To help more companies improve their competitiveness through design the Government has:

◆ *provided funds for 70 Design Counsellors in Business Links, mainly for the benefit of small and medium-sized enterprises*

◆ *worked with the Design Council to establish regional support groups for Design Counsellors*

◆ *funded through the Design Council a new £2 million programme to research and spread best practice in managing design and link it with marketing and technology*

◆ *established Scottish Design to provide design advice to Scottish companies and to promote design awareness in education*

◆ *established the Welsh Design Advisory Service to provide advice to industry and education*

BUSINESS
LINK

....and improve access to know-how in the UK....

11.20 Business can benefit from access to existing know-how through patent searches and links with other companies, business support organisations and universities. Many companies – especially small ones – lack the resources to explore the possibilities quickly. They may need guidance on what is available, what is most suited to their requirements and how best to use it. A range of options is available to help.

◆ Thirty Innovation and Technology Counsellors (ITCs) have already offered technology advice to thousands of firms through Business Links. By the end of 1995 the ITC service will be expanded to cover all 200 Business Links at an annual cost of up to £4.3 million. Complementary services have recently been introduced in Northern Ireland and in Scotland where, as a result of a recent review, responsibility for innovation support has transferred from DTI to the Scottish Office. Similar services will be available in Wales by the end of 1995.

◆ ITCs are establishing their own local service networks (NEARNET) for clients. These include partnerships with local universities and colleges.

◆ DTI has established SUPERNET. This service, accessible through Business Links in England and other routes in Wales and Scotland, helps smaller firms to overcome problems with product or process technology by networking with national centres of technological excellence. Forty-five national centres are now active members of SUPERNET.

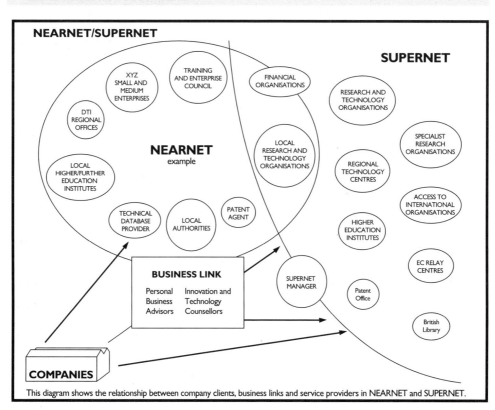

This diagram shows the relationship between company clients, business links and service providers in NEARNET and SUPERNET.

- Technology-based business support organisations, including RTOs, will be developed into a network directing innovation and technology services to smaller firms with Government support of up to £6.4 million over 4 years.

- Patents are the largest single body of technical information, with over 30 million already published and around 1 million new ones each year. The Patent Office makes some 14,000 statutory patent searches each year. In 1993-94 it also implemented nearly 3,000 separate commissions for Government, industry and commerce – an increase of 20 per cent on 1992-93. Business Links are working with the Patent Office to set up regional clinics. They will improve access to patent information by helping small firms with Innovation Credits as announced in the 1994 White Paper.

- DTI and the Economic and Social Research Council (ESRC) are jointly sponsoring a three-year research programme to help firms assess the value of intellectual property rights, and channelling the results to firms through Business Links.

- DTI will pilot the promotion of visits by business people to companies which can show how they have successfully exploited the results of collaboration with universities and other research organisations.

Before the end of this year, the combination of these networks and resources with 200 Business Links will provide local delivery of innovation and technology advice on a scale previously impossible.

11.21 The Government is further assisting technology transfer by providing additional funds up to £7.4 million over 3 years.

- The Teaching Company Scheme (TCS) supports 514 partnerships between universities and companies involving 970 postgraduate associates. To increase participation by smaller firms, 11 TCS centres have been opened. By the end of 1995 this will increase to 17 and cover the whole of the UK.

- A programme is to be developed to bring new technologies to the attention of small firms around the country through Business Links.

- The Postgraduate Training Partnership scheme (PTP) involves collaborative partnerships between universities and RTOs. It will be extended to about 200 industrially-relevant projects.

- The Shell Technology Enterprise Programme, started in 1992, now places over 1000 second year undergraduates in smaller firms each year, and will be extended for three more years to enable the programme to cover the whole country.

....and from overseas.

11.22 The UK is extending its links with overseas sources of know-how, through international trade, inward and outward investment in manufacturing, service and research activities, and interchange of scientific information between universities in the UK and overseas.

11.23 Most scientific and technological advances are made overseas. Contacts between researchers in the UK and other countries are therefore a major advantage. These are being strengthened, for example through Northern Ireland's Joint Statement on Technology Transfer with the US. Under the Brinord scheme, UK and Norwegian companies and researchers have identified opportunities for collaboration on R&D. The Learning from Japan Initiative, overseas visits, and dissemination of technical information from diplomatic posts are among other means by which the Government endeavours to acquire and disseminate knowledge for the UK.

11.24 To increase the inward flow of know-how, the Government plans to:

◆ create a pilot network of international technology promoters to cover Japan, the US, Germany and France, with subsequent expansion to South East Asia at a cost of up to £1.9 million of additional expenditure over 3 years. Through Business Links and other networks, including Trade Associations, they will put firms in contact with innovation and technology developments overseas. They will help to develop business alliances for products and services in future markets;

◆ develop the Engineers to Japan scheme, applying it to other markets and disciplines, involving secondments to and from the UK; and

◆ offer technical information from overseas to UK firms over the Internet.

In guiding technology development, partnership with the rest of Europe can provide resources...

11.25 The EU's Fourth R&D Framework programme aims to improve the competitiveness of European industry. Funding is provided for research projects which stimulate collaborative links across the EU in fields such as biotechnology, industrial materials and technologies, and information technologies. The UK had the highest rate of participation of any Member State in the last programme, and won 18 per cent of the funding.

11.26 EUREKA promotes co-operation among companies in 21 European countries which can lead to profitable partnerships. Over 550 UK organisations (a quarter of them small or medium firms) have taken part in EUREKA projects. DTI's financial commitment to these projects totals over £135 million.

11.27 The European Regional Development Fund (ERDF) can fund technology acquisition in targeted areas of the UK, involving expenditure of up to £80 million a year.

11.28 The Government will use Foresight reports to:

♦ identify areas where European collaboration would be fruitful and encourage UK companies to propose appropriate projects; and

♦ develop its position for the EU's Fifth Framework Programme from 1998.

..alongside UK support for smaller firms.

11.29 It is often the smaller firms which have the greatest need of help – including financial help – to develop ideas and bring them to market. Over 1000 small firms have already developed innovative products and processes with help from SMART and SPUR Award schemes. Since 1986, over 1,200 SMART projects have received Stage 1 financial support and half of these went on to receive more at Stage 2, totalling £80 million in grants from DTI. In addition, SPUR grants of £46 million have helped over 500 projects.

11.30 The Government is improving these services by:

♦ combining and simplifying the existing SMART and SPUR schemes. A new combined programme, with a budget of £76 million (including £7 million of extra funding) over the next three years, will also provide for winners to get business advice from Business Links. The new funding will allow for larger projects in high technology areas with global promise; and

♦ piloting a specialist pre-finance evaluation service at an initial cost of up to £1.8 million over 3 years to help smaller businesses with the difficulties they encounter in raising medium and long-term finance for innovative and high technology projects.

Our university research base is a strength....

11.31 Maintaining and improving the strength of research in our higher education institutes is vital to national competitiveness. Research helps to:

♦ meet industry's need for highly skilled people, as well as innovative ideas for technological development;

BUSINESS LINK

SMART, SPUR, LINK AND EUREKA: SUCCESS STORIES

Optimised Controls, a small company, used a **SMART** *Award to help develop a range of innovative motor controllers. It expanded from a 2-employee consultancy to a 32-employee manufacturing company. Since 1988 the company has grown by over 40 per cent a year and has an annual turnover of £3 million.*

SPUR *helped another small company (TRL Technology) to develop a modem and fax interface for personal mobile communications over the Inmarsat satellite in parts of the world beyond the reach of fixed or cellular communication networks. Exports of these products have helped increase TRL turnover more than five-fold.*

LINK *helped Deakin Davenset Rectifiers Ltd collaborate with scientific partners to produce a commercial success. They developed a new battery charger which they expect to double their share of the UK market within two years.*

Between 1991 and 1994 **EUREKA** *helped the formation of the UK-based Cimulation Centre (TCC), through which firms and universities from the UK, Austria, Denmark and France collaborated to develop innovative software tools for the control of manufacturing processes. Since October 1993 more than 30 systems have been installed, and sales of related products have started.*

◆ keep the UK abreast of research undertaken elsewhere; and

◆ solve practical problems – environmental, medical, social – in all parts of the economy and society.

11.32 The Government will use the Foresight findings in making decisions on the future direction, balance and content of science and technology financed by the public sector. The Research Councils will also take account of Foresight findings in making funding decisions. Government looks to the Higher Education Funding Councils and to universities to use Foresight in this way.

11.33 Measures to develop the links between industry and universities include:

◆ extending the Realising our Potential Awards scheme which rewards researchers for their ability to attract research funding from industry;

◆ taking greater account of industrially-relevant work in the Higher Education Funding Councils' (HEFC) forthcoming research assessment exercise, which will form the basis for funding university research from 1997-98; and

◆ doubling, to £20 million in 1995-96, the financial rewards which the HEFC for England can allocate for generic collaborative research with industry. The HEFC for Scotland will allocate some additional funds to those who are most successful in generating funds from the private sector.

> ### REALISING OUR POTENTIAL AWARDS SCHEME
>
> *Examples of projects*
>
> ◆ *Research into harder-wearing, corrosion-resistant stainless steels. They might be used eventually in turbine blades for generating electrical power, and gears for processing foods*
>
> ◆ *Investigating the potential of a special type of protein molecule for use in blood tests. The protein is not only cheap to produce, but also highly sensitive. One application might be the development of improved diagnostic tests for viral infections*
>
> ◆ *Examining ways of using micro-organisms for removing toxic heavy metals from aqueous waste streams to protect and clean up the environment*

....and research programmes in Government Departments can contribute to competitiveness.

11.34 Departments are making progress in incorporating competitiveness into their science and technology programmes. The Annual Forward Look[7] published in parallel with this White Paper illustrates their activities. Each year, the Forward Look provides industry and the research community with a comprehensive statement of strategy for publicly-funded science, engineering and technology.

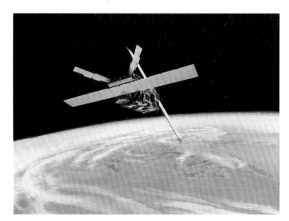

ESR 1, Europe's first RADAR satellite, monitors a range of factors, from oil slicks to global climate change.

[7]*1995 Forward Look of Government-funded Science, Engineering and Technology* [HMSO] (1995)

RESEARCH AND COMPETITIVENESS IN DEPARTMENTS

The Ministry of Defence ensures that its research plans are communicated to industry and, through its Defence Evaluation and Research Agency (DERA), seeks collaboration with industry for the benefit of both. Dual-Use Technology Centres (DUTCs) are being established to allow industry and universities to work with the DERA on technologies with both civil and defence applications. DUTCs have been opened in the fields of structural materials and supercomputing; others will open shortly.

The British National Space Centre is collaborating with suppliers and potential users of Earth Observation data on work to identify new applications: for instance, the ability to predict sugar beet yields and the process of coastal erosion.

MAFF has established Regional Technology Transfer Centres for the food industry. Through the LINK programme on Advanced and Hygienic Food Manufacturing, it will encourage collaborative R&D to develop advanced hygienic manufacturing techniques and technologies. The first MAFF Fellowship in Food Process Engineering will provide a centre of academic excellence to meet the strategic needs of the food industry.

The Department of Health has created an Industry Research Advisory Group to improve links between Government and the health and medical industries, and has launched the MEDLINK programme to promote research in new technologies with the medical devices industry.

DTI has helped to formulate the Land Transport Programme, part of the Innovative Manufacturing Initiative. The programme will bring together industry and universities to work on future vehicle technologies. These include telematic systems to help drivers find their way and avoid collisions, and the use of advanced materials in vehicle design and manufacturing.

The Department of the Environment's Whole Industry Research Strategy has been developed in collaboration with the construction industry, to encourage the best use of technology to improve competitiveness, client satisfaction, quality of life, profitability and public perception of the industry. Task groups will find novel ways to solve construction problems, meet regulatory requirements and manage information.

11.35 The Ministry of Defence (MOD) has made further progress over the last two years in transferring technology from its science and technology programmes. Later this year, it will present its longer-term technology strategy to industry to encourage greater alignment of interests and further collaboration in research. MOD, other Government Departments and the Research Councils are now seeking to improve their co-ordination in pursuing shared technology objectives. The Government will set up a new working forum between MOD, OPSS, DTI and the Research Councils to identify further opportunities for a co-ordinated approach to the planning of civil and defence science and technology. The forum will be informed by the outcome of the Technology Foresight Programme and in particular will aim to identify areas for collaboration involving industry.

11.36 We must maintain a strong emphasis on innovation as a key component of competitiveness, foster more effective partnerships between public and private sectors, and ensure that all partners have access to the necessary resource. Then the UK will make a success of change.

FAIR AND OPEN MARKETS

12.1 Britain is one of the world's greatest trading nations. Trade accounts for 25 per cent of our GDP – compared with 10 per cent in the US and 9 per cent in Japan. We make up only 1.1 per cent of the world's population but are responsible for 5 per cent of world trade in goods.

12.2 Fair and open access to markets throughout the world is therefore vital to our prosperity. Without it, UK business cannot translate its competitiveness into exports and wealth. The openness of our home market brings wider choice at competitive prices.

12.3 This Chapter sets out the Government's policies towards:

◆ opening markets abroad;

◆ helping UK business to exploit market opportunities, through exporting and outward investment; and

◆ making the UK the first choice for inward investors.

TRADE POLICY

Multilateral trade

12.4 When the 1994 Competitiveness White Paper was published, the Uruguay Round of GATT trade talks had just reached a successful conclusion – offering global benefits estimated at $510 billion in the year 2005. With the establishment of the World Trade Organisation (WTO) on 1 January 1995, strong and comprehensive rules for the multilateral trading system are in place – the task now is to make them work.

MULTILATERAL TRADE: THE NEW AGENDA

The Government seeks to open markets and resist any slide into protectionism, whether overt or disguised. Its post-Uruguay Round agenda includes:

◆ *pushing forward work in areas left incomplete at the end of the Uruguay Round (financial services, shipping, telecommunications and aerospace) or which were included in the Round, but where more remains to be done - such as tariffs, standards, intellectual property and Government procurement*

◆ *ensuring the 25 or so new applicants to the WTO meet the requirements for membership. Several applicants are of great economic significance: China and Russia alone represent potential markets of about 1.5 billion consumers*

◆ *ensuring that the WTO's strengthened dispute settlement procedures work effectively - and making use of them where necessary*　　　*Continues...*

MULTILATERAL TRADE: THE NEW AGENDA continued

◆ *rapid progress on a new Multilateral Agreement on Investment, on which work is already underway in the OECD*

◆ *developing the international taxation framework, at OECD and bilaterally, to remove tax impediments to free world trade*

◆ *new elements, such as promoting deregulation, tighter subsidy disciplines and increased international co-operation in competition policy*

◆ *opposing attempts to use non-trade issues - such as environmental protection, or labour standards in developing countries - as an excuse for protectionism*

12.5 The Government plans to build on the success of the Government and business relationship in the GATT Uruguay Round by setting up, by the summer of 1995, a trade policy consultation forum to enhance and improve the exchange of views between Government, business and other interests on trade policy issues.

Trade barriers

12.6 Negotiations in the WTO offer the best long-term prospect for removing external barriers to UK business. But they need to be backed by more immediate action. That is why the President of the Board of Trade announced a new initiative on trade barriers in November 1994. Its objectives are to:

◆ identify which barriers most restrict exports and investment by the UK – in particular, barriers that apply across a number of sectors and in a large number of countries, and that affect the UK's top 80 export markets; and

◆ concentrate on removing those barriers, particularly where there is a reasonable chance of success, rather than waste resources on problems that cannot be solved.

12.7 Trade bodies representing our major export sectors have told the Government which barriers most concern industry. Analysis of the results will give the sharpest ever picture of priorities.

12.8 The Government will tackle these by:

◆ using the Commission's enforcement powers for barriers within the EU;

◆ mobilising the Commission and other Member States to act through multilateral fora such as the WTO and bilateral agreements with third countries; and

◆ using bilateral contacts with other countries to tackle both internal EU barriers and external ones.

12.9 The Government will hold regular discussions with the trade associations representing main export sectors to update its database of barriers and to ensure it continues to reflect their concerns. It will issue regular progress reports on the initiative.

European trade

12.10 Within the EU, the Government seeks to extend the benefits of the Single Market – for UK businesses and consumers alike. It aims to:

◆ consolidate what has already been achieved by making the Single Market work;

◆ bring new sectors within the Single Market; and

◆ extend membership of the Single Market to new countries.

Making the Single Market work

12.11 The benefits of the Single Market will not be fully realised until competitive distortions from state aids are eliminated. Large amounts of aid are still given

---

THE UK IN EUROPE

The EU is the world's largest trade grouping - its members accounting for 40 per cent of world exports. Membership of that bloc is crucial for UK jobs, investment and prosperity.

Our exports to the EU have grown dramatically since we joined:

◆ *the EU now takes nearly 60 per cent of our visible exports, compared with about 40 per cent to the same countries in 1973*

◆ *eight of the top ten UK export markets are EU partners*

◆ *the UK is the number one choice for companies wishing to invest in the EU, with one third of all inward investment into the EU*

◆ *UK financial and other business services have tripled their trade surplus with the rest of the EU 12 from £1 billion in 1983 to £3 billion in 1993*

Moreover, this new business has not been at the expense of reduced exports to non-European countries like the US and Japan. These too have expanded. The increased EU trade reflects improved market access and the reduced costs of trade which flow from EU membership - particularly since completion of the Single Market. The EU, not just the UK, is now the home market for UK companies. Details of trade with our top 80 export markets, including the EU, are set out in Chart 12.1.

Membership of the EU also enables the UK to exert a significant influence in European policies. The Government has been able to:

◆ *achieve greater success in the GATT trade talks, by persuading the EU to adopt many of its objectives*

◆ *promote UK business' interests within the EU - by pushing for more liberalisation, deregulation, and the elimination of unfair state aids and trade barriers*

by many Member States. The 1994 White Paper identified priorities for tackling this. The Government is working on these with the Commission, focusing on four major challenges:

- stopping subsidy auctions between Member States for internationally mobile investments;

- ensuring that rescue and restructuring packages, particularly for state-owned enterprises, are tightly controlled;

- improving the Commission's procedures to ensure effective handling of cases and complaints; and

- achieving effective controls through the WTO and in the Central and East European countries wanting to join the EU.

12.12 The Government is working with the Commission to promote co-operation between enforcement agencies. More enforcement problems could be solved through contacts between national agencies rather than through expensive legal proceedings.

FIGHTING STATE AIDS IN THE COURTS

In parallel with UK industry, the Government challenged in the European Court of Justice the Commission's decision to approve FF 20 billion of aid to Air France. The case will be heard later this year. It could set important legal precedents for the appraisal of future restructuring aid cases.

12.13 Where a company is affected by infringement of Single Market rules by another Member State, DTI's Single Market Compliance Unit (SMCU) takes up the problem with the Commission, the Member State or both. The SMCU seeks out such barriers, promoting its services to firms and commissioning detailed studies of potential problem areas. The Government is currently reviewing how the SMCU's activity could be boosted.

Extending the Single Market to new sectors

12.14 Liberalisation of protected sectors creates investment opportunities and pushes prices down. In November 1994, the Council of Ministers affirmed its commitment to liberalisation in electricity and gas and set a firm timetable for telecommunications. The UK is pressing for rapid action (see Chapter 14).

Extending the Single Market to new countries

12.15 Austria, Finland and Sweden joined the EU at the beginning of this year. All were previously in the Single Market as European Economic Area (EEA) members. The UK has welcomed the applications of Hungary and Poland and would like to see them and other Central and Eastern Europe countries join as soon as

SMCU intervention in 1994 resulted in changes to Spanish regulations on bottle sizes, allowing UK drinks manufacturers such as HP Bulmer Ltd to continue supplying the Spanish market. Other successes include relaxation of French regulations on the bulk import of fertilisers, which had been harming UK exporters.

possible. Consolidation of political and economic reform in these countries remains a challenge for the next decade. Their accession to the EU would be a huge step forward. It would also open markets, extending the Single Market to a further 100 million consumers.

EXPORT PROMOTION

12.16 Export promotion is a vital component of the Government's support for fair and open markets. Our Overseas Trade Services (OTS) help UK firms to overcome information gaps, cultural barriers and other obstacles to full participation in international trade.

12.17 Last year UK exports reached record levels in both manufacturing and service industries, with our exports growing faster than world trade, indicating an increase in our market share.

12.18 Our key export challenge is now to penetrate expanding markets, particularly in Asia and Latin America – where our market share is only 2.7 per cent and 2 per cent respectively – whilst at least maintaining share in our major markets elsewhere in the world. At present growth rates, the Asian and Latin American markets may account for 40 per cent of world income by 2025, compared with 28 per cent in 1993.

Review of progress

12.19 The 1994 White Paper set out the Government's aim of providing the world's best support to exporters. A key milestone in this was the completion of Market Plans to focus and direct the Government's export drive for each of the UK's top 80 export markets. Chart 12.1 illustrates how our position has changed in these markets over the last year, and how our share of world trade to the markets has changed over the ten years from 1983.

12.20 Other achievements include:

◆ extension of the Business Link network in England. All core Business Links will deliver Overseas Trade Services. The Government is supporting the recruitment of 70 experienced exporters as Export Development Counsellors to strengthen Business Links. We aim to have all 70 in place by the end of the year;

◆ DTI's 100 Export Promoters, secondees from the private sector. They have helped over 25,000 UK companies, many as a result of contacts made by overseas Posts;

◆ in 1993-94, Posts received nearly 87,000 business visitors and made 55,000 calls on foreign companies;

◆ a successful language initiative with the private sector, including a National Languages for Export award attracting over 450 applicants and consultancy

BUSINESS
LINK

CHART 12.1 EXPORT PERFORMANCE IN THE UK'S TOP 80 MARKETS

	UK Exports 1994 £ million	Change in UK exports, 1994 on 1993, %	Balance of trade 1994 £ million	Change in Balance of trade 1993 to 1994, £ million	UK share of world exports to country in 1993, %	Change in UK share of world exports to country 1993 on 1992, %	Change in UK share of world exports to country 1993 on 1983, %
Unified Germany	17,704	11	-4975	-791	7	-10	-3
USA	16,783	9	-944	59	4	-2	-19
France	13,684	13	-1980	-452	8	-6	-2
Netherlands	9,777	21	-369	668	9	-9	-21
Belgium/Luxembourg	7,727	9	406	76	9	16	19
Italy	6,966	15	-385	315	6	-1	28
Irish Republic	6,730	6	870	71	42	-7	-19
Spain	5,087	17	1291	198	8	-2	18
Sweden	3,348	16	-812	-81	11	19	-27
Japan	2,991	13	-5850	32	2	-1	68
Switzerland	2,456	8	-2361	87	5	10	-19
Hong Kong	2,298	6	-782	46	3	15	-40
Norway	2,021	33	-1689	962	10	0	4
Canada	1,917	4	36	46	2	-7	-21
Australia	1,914	20	851	249	6	-6	-14
Denmark	1,771	10	-340	217	7	-14	-39
Singapore	1,769	24	-128	57	3	-9	6
Saudi Arabia	1,515	-17	776	224	8	-19	38
South Africa	1,411	25	440	314	12	-11	-21
India	1,311	16	23	-19	7	-15	-10
Malaysia	1,305	35	101	533	3	-1	22
Finland	1,297	15	-956	-181	10	13	46
Portugal	1,256	-8	-10	-122	7	2	-5
Austria	1,035	14	17	76	3	7	29
Israel	1,032	18	459	133	7	22	2
South Korea	971	22	-125	156	2	-1	24
Greece	936	2	577	-12	6	0	55
China	845	14	-797	-209	1	11	-25
Turkey	814	-22	185	-329	6	2	29
Thailand	746	13	-168	-56	2	2	15
Taiwan	735	10	-846	104	1	-4	26
Russia	708	28	-97	173	3	N/A	N/A
Poland	703	-2	158	-111	5	-7	141
Dubai	612	-9	480	-64	N/A	N/A	N/A
Brazil	525	27	-394	94	2	12	60
Nigeria	458	-28	333	-189	14	4	-12
Brunei	418	29	123	106	20	8	-1
New Zealand	411	24	-128	35	6	0	-34
Mexico	389	16	150	-21	1	-4	-27
Czech Republic	374	30	96	54	N/A	N/A	N/A

	UK Exports 1994 £ million	Change in UK exports, 1994 on 1993, %	Balance of trade 1994 £ million	Change in Balance of trade 1993 to 1994, £ million	UK share of world exports to country in 1993, %	Change in UK share of world exports to country 1993 on 1992,%	Change in UK share of world exports to country 1993 on 1983, %
Egypt	368	9	116	-33	4	8	-12
Indonesia	366	11	-417	-47	2	-13	-24
Oman	362	19	284	61	12	3	-64
Philippines	355	16	111	81	2	2	24
Pakistan	355	5	-4	-18	5	-16	1
Abu Dhabi	333	-38	262	-182	N/A	N/A	N/A
Kuwait	312	0	73	-2	8	4	24
Puerto Rico	309	64	232	151	N/A	N/A	N/A
Iran	389	-42	156	-95	5	8	-10
Hungary	259	26	19	-34	2	-5	31
Cyprus	245	4	124	25	11	24	-17
Colombia	231	121	40	111	2	2	0
Argentina	225	25	54	16	2	11	1126
Malta	205	0	130	-13	12	5	-30
Venezuela	197	-13	63	-38	3	13	33
Kenya	196	29	29	49	12	-2	-2
Libya	195	-29	47	-71	N/A	N/A	N/A
Morocco	194	15	-7	7	3	14	-16
Ghana	191	-11	52	-90	18	-5	-3
Sharjah etc	169	68	141	66	N/A	N/A	N/A
Sri Lanka	154	22	-32	-16	5	-2	72
Chile	153	8	-42	64	2	-7	-19
Bahrain	150	0	125	26	6	-24	-27
Lebanon	139	2	131	6	5	23	37
Qatar	128	-11	120	-2	13	6	-38
Romania	127	35	-19	-20	2	11	19
Canary Islands	126	20	34	-22	N/A	N/A	N/A
Jordan	115	-18	91	-28	7	13	-17
Iceland	110	-25	-130	-27	17	68	23
Zimbabwe	105	26	-41	-3	9	-23	-48
Syria	102	37	4	35	3	-4	9
Ukraine	86	18	68	8	N/A	N/A	N/A
Bulgaria	86	2	16	8	4	15	87
Tanzania	82	-24	60	-23	13	29	9
Tunisia	81	30	35	12	2	13	-35
Mauritius	75	3	-217	-9	8	0	-24
Gibraltar	75	-28	70	-30	N/A	N/A	N/A
Yemen	74	-13	69	0	6	0	6
Trinidad & Tobago	72	2	24	-4	8	-6	1
Zambia	45	-40	32	-30	14	-4	-27

grants for companies to review their language needs;

◆ improved ECGD cover for project and capital goods exports. Premium rates for political risk have been reduced by 10 per cent on average since 1994, following reductions of more than 25 per cent over the previous two years; and

◆ re-structuring of Scottish Trade International (STI), the Government's export body for Scotland, to concentrate on key export markets. STI is leading the preparation of an Export Development Strategy for Scotland.

12.21 The business-led Overseas Projects Board targets overseas projects in water, power, healthcare, telecommunications, education and training, airports and railways, through sector groups which advise on tactics, and where necessary help to direct Government support to a single UK bidder. Initiatives now being introduced – with a budget of nearly £3 million over the next four years – include export help for UK education and training providers, and assistance for companies pursuing major contracts to develop associated training initiatives.

12.22 Export promotion involves all of Government. Last year, Ministers from 14

SECTORAL INITIATIVES

◆ *DTI has signed a Memorandum of Understanding with the Brazilian state oil company, to help UK oil and gas companies exploit the opportunities offered by liberalisation of the Brazilian market. Twenty five UK suppliers have already visited Brazil*

◆ *STI has helped Scottish software companies win orders of £3 million in the US, with a further £4 million on the way*

◆ *DOE helped nearly 600 businesses through its export promotion programme for the construction and water industries last year. An enhanced programme is planned for 1995-96. Exports and overseas contracts totalled about £7 billion last year and are set to grow further*

◆ *In Northern Ireland, the Industrial Development Board established a unit to promote greater exports by the food processing industry. Since then, exports have grown by 30 per cent*

◆ *MOD's Defence Exports Services Organisation provides specialist advice and assistance to British defence companies in marketing and exporting their goods and services throughout the world*

◆ *The Treasury will set up, in mid 1995, a dedicated unit to promote exports of UK expertise in privatisation*

◆ *MAFF, in partnership with Food from Britain, helped 170 British food companies win business worth up to £56 million at this year's SIAL food exhibition in Paris*

◆ *The Welsh Office has taken 194 SMEs - of whom 111 were first time exporters - to new markets since April 1993. This successful programme is to be extended until 1999*

Departments went on over 80 trade promotion missions to more than 50 countries, accompanied by over 1000 business people.

The challenge

12.23 Despite progress, many export opportunities are still missed. The Institute of Export estimates that only around 100,000 of the 2.8 million UK companies are exporters. Many more UK businesses could export, and to more markets.

12.24 The Government intends to work in partnership with business to meet this challenge. Working with the export teams in Business Links, it aims to introduce at least 30,000 new exporters to foreign markets by the year 2000.

Meeting the challenge

12.25 Both Government and business will need to improve to meet this target. The Government will raise the level of professionalism of civil servants doing trade promotion work by increasing secondments between the public and private sectors, enhancing civil servants' language skills and extending their training.

12.26 In improving services for exporters, DTI will commit nearly £40 million extra over the next four years, of which over £20 million will be additional Government expenditure.

12.27 The Government will use Business Links in England to reach companies that have never before used its services. It will increase the provision of export services and training through Business Links, and by the end of 1995 bring in a package of financial and other incentives to help SMEs. It will also examine ways in which Business Links could assist SMEs in applying for export credit insurance.

12.28 In addition DTI will increase support for Trade Fairs and for Inward and Outward Missions by nearly £30 million over the next four years. It will work with sponsors to ensure that companies follow best practice and derive maximum benefit from participation.

BEST EVER DTI EXPORT SUPPORT PLANNED FOR 1996-97

- *400 Trade Fairs, up from 334 in 1994-95*

- *280 Outward Missions, up from 145 in 1994-95*

- *30 Overseas Seminars, up from 16 in 1994-95*

- *20 supported inward VIP visits, up from 11 in 1994-95*

- *60 Inward Missions, up from 34 in 1994-95*

- *22 Store Promotions, up from 13 in 1994-95*

EXPORT VOUCHERS

SMEs are often daunted by the prospect of exporting and unsure of the value of buying in assistance. To help overcome these problems, the Government will provide the 70 Export Development Counsellors in Business Links with vouchers to give to SMEs, starting in September 1995. After a free initial consultation, the vouchers will be exchangeable for additional services such as:

BUSINESS LINK

- *diagnostic checks on exporting potential*

- *professional development of a Business Plan for exports*

The scheme's budget will rise to £2 million a year over the next three years.

12.29 At the Britain in the World conference in March, there was much emphasis on the need to present the UK's strengths more positively abroad. In the commercial field, the Government will mount a rolling programme of major all-British exhibitions to promote the best of our commercial expertise to selected markets, on the lines of the recent successful Partners in Progress fair in Jeddah. The events will cost £11 million over the three years from April 1996.

A 'North America Now' showcase event, one of a series being held around the country.

12.30 The role of commercial staff overseas is crucial. The FCO already devotes 30 per cent of its frontline overseas staff to commercial work – its largest overseas activity. The FCO now plans to strengthen its support for exporters during 1995. This will include:

◆ fourteen new Posts in the former Soviet Union and in emerging markets in Asia and Latin America;

◆ more than 100 extra commercial staff overseas (an increase of over 9 per cent);

◆ rapid-response funding to ensure swift deployment of staff to meet temporary surges in demand; and

◆ piloting video-conferencing and electronic mail systems to link Posts with staff engaged in export promotion work in the UK, including Business Links.

12.31 Business also needs to play its part. In particular, business support organisations could do more to develop the international competitiveness of the sectors they represent. The Government is therefore announcing an "Export Challenge" to trade associations.

BUSINESS LINK

THE EXPORT CHALLENGE

The Government will invite trade associations to put forward proposals to improve the international competitiveness of the sectors they represent.

Ten successful associations will receive awards this year of up to £50,000 each to part-fund innovative, practical initiatives offering the prospect of long-term export benefits.

INWARD AND OUTWARD INVESTMENT

12.32 Successful companies source, produce and market their products across the world. Often, they invest directly overseas.

12.33 The world's stock of Foreign Direct Investment (FDI) has grown rapidly, increasing some twenty-fold since the late 1960s – from $104 billion to $2.1 trillion in current prices.

12.34 FDI is increasingly linked with exporting, as companies use both to gain competitive advantage. For service companies, direct investment is often the only way to sell in overseas markets.

12.35 The Government's policy is to encourage both inward and outward investment.

Inward investment

12.36 Inward investors are of huge importance to the UK economy. Foreign-owned manufacturers provide:

◆ a third of manufacturing investment;

◆ nearly a fifth of manufacturing employment;

◆ over a fifth of manufacturing output; and

◆ around two-fifths of UK manufactured exports.

12.37 Inward investment brings not just jobs, but a wide range of additional benefits. A recent study commissioned by DTI[1] reveals a positive impact on the performance and competitiveness of UK suppliers, particularly on their production processes, including quality assurance systems, plant and machinery, delivery times and cost control methods. Product development is also strengthened. Inward investors stimulate UK exports: the study suggests that less than a quarter of inward investors' overseas sales would have been won by other UK firms.

12.38 The UK's stock of inward investment has risen from nearly £52 billion in 1986 to £131 billion. DTI's Invest in Britain Bureau (IBB) has recorded 4,096 inward investment decisions since 1979, creating and safeguarding nearly 700,000 jobs – over 367,000 jobs in the past five years alone.

CASE STUDY OF AN INWARD INVESTOR TO THE UK

Fujitsu launched its operations in the North East of England in early 1991 with the aim of exporting to customers in Europe. A good relationship was established with local agencies, acting in partnership, who put together an attractive package of incentives. The 300,000 square foot factory was built and commissioned in world record time. It now represents investment of some £325 million and is a leading producer of electronic memory devices used in computers and other IT equipment.

The company's performance has been impressive. In 1993, the North East plant was designated the best of 400 Fujitsu units worldwide. Over 500 jobs are available to local people. Employment and turnover have more than doubled in three years. Virtually all output is exported, primarily to Europe.
Continues...

[1] *Assessment of the wider effects of foreign direct investment on manufacturing in the UK.*
[PA Cambridge Economic Consultancy] (1995)

CASE STUDY OF AN INWARD INVESTOR TO THE UK *continued*

Its strong presence in the North East has helped improve the region's competitiveness:

- *the emphasis on training and standards has helped stimulate and improve local training provision, particularly for technical skills*

- *work force skills have been enhanced, particularly those of young people, with a greater focus on NVQs and GNVQs. Some 35 per cent of the workforce are involved in further and higher education courses*

- *the technological base of the area has been strengthened through an upgrading of the capital stock and local expertise*

- *high quality site investment has helped to regenerate the area physically and improve the environment*

- *the company's good reputation, together with the scale of its investment and success, has helped improve the image and visibility of the North East*

- *Fujitsu has placed importance on collaboration with local agencies. It works as a partner with local and regional Government bodies to champion the North East and stimulate further investment and economic success*

- *it has positive links with Further Education Colleges and the TEC which have strengthened training provision in technical skills and computing. Its links with local schools have raised awareness of the world of work for young people and teachers, with whom it has worked jointly on the school curriculum. Universities have participated in joint research on technical issues and marketing*

- *it has worked with professional organisations to shape industry standards*

Fujitsu also has a presence in Northern Ireland where it has recently expanded its operations.

Competition in attracting and retaining inward investment

12.39 Foreign investors are looking for an environment which offers a sustainable competitive advantage. Over many years the UK has attracted the largest share of foreign direct investment in the EU – more than France and Germany combined.

- Britain is the second largest recipient of foreign direct investment worldwide (Chart 12.2).

- Our principal sources of investment are the US, Japan and Germany. There are now over 4000 US and over 210 Japanese manufacturing companies in the UK. Around 20 per cent of the stock of French and Dutch investments

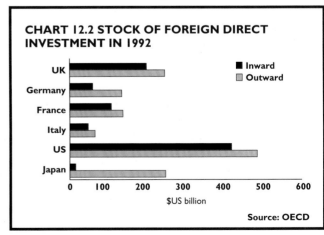

CHART 12.2 STOCK OF FOREIGN DIRECT INVESTMENT IN 1992

Source: OECD

in the EU and some 13 per cent of the stock of German investment is located in the UK.

◆ The UK continues to be more successful at attracting US and Japanese investment than any other European country (Chart 12.3).

◆ Growing investors are also attracted to the UK. For example, 27 per cent of Korean investment in the EU comes to the UK.

12.40 Inward investors are attracted to the UK because it offers a competitive environment, with:

◆ an open market and stable economy;

◆ a world-class science base;

◆ low taxes;

◆ superior international communications;

◆ a skilled workforce and excellent labour relations;

◆ a regulatory regime which encourages innovation, making the UK a world-class centre for high technology industries such as telecommunications, pharmaceuticals and bio-technology; and

◆ a cultural heritage which helps to make the UK an attractive place in which to live and work.

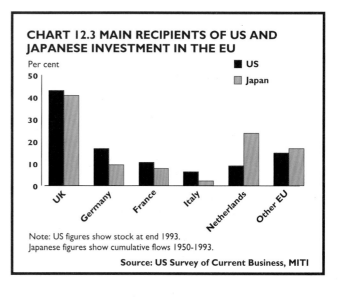

CHART 12.3 MAIN RECIPIENTS OF US AND JAPANESE INVESTMENT IN THE EU

Note: US figures show stock at end 1993.
Japanese figures show cumulative flows 1950-1993.

Source: US Survey of Current Business, MITI

Review of progress

12.41 Over the last year the Government has:

◆ appointed a new Chief Executive for the IBB from the private sector;

◆ launched sectoral initiatives to promote inward investment in the vehicles, vehicle components, pharmaceuticals and electronics industries. Outward missions have already visited China, Japan, Korea and the US;

◆ increased the funding of the English Regional Development Organisations (RDOs) to over £9 million in 1995-6, increased their number from

The President of the Board of Trade, flanked by Dr John Bridge, Chief Executive of Northern Development Company, and Vice Chairman Kim of Samsung, at the ground breaking ceremony for Samsung Industrial Park. The investment is worth £450 million and should bring more than 3,000 jobs to the North East.

INWARD INVESTMENT OVER THE PAST YEAR

- *Samsung Electronics Company - £450 million electronics investment in the North East, with over 3000 jobs*

- *Motorola - £250 million investment in silicon chip manufacturing in Scotland, with 250 jobs*

- *Toyota - £200 million investment in motor manufacturing in the East Midlands, with 1000 jobs*

- *Nippon Electric Glass - £194 million investment in TV component manufacture in Wales, with 750 jobs*

- *NEC - £530 million investment in semi-conductor fabrication in Scotland, with 430 jobs*

- *Honda - £330 million investment in motor manufacturing in the South West, with 2000 jobs*

- *Daewoo Electronics - £17 million investment in production of video cassette recorders in Northern Ireland, with 250 jobs*

WHAT INVESTORS SAY ABOUT THE UK

- *"Structural change has made Britain by far the most attractive place to invest in Europe"*
  Herr Berndt Pischetsrieder, Chairman of the Executive Board, BMW

- *"We could have located this expansion elsewhere in Europe, but we have been delighted with the standard and dedication of the local workforce here."*
  Mr Katsunori Kubo, Managing Director, SEH Europe Ltd

- *"A truly European Bank must have an integrated pan-European management operating from its largest market - that is London for international products."*
  Herr Hilmar Kopper, Chairman, Deutsche Bank

---

six to eight and set aside a further £400,000 to enable Government Offices to provide a better investor service in the remaining regions (the East and South East);

- re-inforced existing aftercare programmes in Scotland, Wales and Northern Ireland; and

- re-structured the Welsh Development Agency's inward investment activities with additional resources overseas. At home, its resources have been refocussed to provide a more coherent service to potential and existing customers.

A forward look

12.42 But others in Europe are determined to increase their share of inward investment (see Chart 12.4). They are becoming far more active in overseas markets and more receptive to investors' demands.

12.43 There is room for further improvement, with more emphasis on:

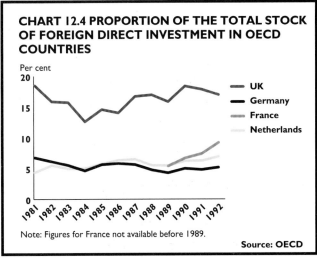

CHART 12.4 PROPORTION OF THE TOTAL STOCK OF FOREIGN DIRECT INVESTMENT IN OECD COUNTRIES

Note: Figures for France not available before 1989.

Source: OECD

- markets which offer longer term potential. The US will continue to provide the major source of inward investment. Japan, Korea and Taiwan all have companies investing internationally;

- satisfying potential investor needs and understanding companies' strategic objectives. Rationalisation of multi-plant activities is likely to continue, with parent companies forced to take hard decisions on the relative merits of different European locations. A better understanding of companies' strategic thinking will enable the Government to assist local management argue the case for concentrating activities in the UK; and

- attracting headquarters operations to the UK, in addition to manufacturing and service sector projects.

New initiatives

12.44 To address these issues, the Government will:

- re-structure the IBB to allow greater focus on potential investors from key markets and on "aftercare" for existing investors. The detail of this re-structuring will be announced in the IBB's Annual Report for 1994-95;

- increase IBB's staff by over 20 per cent; and

- allocate five additional FCO staff to inward investment work in Europe, North America and Asia Pacific.

12.45 In addition the Government will examine with existing companies the prospects for developing an action plan to encourage new inward investment in the food industry.

OUTWARD INVESTMENT

UK performance in world markets

12.46 The UK stock of FDI ranks second only to the US, just ahead of Japan. As a proportion of GDP, it is more than double that of any other major investor. These investments returned £6.5 billion to this country in 1993, and generated further profits of about £10 billion which were re-invested overseas.

Review of progress

12.47 In the 1994 White Paper, the Government outlined commitments to help outward investors by improving the framework within which decisions to invest overseas are made. Achievements include:

- agreement on 14 new or revised double taxation treaties, which minimise tax barriers to UK overseas trade and investment. The UK has the world's largest network of bilateral tax treaties, numbering nearly 100. Twenty treaties are currently under negotiation;

- conclusion of 26 Investment Promotion and Protection Agreements (IPPAs) since 1993, including those with India, Brazil, South Africa and Cuba. Over 75 have been signed since 1975;

- review of ECGD's Overseas Investment Insurance Scheme, which currently insures investments in 31 markets with total exposure of £205 million. The review has led to a 30 per cent cut in average premium rates. Portfolio control is now more closely tied to the level of risk. In some markets ECGD now considers insurance for exposures of more than £100 million; and

- introduction of a Strategic Alliance Programme to provide help towards consultancy costs for companies seeking to establish a permanent presence in North and South America.

A forward look

12.48 The Government will:

- push forward negotiations in the OECD on a Multilateral Agreement on Investment, to

EXAMPLES OF OUTWARD INVESTMENT

- *Cadbury Schweppes' purchase of Dr Pepper has made them the third largest soft drinks manufacturer in the US after Coca-Cola and Pepsi*

- *BT has invested $4 billion in MCI, giving it a 20 per cent stake in the second largest international and long distance telecommunications company in the US*

- *Glaxo completed a $26 million manufacturing plant in Jeddah last September. The company's capital expenditure overseas in 1994 was £239 million, 44 per cent of its total capital expenditure*

- *Consortia led by North West Water and Severn Trent Water have won contracts valued at £517 million to provide water services for over 4 million people in Mexico City*

- *Last year the BBC entered a "global strategic alliance" with Pearson plc, which aims to launch commercial satellite and cable services around the world. £30 million has been invested to date*

secure comprehensive, transparent and legally binding rules to promote and protect foreign investment. It will seek high standards of liberalisation and investor protection and effective enforcement procedures, in an agreement open to both OECD and non-OECD members;

◆ expand further the network of Double Taxation Agreements, and modernise existing ones, targeting the economies offering greatest growth potential for UK business;

◆ expand further the network of bilateral IPPAs, giving priority to developing countries in the top 80 UK export markets;

◆ by September 1995, improve collection and dissemination of information on investment opportunities overseas, making it widely available to UK companies; and

◆ also by September 1995, launch a pilot initiative to promote networking and joint marketing between British companies overseas.

12.49 In addition, the Government will carry forward the work on the study on outward investment announced in the 1994 White Paper. Preliminary results from the study suggest that the Government could offer further assistance to outward investors, for example by:

◆ issuing a best practice guide;

◆ improving sign-posting to information and advice networks; and

◆ improving publicity for existing initiatives, including the facts about IPPAs.

12.50 It will address these issues, and further results from the study when it is completed, during 1995.

FINANCE FOR BUSINESS

13.1 Access to finance is essential for business development. The 1994 Competitiveness White Paper highlighted a number of features of UK financial markets. This Chapter:

- analyses developments and progress over the past year; and

- sets out future plans to encourage the successful flow of finance to industry.

The framework

13.2 In 1993, the Chancellor launched the Industrial Finance Initiative (IFI), which analysed the impact of the fiscal and regulatory regime on the flow of savings to business. Businesses and finance providers were consulted. It concluded that:

- investment of risk capital in SMEs should be encouraged;

- increased competition in the provision of finance was desirable; and

- improvements in SME financial management were required.

13.3 Also in 1993, the Governor of the Bank of England launched an initiative involving the banks, the CBI, small firms' representatives, Government and academics to consider finance for small firms. This has led to two reports by the Bank[1,2], the most recent in January 1995.

Large firms

13.4 The UK financial system is exceptional in its concentration of shareholding in the hands of major financial institutions. Insurance companies and pension funds account for three-fifths of all share ownership. This partly reflects favourable tax treatment of pension funds.

Larger companies face little difficulty in raising finance.

13.5 The financial strength of these institutions gives large companies ready access to new equity capital. Larger firms also face little difficulty in securing bank finance.

13.6 However, the UK bond market is under-developed compared to the US. To give companies better access to capital markets, the Government will:

- loosen restrictions later in the year to make it easier for companies to issue bonds; and

- allow preference shares and bonds of non-financial companies into Personal Equity Plans.

13.7 International comparisons of the cost of capital are difficult to make with precision because of differences in financial structures and tax systems. Evidence suggests that the real costs of debt and equity in the UK are not significantly different from those in other

[1]*Finance for Small Firms* [Bank of England] (January 1994)
[2]*Finance for Small Firms: A Second Report* [Bank of England] (January 1995)

countries, and companies here also benefit from low rates of tax. However, UK firms use more equity finance, which is relatively expensive, and less debt than firms abroad. As inflationary expectations fall, so should the cost of capital.

13.8 The Government welcomes the various initiatives to improve relations between the City and industry, and to improve corporate governance. These include the Cadbury and Greenbury committees and the Myners Group.

Dividend policy

13.9 The proportion of profits paid out in dividends by UK companies is high by international standards, although it has fallen as the economic recovery has strengthened (Chart 13.1).

13.10 Analysis suggests that dividends are more flexible than is apparent from the aggregate data: for example, one survey[4] showed 22 per cent of firms cut their dividends in 1992.

SMEs

13.11 SMEs face more problems than larger firms in the following areas:

- equity capital;
- loan finance;
- late payment; and
- financial management.

13.12 In each area, the Government is working with others to improve the situation.

Equity capital

13.13 UK financial institutions invest relatively little in smaller firms, considering the substantial contribution of SMEs to private sector output. Yet it is smaller

---

MYNERS GROUP REPORT

- *The report[3] was published in February 1995 by a joint City and industry working group, supported by DTI*

- *It recommends that companies and investing institutions work in partnership to ensure UK industry invests for the long term*

- *It identifies best practice for companies, institutions and trustees:*

  - *companies should articulate their strategic objectives, and develop clear communications, for example through more effective AGMs*

  - *institutional shareholders should be more open with company management about its performance, play an active role in corporate governance, and improve fund managers' industrial and commercial knowledge*

  - *trustees should encourage fund managers to take a long-term view of companies they invest in*

- *Industry's response has been encouraging, and indicates a willingness to adopt and improve the best practice set out in the report*

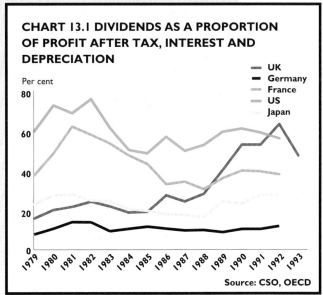

CHART 13.1 DIVIDENDS AS A PROPORTION OF PROFIT AFTER TAX, INTEREST AND DEPRECIATION

— UK
— Germany
— France
— US
Japan

Per cent

Source: CSO, OECD

---

[3]*Developing a Winning Partnership – How companies and institutional investors are working together* [Report by the Myners Group] (Feb 1995)

[4]Data from Datastream International. See K. Wright; *Company Profitability and Finance* [Bank of England Quarterly Bulletin] (August 1994)

dynamic companies which are most likely to need risk capital. Only 0.7 per cent of institutional funds is invested in unquoted securities[5], and only 2.7 per cent in quoted companies with a market capitalisation of less than £40 million[6]. One reason for this may be the cost of appraisal and subsequent management, which is proportionally greater for investment in small firms.

13.14 Innovative and technology-based start-ups and smaller firms with growth potential are particularly disadvantaged. This is because real and perceived risk to reward ratios are high and the timescale for returns is long. There may also be a lack of understanding of the technology and market prospects by finance providers.

13.15 The Government is encouraging the retention of capital within growing firms by reducing taxation.

- Capital Gains Tax (CGT) roll-over relief defers tax on disposals of business assets where the proceeds are reinvested.

- CGT retirement relief reduces liability on gains from business assets of up to £1 million.

- Inheritance Tax relief enables many small businesses to be passed on tax-free.

13.16 The Government is encouraging investment in smaller companies through:

- Venture Capital Trusts (VCTs);

- the Enterprise Investment Scheme, which gives reliefs similar to those available for VCTs, and which was enhanced in the 1994 Budget to make it more attractive for both companies and investors;

- CGT reinvestment relief, which defers tax on gains invested in unquoted shares;

- single company Personal Equity Plans (PEPs), which may include unquoted shares emerging from approved all-employee share schemes; and

- the relaxation of valuation rules for unquoted shares held by insurance companies.

VENTURE CAPITAL TRUSTS

- *Small companies will be able to raise up to £1 million a year from a VCT*

- *VCTs will invest in a range of companies to enable investors to spread risk*

- *Individual investors who hold shares in a VCT will enjoy the following benefits on investments of up to £100,000 a year:*

  - *exemption from income tax on dividends*

  - *freedom from capital gains tax on disposals*

Those who buy new shares, and hold them for five years, will also be entitled to:

  - *income tax relief at 20 per cent*

  - *defer tax on capital gains where the gain is reinvested in a VCT*

13.17 Business angels often bring professional expertise to a business as well as capital. Five informal investment demonstration projects supported by DTI have been successfully concluded. The lessons learned from the projects are being collated, and best practice examples will be disseminated later this year.

[5] [CSO]
[6] [The WM Company]

The Government is currently examining the scope for relaxing the Financial Services Act to improve the supply of information on smaller investment opportunities.

13.18 DTI and the Treasury will participate in a panel set up by the private sector to encourage the development of a UK business incubator movement. Incubators will provide shared services at a common location and continuing advice and support to companies.

13.19 Measures to encourage investment in growing companies are not enough. Many investors in smaller companies find it difficult to withdraw their investment. The existence of an active market in medium-sized company shares would make investment in potential growth companies more attractive and would improve access to capital for the medium-sized companies themselves. A number of initiatives are being developed to provide such facilities.

- The **Alternative Investment Market (AIM)** is due to be launched in June by the London Stock Exchange. Initial responses to countrywide marketing and seminars on the new market indicate significant interest from small and growing companies in using AIM to access new capital and from professional advisers in providing assistance to potential entrants. The Government has confirmed that AIM securities will be eligible investments for the new Venture Capital Trusts and will be eligible for the full range of "unquoted" tax reliefs.

- **Tradepoint** is planning an electronic market place to compete with the London Stock Exchange, and has applied for recognition from the Securities and Investments Board (SIB).

- **Electronic Share Information (ESI)** intends to apply for recognition this year: it plans a facility to enable the general public to deal in smaller company shares using home computers.

- **EASDAQ** may also apply for recognition from the SIB: it plans a version of the American NASDAQ market to provide a Europe-wide market for shares in growing companies. Its target date for launch is January 1996.

Loan finance

13.20 Small and growing companies remain largely dependent upon banks for external finance. Bank relationships have been cited as an area of

> ### DEVELOPMENTS IN SCOTLAND AND NORTHERN IRELAND
>
> *A 1993* **Scottish Enterprise study**[7] *identified finance as a major factor in the relatively low level of business creation and growth in Scotland. As part of its strategy to help create 25,000 more businesses by the year 2000, Scottish Enterprise is:*
>
> - *piloting with Scottish banks a £100 million capped-rate loan scheme for small businesses. Since its launch at the end of 1994, £16 million of loans have been authorised*
>
> - *working with others to put business angels in touch with small companies*
>
> - *developing with the financial sector a Scottish Venture Fund to provide equity to small firms, underpinned by aftercare from business advisers*
>
> *The Department of Economic Development in* **Northern Ireland** *launched in March 1995 a £10 million Development Capital Fund financed equally by the EU and the private sector. The Fund will be managed by Hambros.*

[7]*Improving the Business Birth Rate – A Strategy for Scotland* [Scottish Enterprise] (October 1993)

competitive weakness, but there has been improvement.

- ◆ Banks are making serious efforts to understand better the needs of smaller business customers. They have introduced voluntary codes of practice governing relations with SMEs. They have invested in staff training and have produced targeted material for customers. Some have offered inducements to SMEs to improve financial management.

- ◆ The Bank of England reports that the ratio of term loans to overdrafts has risen from 2:3 to 3:2 over the last three years.

- ◆ Banks increasingly offer alternative kinds of finance. For example, latest figures show that factoring and invoice discounting to all customers increased by 22 per cent[8] in 1994.

13.21 Despite these improvements, some smaller firms remain critical of banks. Accordingly, the Government will encourage greater competition in the provision of finance to SMEs, both in equity finance (see above) and loan finance. For example, since April, building societies have been allowed to lend to businesses without land as collateral, and the extension of PEPs to corporate bonds (see above) will help to develop new sources of finance.

13.22 Business Links will play a part in informing businesses about the range and relative merits of different kinds of finance. They will deliver a new Government-funded service which will help growing businesses get access to the most appropriate finance package. Banks are being encouraged to refer customers to Business Links for information and counselling services.

Smaller firms can now turn to Business Links for advice on financing their business.

13.23 The Small Firms Loan Guarantee Scheme facilitates lending to companies who would not otherwise meet lenders' collateral or track-record requirements. Take-up of the scheme increased dramatically from £52 million in 1992-93 to £240 million in 1994-95. The scheme is being reviewed to improve its effectiveness. Any changes will be implemented this year.

Late payment

13.24 Trade credit is an important source of funds to small firms. It is often abused through late payment. The 1994 White Paper indicated that there was no clear mandate for legislation, but that the case would be reviewed after two years. However, it announced several initiatives to encourage prompt payment by Government and the private sector.

13.25 Several sources show that payment times are reducing, although this might be expected during an economic recovery. The Grant Thornton and BSL European

---

[8]*Annual Statistical Review* [Association of British Factors and Discounters] (January 1995)

TACKLING LATE PAYMENT

◆ *Government Departments have been instructed to abide by the CBI prompt payers' code and to publicise their payment practices. On available information, over two-thirds of Departments improved their payment performance in 1994-95. The Government is committed to further improvement*

◆ *A CBI-led working group to develop proposals for a British Standard for prompt payment is expected to report by July 1995*

◆ *The Government issued a consultative document on company payment policy[9]*

◆ *Changes to court procedures for debt recovery are now being implemented and the scope of the small claims court is under review*

◆ *"Make the Cash Flow", a guide to credit management, was published[10] by the Government in November 1994*

Business survey indicates that average payment periods by UK firms shortened from 52 days in 1993 to 48 days in 1994, compared with an EU average of 63 days.[11]

Financial management

13.26 Financial management in small firms, particularly those that are growing rapidly, is often inadequate.

13.27 The Government has issued a consultative document on the proposed introduction of a financial management certificate. This is aimed at making it easier for finance providers to assess a company's prospects.

13.28 The Enterprise Investment Scheme (EIS) allows investors to participate in the management of firms. This should improve the quality of management. Over one half of recent EIS issues has involved a business angel.

13.29 The Government assists financial training. Business Links provide counselling on financial skills, help small firms with the costs of employing outside consultants, and guide SMEs to training most suited to their needs. The "Money and Machines" initiative[12] will help SMEs to plan and finance good quality capital investment.

"MONEY AND MACHINES"

The guide is the result of a partnership between City and industry. It aims to improve the quality of UK manufacturers' capital investment by:

◆ *highlighting the importance of a well-thought out business plan when making investment decisions*

◆ *emphasising the benefits of improved understanding between lenders and businesses*

◆ *advising on capital investment plans, financial appraisal techniques, appropriate financial packages and on dealing with finance providers*

Since its publication in February 1995, over 100,000 copies have been issued to firms, trade associations and lending institutions.

BUSINESS
LINK

---

[9]*Tackling Late Payment: Stating Payment Policies in the Directors' Report* [DTI] (February 1995)
[10]*Make the Cash Flow [DTI] (November 1994)*
[11]*Grant Thornton European Business Survey* [Grant Thornton International and Business Strategies Ltd] (Spring 1994)
[12]*Money and Machines: A Guide to Successful Capital Investment in Manufacturing* [DTI] (February 1995)

COMMUNICATIONS AND PHYSICAL INFRASTRUCTURE

14.1 The industries considered in this chapter are fundamental to the effective performance of business. Most have been privatised, and their relationships with their customers have changed significantly. The Government's approach has excited interest and emulation in many other countries, bringing enormous opportunities in other markets for the privatised companies and their advisers.

14.2 The Government's approach has been to:

♦ privatise public sector companies, opening markets to new entrants and introducing competition where possible. This has promoted choice, investment, and lower prices;

♦ introduce regulatory regimes where necessary to encourage the development of competition and represent the interests of consumers;

♦ help the privatised companies to secure business overseas (see Chapter 12); and

♦ extend privatisation and liberalisation throughout the EU.

COMMUNICATIONS AND BROADCASTING

Telecommunications

Liberalisation and competition

14.3 In 1984, the telephone network in the UK was owned and operated by British Telecom (BT) as a public sector monopoly. Since then the Government has privatised BT, liberalised the supply of apparatus and services, and encouraged the development of effective competition in all segments of the market. The initial BT/Mercury duopoly ended in 1991. The results have been dramatic:

♦ there is now extensive competition, with 150 public telecommunications licensed operators, leading to a substantial improvement in the quality and range of services;

♦ BT has invested over £22 billion in its network since privatisation, and over 99 per cent of its customers are now connected to modern exchanges (compared to 47 per cent in 1990). Other public telecommunications operators in the UK are also investing large sums. Cable companies, most of whom offer telephony services as well as television, are currently investing over £2 billion annually in new networks and adding 260,000 miles of optical fibre each year. BT's existing network has 1.6 million miles of fibre; and

♦ prices have fallen substantially. Since privatisation, BT's tariffs have fallen over 35 per cent in real terms. Other UK operators are even cheaper. As a result, UK call charges are now amongst the lowest in the world (Chart 14.1).

14.4 The competitiveness process continues. Since the 1994 Competitiveness White Paper, four new public operators and 24 others have been issued with telecommunications licences. In the year up to 1 August 1995, BT will have made price cuts of around £300 million. The Government has also sought to open up telecommunications services and infrastructure in other markets to help spread the benefits of liberalisation worldwide:

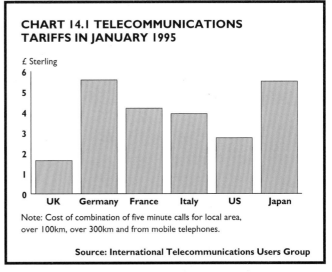

CHART 14.1 TELECOMMUNICATIONS TARIFFS IN JANUARY 1995

Note: Cost of combination of five minute calls for local area, over 100km, over 300km and from mobile telephones.

Source: International Telecommunications Users Group

- the provision of EU telecommunications services over satellite links was liberalised in November 1994, and all telecommunications services and infrastructure are to be liberalised by January 1998;

- telecommunications between the US and UK were made more competitive in October 1994, bringing down transatlantic prices. The US Administration has also announced plans to end the 20 per cent foreign ownership limit in communications companies in respect of countries such as the UK which have opened their markets; and

- the Government is working within the World Trade Organisation to open up competition in network infrastructure around the world to allow the information society to take off.

14.5 Telecommunications software is an increasingly important part of telecommunications services and supply. The industry has about 17,000 employees, with a turnover of £1.2 billion. DTI published in May 1995 a study into the competitiveness of the sector[1]. This put forward an agenda to tackle the current weaknesses of the industry through action by both Government and companies themselves.

Information superhighways and multimedia

14.6 Last year's Broadband Command Paper[2] set out the Government's vision for the development of information superhighways and multimedia services. Its policies are succeeding. The UK's telecommunications, IT and multimedia industries are expanding rapidly and investing heavily. The Government's early liberalisation of telecommunications has given the UK an edge in developing networks for new services. The Cable Communications Association said recently that "the UK

[1]*Telecoms Software: An Opportunity for the UK?* [DTI] (May 1995)

[2]*Creating the Superhighways of the Future: Developing Broadband Communications in the UK.* Cm 2734 [HMSO] (November 1994)

probably now has one of the best regulatory environments in the world for the development of both multi-channel television and competitive telephony".

MULTIMEDIA AT WORK

Business is changing as the high capacity and low cost of modern computers and communication networks allow the development of new multimedia applications.

- *Using advanced communications networks, John Brown Engineers and Constructors Ltd has created a 24-hour "global office" enabling images and text to be shared, and video-conferences held, between experts in different locations. Commercial benefits include higher quality, lower costs, and shorter lead times for projects*

- *The Nationwide Anglia Building Society is experimenting with the use of multimedia kiosks for customers. In addition to providing direct access to various services, the kiosks incorporate a video link to staff at the company's head office to handle specialist enquiries*

- *Information services which combine local storage of still and moving pictures with real time delivery of text are being developed. In the car sales industry, for example, locally stored pictures and video clips of the model range can be integrated with remotely delivered, up to the minute price information*

- *A series of interactive systems are being developed for the Scottish tourist industry, including information terminals at Glasgow Airport and a multi-seat ride for a tourist orientation centre at Aberfoyle*

- *In rural Wales, the NHS is experimenting with videotelephony equipment for low-cost remote diagnosis and training*

14.7 BT and Mercury are entitled to provide interactive services nationally. They are not permitted to convey or provide broadcast entertainment nationally on their existing infrastructure. On the basis that effective competition continues to develop, it is likely that the restriction on conveying broadcast entertainment will be reviewed in 1998, and the restriction on providing such entertainment in 2001. The Government's commitment to this regulatory framework gives investors in the cable industry the confidence that long term commitments to new infrastructure and services will be rewarded. This confidence has been reflected in successful stock market flotations by UK companies over the past year and an accelerated rate of investment. All telecommunications operators, including BT and Mercury, are encouraged to bid for new local cable franchises.

Radiocommunications

14.8 Radio is vital for competition and choice in telecommunications, broadcasting and multimedia. It contributes over £10 billion to GDP, provides over 300,000 jobs, and generates over £7 billion in user benefits and efficiency gains.

14.9 Radio services depend on the availability of radio spectrum free from interference. Spectrum is a limited resource, and demands on it are increasing as new services are developed. DTI's Radiocommunications Agency is undertaking a number of initiatives to help meet this increasing demand.

14.10 The Agency has already made spectrum available which has:

- allowed the development of a fast-growing market for mobile telephone services. The market grew by 76 per cent last year, and four operators provide six competing networks. The UK now has over 3.5 million subscribers: only the US has more; and

- provided for new local and national commercial radio stations, and for a fifth terrestrial television channel.

14.11 Agreement was reached in NATO at the end of last year to give the emergency services access to spectrum previously used for military purposes. The Home Office is studying the possibility of using this additional spectrum to introduce a digital trunked communications system. This system would be among the first of its kind in Europe. It would offer greatly improved radiocommunications facilities for the emergency services and other Government users. It would also create a substantial home market for digital trunked communications systems, boosting their development in the UK, creating jobs and bringing export opportunities. The release of the spectrum vacated by the emergency services will allow a realignment of frequencies, which will reduce the interference from continental Europe currently affecting some mobile communications in the UK.

14.12 The Agency announced in March 1995 that it would also make spectrum available for low-cost, flexible links between telecommunications-switching centres and customers. These links will improve access to advanced digital services and the information superhighway for SMEs, especially in more remote areas. A consultative document[3] is being published at the same time as this White Paper with details of the procedure for awarding licences and the services to be offered.

14.13 The Agency published in March 1995 the first edition of its long-term spectrum strategy on current and future trends[4]. In addition, a fundamental review of future spectrum management is being undertaken and a National Spectrum Management Committee being established. Decisions on the future management of the radio spectrum are being considered in the light of the responses to the consultative document[5] published last year and will be announced shortly.

[3]*Radio Fixed Access - Increasing the Choice. A Consultative Document* [DTI] (May 1995)

[4]*A Strategy for the use of the Radio Spectrum* [Radio Communications Agency DTI] (March 1995)

[5]*The Future Management of the Radio Spectrum* [Radio Communications Agency DTI] (March 1994)

Broadcasting

14.14 The technology of broadcasting is undergoing change which is possibly as fundamental as the introduction of sound to films. Digitalisation – turning sound and pictures into a stream of electronic impulses – will greatly increase the number of channels that can be broadcast within the available frequency spectrum. This will allow the introduction of new interactive services and a new generation of receiving equipment. The Government attaches importance to helping business take advantage of these opportunities in the UK and overseas. The Department of National Heritage (DNH) is currently developing proposals for the introduction of digital broadcasting and intends to produce a consultation document within the next few months, seeking views on proposals for a regulatory framework for the operation of these services.

14.15 While we are second only to the US in our share of world trade in broadcasting programme material, we are a long way behind. To encourage the industry to improve its competitiveness, the Secretary of State for National Heritage established a Broadcasting and Audio-visual Sponsorship Division in April 1995. Its remit is to develop a dialogue with the industry about issues that affect its international competitiveness and about what action the industry should be taking (with Government support where appropriate) to improve its position.

14.16 The BBC is the UK's largest broadcasting organisation and largest exporter of programme material. It is central to the UK's international success in broadcasting. Last year's White Paper on the BBC[6] proposed that the Corporation should be granted a new Royal Charter for a further ten years. It also proposed that the BBC should exploit international commercial opportunities in partnership with the private sector.

14.17 The Government is encouraged by the way the BBC has responded. The Corporation has established BBC Worldwide to co-ordinate all its international and commercial interests. Within BBC Worldwide, BBC subsidiaries market both individual BBC programmes and TV channels delivered by satellite and cable across the globe. The BBC has also formed a global strategic partnership with Pearson plc and Cox Cable of the US. This has produced two new satellite channels, BBC World, focusing on news and current affairs, and BBC Prime, launched in January 1995 to provide entertainment. They represent a bold new attempt, one that is not funded by the licence fee, to give a significant boost to the BBC's international trading position.

14.18 The Government also welcomes the renewed efforts of the independent TV broadcasters and the UK's many independent producers to promote their products in international markets.

[6]*The Future of the BBC: Serving the Nation, Competing Worldwide.* Cm 2621 [HMSO] (July 1994)

14.19 The EU's Broadcasting Directive has established quotas on the European content of broadcast material. The UK Government has made clear to its European partners that the Commission's proposals to remove the existing flexibility in this quota regime are unacceptable, and that quotas ought to be eliminated or phased out as quickly as possible. No evidence exists that such quotas are effective in stimulating a strong and competitive European programme industry. A more open European broadcasting sector would offer major opportunities to UK media companies which are among the most highly regarded in the world.

Cross-media ownership

14.20 The Government is reviewing the regulations governing ownership of the media. The aim is to ensure that the ownership rules continue to strike the right balance between maintaining diversity and plurality on the one hand, and encouraging the industry to be competitive in national and international markets on the other. A policy document setting out the Government's proposals will be published soon.

Posts

14.21 The Post Office continues to provide valuable services to the business community. Royal Mail handles an ever increasing volume of mail to exacting service standards and at domestic tariffs which continue to fall in real terms. Following an agreement with the Government, Post Office Counters is bringing new clients into the Post Office network, and is investing in new technology to modernise its processes, giving its 19,000 private agency businesses new opportunities.

14.22 The Government announced in May 1995 the outline of a revised control regime which, when fully implemented, will help the Post Office to succeed in a more competitive environment.

ENERGY

Gas

14.23 Since privatisation in 1986, 42 new suppliers of gas have entered the market – five in the last year alone. At the end of 1994 they had 44 per cent of the industrial market, compared with 32 per cent at the end of 1993. Privatisation and increased competition have benefited both the industrial and domestic consumer. By December 1994, the average industrial gas price had fallen by 39 per cent in real terms since privatisation. The average price paid by business in 1994 was 6 per cent

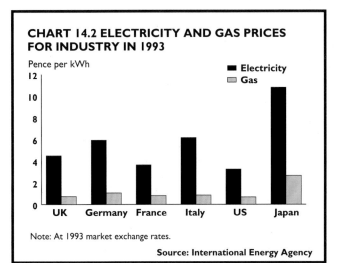

CHART 14.2 ELECTRICITY AND GAS PRICES FOR INDUSTRY IN 1993

Pence per kWh

■ Electricity
☐ Gas

Note: At 1993 market exchange rates.

Source: International Energy Agency

lower in real terms than in the previous year. In 1993, UK prices were the third lowest within the G7 (Chart 14.2).

14.24 The Gas Bill introduced in March 1995 will abolish the existing monopoly in the supply of gas to domestic and small business consumers. Competition will be phased in between 1996 and 1998, providing consumers with a choice of suppliers, stimulating innovation, and exerting further downward pressure on costs and prices. The Bill will provide for separate licensing regimes for the transportation, shipping and supply of gas. The new legislation and licences will include safeguards in such areas as safety, the continuity of supply, and the provision of special services to older and disabled customers. Gas will also be available in Northern Ireland from the end of 1996.

14.25 A consortium of nine companies is proposing to build an interconnector linking the UK and European gas grids by late 1998. This would bring new market opportunities, accelerate the exploration of UK Continental Shelf (UKCS) gas fields, and strengthen the UK's wholesale market. The Government is negotiating a Treaty with the Belgian Government to allow the interconnector to go ahead. It also continues to press within the EU for the liberalisation of gas markets and an end to anti-competitive practices.

OFFSHORE INFRASTRUCTURE INITIATIVE

In 1994, DTI issued a consultative document[7] setting out its concern at the lack of transparency in charges for access to offshore infrastructure, and making proposals for improvements. Most responses supported these proposals, and DTI has asked an industry-wide Steering Group to produce a report by the end of June 1995, including:

♦ *a code of practice for third party use of oil and gas offshore infrastructure and receiving terminals*

♦ *recommendations for standardisation, unbundling and transparency of the terms for third party access to such infrastructure*

DTI will consider whether the current regulatory regime needs to be amended in the light of this report.

Electricity

14.26 Since privatisation in 1990, the market for generation has been opened to competition, and the supply of electricity partially liberalised. National Power, PowerGen and Nuclear Electric together now account for over three-quarters of the market in England and Wales, compared with over 90 per cent in 1990. Furthermore, there are now 22 major generators, including two major independent generators who began production in 1994. Altogether, there were 44 companies supplying electricity in 1994, eight more than in 1993.

[7]*UKCS Competitiveness – Infrastructure* [DTI] (October 1994)

14.27 By the final quarter of 1994, the average industrial electricity price had fallen by 5.5 per cent in real terms since privatisation. The average price paid by industry in 1994 as a whole was 3.5 per cent lower than in the previous year. UK prices were in the middle of the G7 range in 1993 (Chart 14.2).

14.28 A small number of significant users of electricity have faced real price increases. These users received favourable treatment under special schemes before and immediately after electricity privatisation. The undertakings on electricity pool prices given by the main generators to the Director General of Electricity Supply (DGES) have, however, helped to reduce prices for many of these users. The Government also introduced changes to the licensing regime last year which reduced the regulatory burden on small generators and those companies (such as large consumers) who generate electricity for their own use.

14.29 New distribution price controls for electricity in England and Wales came into effect in April 1995. They should deliver savings of 3-4 per cent in real terms on final bills in the first year. In March 1995, the DGES announced that he would consider a possible further tightening of these controls from April 1996. Analogous price controls were proposed in Scotland in September 1994. Work on a price review in Northern Ireland will begin in mid 1995.

14.30 The Government's review of the prospects for nuclear power (para 14.33) concluded that fossil-fuel levy payments to Nuclear Electric should cease at the time of its privatisation. This should reduce electricity prices in England and Wales by about 8 per cent. In Scotland, the premium price charged by Scottish Nuclear was set to decline over the period 1994 to 1998, reducing electricity prices for franchise customers by about 8 per cent in real terms over that period. Ending the premium in 1996 is expected to lead to a price reduction of around 3-4 per cent to franchise customers then.

14.31 Electricity is supplied by an increasing number of private sector companies. Customers with a maximum demand of between 100 kilowatts and one megawatt have been able to choose their supplier since April 1994. All customers, including individual households, will have that choice from 1998. Just under half of all consumption is now open to competition. About a quarter of the newly eligible industrial customers in England and Wales have changed their supplier

> **PFI PROJECT: THE ROYAL DOCKS ENERGY COMPANY INITIATIVE**
>
> *The Royal Docks Energy Company Initiative aims to create a local energy company providing electrical and thermal energy to users in the Royal Docks through Combined Heat and Power (CHP). The costs of providing the energy infrastructure in the Royal Docks will be met by the private sector, not the public sector London Docklands Development Corporation. CHP will be more efficient and effective than conventional methods of supply and will reduce pollution.*

and many have secured lower prices and better contractual terms. Prices for small industrial customers, the group which includes the majority of consumers given the freedom to choose supplier in 1994, were 3 per cent lower in real terms in 1994 than in 1993.

14.32 The Government continues to support the Commission's efforts to liberalise EU electricity markets and end anti-competitive practices.

Nuclear

14.33 The future of nuclear power in the UK will depend on its ability to supply electricity at competitive prices, while maintaining rigorous safety and environmental standards. The Government published in May 1995 the results of its review of the nuclear industry[8]. This announcement included the Government's intention to privatise part of the industry in 1996.

14.34 The Government is committed to opening up the domestic market for dealing with nuclear liabilities. Last year, Government Departments and nuclear operators spent over £400 million on nuclear decommissioning and waste management. UK companies are already winning substantial overseas business in an expanding international decommissioning and waste management market currently worth more than £6 billion a year. With greater opportunity and competition at home, UK companies will be well placed to increase their market share.

Coal

14.35 After almost 50 years in the public sector, the coal industry was returned to private ownership at the end of 1994. Purchasers of the Regional Coal Companies and Care-and-Maintenance Collieries offered for sale included an established UK mining company, and management and employee buy-out teams. Competition in the industry has greatly increased with the addition of nine other former British Coal pits reopened by private sector operators during 1994, alongside an already established private mining sector.

The Rt Hon Tim Eggar MP, Minister for Industry and Energy, visits Tower Colliery, a mine now owned and operated by its workforce following last year's privatisation of British Coal's mining activities.

14.36 Freedom from the constraints of public ownership will allow the coal industry to build upon efficiency improvements made in recent years and to achieve the Government's aim of the largest economically viable coal industry in the longer term. It is expected that coal production in 1995 will be around 47 million tonnes. A new licensing body, the Coal Authority, has been established to encourage viable private sector coal mining and coal bed methane operations.

---

[8]*The Prospects for Nuclear Power in the UK: Conclusions of the Government's Nuclear Review.*
Cm 2860 [HMSO] (May 1995)

Renewables

14.37 New and renewable energy sources contribute to diverse, secure and sustainable energy supplies and reduce the emission of pollutants. The Non-Fossil Fuel Obligation (NFFO) is the Government's principal instrument for stimulating their development, providing a guaranteed market for electricity from renewables. As new sources of supply are developed, the premium price offered for renewable fuels and technologies is being reduced. For example, the prices paid for power from municipal and industrial waste and from large wind projects fell by 20 per cent and 50 per cent respectively between 1991 and 1994.

Energy efficiency

14.38 Business can reduce energy costs by increasing energy efficiency. This also benefits the environment.

14.39 The revised Building Regulations for England and Wales incorporate a simple but reliable indicator of the energy efficiency of homes. Such an approach could also reduce energy costs for business users. The Government therefore proposes to explore with interested parties whether similar benefits could be achieved in the non-domestic sector without imposing additional regulatory burdens.

> **THE PAYBACK FROM ENERGY EFFICIENCY INVESTMENT**
>
> *Stimulated by the Energy Efficiency Office (EEO) "Making a Corporate Commitment" campaign, a manufacturer of telecommunications equipment has:*
>
> - *made fuel savings of £1.4 million, representing a 50 per cent reduction*
> - *made water savings of £200,000, a reduction of two-thirds*
> - *reduced CO_2 emissions by 30,000 tonnes*

WATER

14.40 There has been unprecedented investment in water and sewerage services in England and Wales since privatisation in 1989 (Chart 14.3). Infrastructure has been upgraded, capacity raised, and higher environmental and quality standards attained. The quality of water is now excellent: in 1993, 98.9 per cent of over 3.5 million tests complied with the relevant standards (compared with 98.7 per cent in 1992). Investment of £24 billion over the next decade will raise standards further. Average price rises have been pegged by OFWAT at 1 per cent a year in real terms over the next ten years, so water companies will meet more of the costs of improvement.

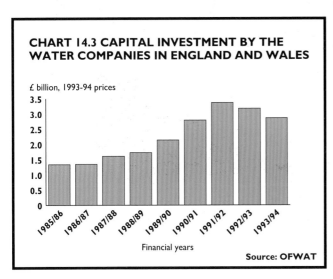

CHART 14.3 CAPITAL INVESTMENT BY THE WATER COMPANIES IN ENGLAND AND WALES

£ billion, 1993-94 prices

Financial years

Source: OFWAT

14.41 There are opportunities for private finance and management expertise in water and sewerage provision in Scotland

and Northern Ireland. Possible PFI schemes in Scottish local authorities over the next 10 to 15 years have a potential value of about £1 billion. In Northern Ireland, a Next Steps Agency will become responsible for water and sewerage services from April 1996 as an interim stage to privatisation.

TRANSPORT

14.42 Quick, reliable, cost-effective transport links play an important role in the competitiveness of British business. The Government's aim is to ensure that the country has the modern transport system that it requires to achieve sustainable economic growth. It seeks to maximise private sector resources and expertise.

14.43 The Government's programme of privatisation and market opening has led to increased competition and better use of infrastructure. These policies have helped develop world class transport services in the UK. Our airports and airlines are world leaders; so too are some of our cruise lines, ferry and container vessel operators. The distribution and logistics sector is highly competitive, with a lower cost structure than Germany, France or the Netherlands (Chart 14.4). Franchising passenger services, privatising British Rail's freight businesses and the flotation of Railtrack will give the railways the opportunity to become world class as well.

Investment

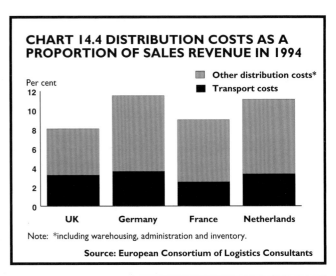

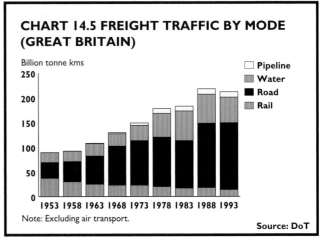

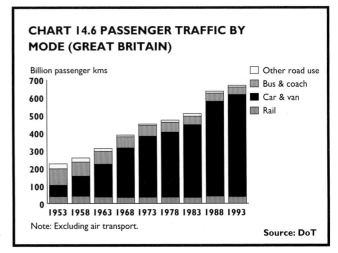

14.44 As the economy has grown, so has its need for transport infrastructure and services. In the last 40 years, passenger traffic has tripled and the volume of freight has more than doubled, placing particular pressure on roads: in 1993, more than 94 per cent of all passenger traffic and 63 per cent of all freight moved by road (Charts 14.5 and 14.6). Although the growth of road traffic levelled off in the early 1990s, it has now resumed. Department of Transport (DoT) forecasts indicate that the volume of road traffic in the next 20 years could increase by 40-70 per cent.

14.45 The growth in demand for transport in the UK has led to calls for more investment in infrastructure from the CBI and others. However a small firms survey published in January 1995 by the British Chambers of Commerce[9] indicated that 85 per cent of those questioned were satisfied with existing UK transport infrastructure.

14.46 Expenditure has increased significantly in real terms in recent years. Capital expenditure by Government in roads and rail over the last five years was some 40 per cent higher than in the previous five years. In the autumn of 1994, the Government decided to reduce previously planned levels of expenditure on roads, but each year of the new plans still provides for more expenditure in real terms than on average during the 1980s. Planned investment in rail in 1995-96 remains unchanged.

14.47 The private sector is increasingly contributing to investment in the nation's transport infrastructure. This has allowed faster progress on major schemes and provided new services more quickly. Over the past year, the private sector has invested some £100 million in the rail network. Substantial developments are also underway with the private sector under the Private Finance Initiative (PFI) – an area where the UK is leading the field in Europe. The privately funded Channel Tunnel opens up vast new opportunities. Other projects, such as the Heathrow Express, will also bring major benefits to business. The PFI is also encouraging the development of new products, for example the new state-of-the-art signalling system for the West Coast Main Line.

PFI CASE STUDY: NORTHERN LINE

The recent £400 million deal for new Northern Line trains is a good example of how the PFI can deliver extra investment. The supplier - GEC/Alsthom - will finance the entire costs of the new trains, be responsible for their maintenance, and take a substantial share of the risks in the project. It will be paid according to the performance of the trains over the 20 year contract. The first trains should enter service in mid-1996.

14.48 Design, build, finance and operate (DBFO) road schemes are further extending private sector opportunities and potential business benefits. Under these schemes, the private sector takes responsibility for the finance, design and building of new or improved roads, and for operating them, in return for payments principally linked to use. Tender invitations for the first four DBFO projects were issued in January 1995, and interested groups submitted bids to pre-qualify for a further four projects in March 1995. The construction elements of these eight projects amount to about £550 million of capital expenditure to be undertaken by the private sector.

[9]*Small Firms Survey: Transport* [Association of British Chambers of Commerce] (January 1995)

14.49 In Scotland, "Competing for Better Roads" sought comments on proposals to develop a more efficient approach to the management and maintenance of the Scottish trunk road network following local government reorganisation in April 1996[10]. One of the key objectives is to introduce competition by enabling the private sector as well as local authorities to bid for contracts. A further document will be published later this year.

Transport and the environment

14.50 Whether investment comes from the public or private sectors, the rapidly increasing demand for transport cannot be met by simply increasing the provision of infrastructure. The Government fully recognises the importance of good transport infrastructure to business and other users. But the economic benefits of additional provision have to be weighed against the costs, including the wider environmental costs.

14.51 Last year's White Paper "Sustainable Development" made clear that the Government believes that transport decisions should address transport needs while preserving or enhancing the environment[11]. In Northern Ireland, the Government announced in January 1995 seven guiding principles for transport planning to help ensure that future transport needs are met in a sustainable way. The Royal Commission on Environmental Pollution has also published a report on the impact of transport on the environment[12].

14.52 Concern about the balancing of these different interests underlay the recent CBI report "Missing Links", which compared transport policy in the UK with policy in three other European countries[13]. It concluded that there was a greater degree of consensus in those other countries on the shaping of transport policies, and that there was a need to improve the public policy process in the UK in view of environmental and public spending constraints. It called on the Government to set out a vision for future transport priorities.

14.53 The building of consensus on transport priorities depends upon interested parties being willing to engage in constructive and well-informed debate, and to take into account the views of other groups. The Secretary of State for Transport has accordingly initiated via a series of speeches a national debate on transport priorities, aimed at focusing attention on the key issues. These speeches will be published shortly, and comments invited from interested parties.

14.54 The Secretary of State has made clear that, while this dialogue develops, he will not hold back plans for improving the UK's transport network and reducing the impact of pollution.

---

[10]*Competing for Better Roads: The Future Management and Maintenance of Scotland's Trunk Roads* [Scottish Office] (December 1994)

[11]*Sustainable Development: The UK Strategy.* Cm 2426 [HMSO] (January 1994)

[12]*Royal Commission on Environmental Pollution: Transport and the Environment.* Cm 2674 [HMSO] (October 1994)

[13]*Missing Links: Setting National Transport Priorities* [CBI] (February 1995)

Cross-modal links

14.55 DoT was reorganised late last year along cross-modal lines to make it easier to take account of links between different transport modes. One part of the Department is now responsible for transport infrastructure, and another for operations. Since most journeys are local ones, the Government is also encouraging local authorities to develop cross-modal transport strategies. £79 million has been set aside in 1995-96 for 37 packages of measures proposed by local authorities outside London to encourage public transport and to offer attractive alternatives to car users. A further £15 million is being provided in 1995-96 for innovative schemes proposed by London boroughs covering both road and rail transport.

Roads

14.56 The Government has invested some £10 billion over the last five years in motorway and trunk road capacity, leading to significant improvements in the road network. For example, the development of the A14 between the A1 and the M1 will improve links between the industrial areas of the West Midlands and the East Coast ports, providing better routes to continental Europe.

14.57 The rapid growth of both freight and passenger traffic has nevertheless led to congestion, particularly on our busiest motorways and in urban areas. Congestion imposes additional costs on business and adds to pollution.

14.58 Additional roads cannot be the whole solution. The Government is therefore taking steps to reduce congestion and make the most of the existing network by:

- targeting expenditure on black spots, including much needed bypasses for towns and villages. Spending on small network improvements will increase from £73 million in 1994-95 to £108 million in 1995-96;

- undertaking a programme of research to improve traffic modelling techniques;

- examining the scope for using information technology to provide more information to road users using both in-car and highway-based telematics (see Chapter 11); and

- undertaking research into congestion charging in urban areas.

MULTI-MODAL TRANSPORT INITIATIVES

- *The Scottish Office is developing a multi-modal transport package to tackle transport problems around Edinburgh and across the Forth. This includes proposals for a privately financed second road crossing of the Forth and improved links to the national road network*

- *The Northern Ireland Office is examining the feasibility of various alternative transport technologies as part of an investigation of public transport options for the congested Belfast to Newtownards corridor. This will include consideration of a full range of public transport alternatives from rail to bus-based schemes*

- *A high-level group chaired by the Minister for Transport in London is to examine the opportunities for improvements, particularly privately-funded improvements, in access to and between London's main airports by rail and through traffic management measures*

14.59 Motorway tolling could contribute to tackling the problem of congestion by enabling more new road capacity to be provided than would otherwise be the case, and by ensuring that we make more effective use of the existing network. The Government is assessing electronic motorway tolling systems. If the assessment justified it, the Government would consider legislation to provide for motorway tolling.

Rail

14.60 The Government's main aim in privatising the railways is to improve the quality of rail services. Private ownership and competition will bring more flexibility of response, greater efficiency of operation, and more attention to rail users' requirements. They will also create new opportunities and new markets for business. Customers will reap the benefits.

14.61 Considerable progress is being made towards implementation of the privatisation plans. Railtrack has been set up as a Government-owned company to own and manage the railway infrastructure. It is to be sold by stock market flotation within the lifetime of this Parliament. The sale process for the first passenger service franchises has begun and contracts are due to be awarded by the end of 1995. The sale of BR's freight businesses and the three rolling stock leasing companies is also moving ahead. The Government is examining the scope for introducing private sector finance and management expertise in to the operation of Northern Ireland Railways.

14.62 Rail freight has been losing market share for decades. It now accounts for less than 10 per cent of surface freight in the UK. Privatisation will bring private sector finance and expertise to the challenge of reversing this decline. The Channel Tunnel will also offer rail an historic opportunity to boost its markets. There are already through freight services to destinations in Italy, Germany and Spain, and the service and range of places served is still growing.

The Channel Tunnel is now open for business. This major project is of enormous significance to business with the Continent.

THE CHANNEL TUNNEL RAIL LINK

The Channel Tunnel Rail Link (CTRL) is a flagship PFI project. A competition is under way to select a private sector consortium to design, build, finance and operate the line. Four consortia submitted bids in March this year. The Government intends to select a winner before the end of 1995.

The high speed railway line will connect London St Pancras and the Channel Tunnel, increasing capacity and reducing journey times to Paris and Brussels by around half an hour. It will also carry domestic passenger services, reducing journey times for commuter services to many parts of Kent by up to 60 per cent. The CTRL Hybrid Bill required to authorise the project is currently being considered by Parliament.

In recognition of its benefits to international and domestic passenger traffic and to the regeneration of the East Thames gateway, the Government is prepared to make a substantial contribution to the project, including the assets of European Passenger Services (the operators of the Eurostar services) and a long lease on Waterloo International. The size and timing of the Government contribution will be determined by the competition.

Other public transport

14.63 Investing in public transport cannot be a complete answer to traffic problems; there is clear evidence that increasing public transport provision alone does not necessarily take much traffic off the roads. Rail, bus, trams and light rail can however contribute sigificantly to the relief of congestion in urban areas. Government funding has already supported the construction of the Docklands Light Railway, the Greater Manchester Metrolink, and the South Yorkshire Supertram. The Government has also provisionally set aside funding for Croydon Tramlink and Midland Metro Line One: in both cases there will be private sector finance. The London Underground Jubilee Line is currently being extended to Docklands at a cost of £1.9 billion, with financial contributions from the private sector.

14.64 In Wales, five new stations have been opened over the past five years enabling local services to be reintroduced on the mainline between Bridgend and Swansea. Elsewhere, resignalling work is taking place to allow greater capacity on lines in the South Wales Valleys. Investment of £8.5 million is being made by West and Mid Glamorgan County Councils. Support has also been given by the European Regional Development Fund.

14.65 Buses can be efficient users of road space. They can be helped by being given priority on congested routes. Trials of guided bus-ways, priority measures for buses, and other techniques which may help buses are currently being conducted. In London, the Government is supporting co-ordinated plans by the London boroughs for a 400 mile network of bus priority routes. In Scotland, Lothian Regional Council has plans for a "Greenways" Order which will enhance bus priority on key routes in and out of Edinburgh.

Airports

14.66 The Government is firmly committed to enabling the development of additional airport capacity where this makes economic, social and environmental sense. Good quality airport infrastructure assists trade and employment by linking the UK with international markets, and by attracting business and tourists to the UK. It also helps regional development: internationally mobile firms value ready access to international air networks. Airports in the South East underpin the world position of London as a centre for tourism and business.

14.67 The Government responded in February 1995 to the report[14] it had commissioned on the provision of additional runway capacity in the South East. Its response acknowledged the strong case for additional capacity, but recognised the need to take account of environmental impacts. It concluded that the options considered for an additional full runway at Heathrow or Gatwick should not be pursued, and that further work was needed on other alternative measures, such as a close parallel runway at Gatwick and possible enhancement to Heathrow's existing runways.

[14]*Runway Capacity in the South East: A Report by the Working Group* [Department of Transport] (July 1993)

14.68 The Government welcomes the growth in traffic at regional airports over the past decade, and expects the range and frequency of services to continue to increase. It announced in October 1994 that access to regional airports for services to and from the US was to be liberalised, thus giving further opportunities for growth.

INVESTMENT BY THE CIVIL AVIATION AUTHORITY

The CAA plans to invest over £450 million over the next three years, much of it on infrastructure projects to increase airspace capacity over the UK and to meet an anticipated increase in demand of 5 per cent per year over the next ten years. PFI projects will account for a third of this investment, including the New Scottish Centre and the Oceanic Flight Data Processing System.

14.69 The Government believes that continuing growth can best be achieved under private management. Since 1990, six local authority airports in England and Wales have been sold, two of them in the past three months. This process will be further encouraged by the two-year relaxation of the "set-aside" rules announced in April 1995. This will allow local authorities to spend 75 per cent of the receipts from sales to the private sector on new capital projects. In Northern Ireland, the sale of Northern Ireland Airports Ltd was achieved in July 1994 through a management and employee buy-out.

14.70 The Government has responded to concerns expressed by business aviation users about the shortage of slots in the South East. A discussion document last year proposed a civil enclave at RAF Northolt, but respondents thought this would not be viable. The Government therefore announced in April 1995 that it would seek views in the next few months on alternative ways of extending and improving the services offered at RAF Northolt to business users. It has also recently underlined the importance of retaining capacity for business aviation at the MOD airfield at Farnborough.

Shipping

14.71 In spite of the subsidies available to some other fleets, the UK shipping industry has remained efficient, safe and competitive. It includes a number of world leaders, particularly in the cruise, ferry and container sectors of the market. The latest indications suggest that the decline in the size of the UK fleet seen in recent years may at least be levelling out.

14.72 Significant new opportunities will flow from the removal in 1999 of almost all remaining restrictions on EU internal shipping services. This, and the debate on transport priorities (para 14.53), should also increase awareness of the scope for developing the competitive role of coastal shipping in the movement of internal freight.

14.73 Organisations representing UK shipping companies, shipbuilders and repairers, and marine equipment manufacturers have agreed to collaborate further to help improve the competitiveness of their respective industries. This agreement will provide for better exchange of information between ship owners, builders and equipment manufacturers, prior to the placing of orders for the construction of new vessels, major repair work, and major equipment purchases.

Ports

14.74 Over 90 per cent of UK overseas trade by weight goes through UK ports. Following the success of the privatisation of five trust ports in 1992, the Dundee Port Authority is moving towards voluntary privatisation. The significant increase in the profitability of the ports privatised in 1992 is clear evidence of the greater operating efficiencies introduced by private sector management.

Trans-European Networks (TENs)

14.75 TENs are large-scale EU infrastructure projects. They seek to improve the working of the Single Market. In addition to national government and private sector funding, TENs can be financed by EU grants for feasibility studies, by interest-rate support and by loan guarantee premiums, as well as by loans from the European Investment Bank.

14.76 The UK's interests in TENs projects include:

Transport

- the Channel Tunnel Rail Link;
- the West Coast Main Line improvement;
- the upgrading of the Cork-Dublin-Belfast-Larne-(Stranraer) rail link; and
- the Ireland-UK-Benelux road link, including a spur from Stranraer to Birmingham.

Energy

- gas interconnectors linking Northern Ireland to Great Britain, and the UK to European gas grids; and
- an electricity interconnector between Scotland and Northern Ireland.

LIVERPOOL DOCKS

The Port of Liverpool is a good example of how many UK ports have prospered since abolition of the restrictive practices of the former Dock Labour Scheme in 1989. Having recovered from bankruptcy brought about by overmanning and trade losses, this previous trust port became a statutory company in 1971 and completed its financial reconstruction in 1989. Abolition of the Scheme that year resulted in increases in productivity throughout the port - over 40 per cent in some sectors. In 1993, the company was able to announce record trading: compared with 1992, trade had increased by 1.5 million tonnes to its highest level for over 20 years; profits by 38 per cent to £15.2 million; and turnover by 14 per cent to £98 million. The Euro Rail terminal and the successful Freeport are likely to mean continuing expansion.

COMMERCIAL FRAMEWORK

15.1 As set out in the 1994 Competitiveness White Paper, the Government is determined to:

♦ reduce the cost burdens that excessive regulations and enforcement place on business; and

♦ maintain and develop a clear, effective legal framework in which businesses can operate responsibly.

DEREGULATION

15.2 Deregulation is vital to competitiveness. Rules can act as a deterrent to market entry, unnecessary requirements impose costs on business, and the burden of official forms and paperwork wastes management time. Bad regulation stands in the way of innovation, investment and jobs.

15.3 As well as cutting back unnecessary old regulations, the Government weighs up carefully the need before introducing new ones. But not all regulations are bad. Some are tools of deregulation. One statutory instrument can only be improved or abolished by means of another. Of the regulations made in 1994, 15 per cent were repeals, more favourable regimes or market opening measures; a further 52 per cent were in areas with no impact on business, for example, regulations concerning police conditions of service.

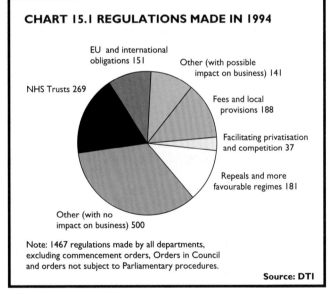

CHART 15.1 REGULATIONS MADE IN 1994

EU and international obligations 151

NHS Trusts 269

Other (with possible impact on business) 141

Fees and local provisions 188

Facilitating privatisation and competition 37

Repeals and more favourable regimes 181

Other (with no impact on business) 500

Note: 1467 regulations made by all departments, excluding commencement orders, Orders in Council and orders not subject to Parliamentary procedures.

Source: DTI

15.4 To bring about change, the Government:

♦ uses the powers in the Deregulation and Contracting Out Act 1994;

♦ works with its European partners and business to improve European regulation;

♦ improves regulation through consultation and compliance cost assessment;

♦ helps new businesses understand how the law affects them; and

♦ ensures that the way that regulation is administered and enforced is more business-friendly, consistent and transparent.

15.5 To ensure a business focus, the Government asked eight Task Forces covering business and charities, led by Lord Sainsbury, to advise on priorities for action. They made almost 800 recommendations[1]. Of these, 521 have been accepted, 178 rejected and 96 are under consideration. A new Task Force under Francis Maude is making further recommendations to Government. This ensures the private sector's views are heard at the heart of Government.

15.6 To ensure that deregulation has a high priority, a new Cabinet sub-committee chaired by the President of the Board of Trade will be set up to drive forward work on deregulation. The Government has already given a Minister in each Department responsibility for deregulation: each Minister is supported by a team of officials.

15.7 Over 1,000 regulatory provisions have been earmarked for repeal or amendment by Departments. By the end of 1995 nearly 500 of these changes will have been implemented. The improvements include simpler accounting for small firms, protection of trade marks, improvements in charity legislation, improvements to the planning system, plans for commercial and company law reform, encouraging development of the biotechnology industry and reform of shopping hours. Some measures are of particular value to small businesses, notably changes in tax and changes to sweep away prescriptive and out-of-date health and safety regulations.

Deregulation and Contracting Out Act 1994

15.8 This Act received Royal Assent in November 1994. It has four major features:

- over 30 specific deregulatory measures;

- powers to allow the amendment or repeal of primary legislation, subject to special new Parliamentary scrutiny procedures. The first Order was laid on 5 April 1995. Fifty-five candidates for use of this power have already been announced. Many further proposals are being developed;

> **EXAMPLES OF CHANGES ARISING FROM THE DEREGULATION ACT**
>
> - *Less paperwork for road hauliers*
> - *An end to licensing for employment agencies*
> - *Improvement to competition law*
> - *Improvement to redundancy law*
> - *Allowing children into suitable pubs*
> - *Allowing charging for Sunday sporting events*

- new powers to improve the way the law is applied and enforced. The objective is to enable businesses to be given the right to clear, written explanations of what action is required of them and why. Unless immediate action is needed, they can be given a right to have their arguments heard first; and

- provision to develop a new model-appeals procedure. A consultative document[2] is being published on the same day as this White Paper. This provision will be particularly important to small businesses.

---

[1]*Deregulation Task Force Proposals for Reform* [Business Deregulation Task Force] (1994)
[2]*Enforcement: The Model Appeals Mechanism* [Deregulation Unit] (1995)

Europe

15.9 The EU has a key role. The Government is, therefore, driving a number of initiatives in Europe, working with the Commission and other Member States to embed deregulatory principles and practices in European policy-making.

♦ A group of independent national experts (the Molitor Group) was set up last year to examine the impact of legislation on employment and competitiveness. The Group, which includes Sir Michael Angus, chairman of Whitbread plc, will report to the European Council in June 1995.

♦ The Commission has asked UNICE (Union of Industrial and Employers' Confederations of Europe) to examine how legislation affects competitiveness and employment in a dozen key sectors of industry. Results are being fed into the Molitor Group, and a full report is due in June 1995.

♦ A new Commission committee, which includes small firms' representative bodies, is assessing how to improve and simplify the business environment for SMEs. It is identifying best practice benchmarks, focusing initial work on new business start-ups.

♦ Following a meeting between the President of the Board of Trade and Dr Rexrodt, Germany's Minister of Economics, a group of senior businessmen from both countries was set up at the Anglo-German summit in 1994. The Group's report[3] in March 1995 was welcomed by the Prime Minister and Chancellor Kohl. It highlighted the damaging effect on competitiveness of the cumulative burden of European regulation. It called for a Commissioner to spearhead deregulation, a more effective business voice in Europe, a checklist to improve regulation, and the repeal or amendment of a number of specific measures.

Good regulatory practice

15.10 New regulation will still be needed. But the Government is determined to ensure that costs are kept to a minimum. An assessment of compliance costs is now required when proposals are first considered and again when they are brought forward. Proper consultation is an essential part of the regulatory process. To emphasise the "think small first" message, a small business litmus test was introduced last year. This requires all compliance cost assessments to include a section outlining the impact of regulatory proposals on a few small businesses.

15.11 The Government will be using the new powers in the Deregulation and Contracting Out Act to make enforcement procedures more business-friendly.

15.12 The Code[4] for Enforcement Agencies "Working with Business", based on Citizen's Charter principles, has been adopted by over 70 Central Government Agencies and is being extended further.

[3]*Deregulation Now* [Anglo-German Deregulation Group] (1995)
[4]*Working with Business – A Code for Enforcement Agencies* [Deregulation Unit and Citizen's Charter Unit] (1993)

15.13 Forty local business partnerships have been established to improve communications between local authorities and business. The aim is to establish a further 100 by March 1996. They make it easier for business to comply with regulation by providing clear advice and guidance and by jointly tackling problems.

ENVIRONMENTAL FRAMEWORK

15.14 The Government is committed to sustainable development (see Chapter 6). The best guarantee of our environment is a prosperous economy, an efficient market with appropriate price signals, and voluntary action by forward looking firms. But where the market does not fully reflect environmental costs, action by Government is often necessary, following internationally recognised principles.

- Ecological impacts must be considered, particularly where effects may be irreversible.

- Decisions should be based on the best possible scientific information and analysis of risks.

- Where there is uncertainty and potentially serious risk, precautionary action may be necessary.

- The costs and benefits must be assessed.

- Costs should fall on those responsible (the polluter pays principle).

15.15 Policy decisions are based on dialogue, predictability, clear priorities and sensible timing, so that business is best able to maintain and enhance its competitiveness.

15.16 Where appropriate, the Government will use economic instruments rather than regulation. They allow business greater flexibility in responding to environmental requirements and are likely to be more cost effective than regulation alone. They give firms an incentive to develop less expensive methods of pollution control.

15.17 In the 1994 Budget, for example, the Chancellor announced his intention to introduce a landfill tax in 1996 to encourage manufacturers to minimise waste and increase recycling. Other proposals being considered include tradeable permit systems for sulphur emissions and economic instruments for water pollution.

15.18 However, regulation is sometimes unavoidable, for example to outlaw a damaging substance, as with CFCs, or guarantee minimum standards. In such cases the Government's preferred approach is to establish environmental quality targets and performance standards, allowing companies the freedom to achieve them as cost-effectively as possible.

15.19 In weighing the costs and benefits of Government action on the environment, economic as well as environmental benefits must be considered. Higher environmental standards can stimulate innovation and improve firms' efficiency. Appropriate regulation and an innovative response by industry can create new markets (see Chapters 4 and 6). In certain circumstances UK industry may be better placed to exploit these opportunities in world markets if the UK moves early to tackle recognised environmental problems. The Government considers the economic benefits case by case, taking into account the UK's underlying strengths and the international context.

15.20 Business must be confident that regulation will be enforced consistently. The Government has introduced legislation to establish an Environment Agency for England and Wales and a Scottish Environment

---

DIALOGUE WITH INDUSTRY

The Government recognises the importance of regular dialogue with business on environmental issues. Two particular initiatives are:

- *the Advisory Committee on Business and the Environment (ACBE) – a high level business committee appointed by Ministers to consider strategic environmental issues and make recommendations to business and Government. ACBE has studied issues such as contaminated land and liability, a landfill tax, and corporate environmental reporting*

- *the sector dialogue initiative – which brings together industry, technology suppliers, regulators, researchers and Government to discuss the likely direction of environmental pressures and policy over the next 15-20 years. A dialogue with the chemical industry is under way; others with the construction and textiles industries will follow shortly. This fulfils a commitment in the 1994 White Paper*

In Northern Ireland a business-led working group on industry and environment issues presented a report[5] to the Government at the end of 1994. The Government will shortly be publishing its response to the recommendations.

---

[5]*Recommendations to Government and Industry* [Green Economy Working Group] (1994)

LIABILITY

Business needs a sensible, fair and clear framework of environmental liabilities. The Government[6] has therefore:

◆ *published "A Framework for Contaminated Land"*

◆ *proposed legislation to clarify the powers of regulators over contaminated sites*

Protection Agency. These will bring a number of environmental regulators together to provide a single point of access for business and promote consistency of enforcement. A Heritage and Environment Agency for Northern Ireland is planned for April 1996. In the EU, the UK has been a driving force behind a network of pollution inspectorates, known as the Chester network or IMPEL, which aims to improve consistency of enforcement in different Member States.

PLANNING SYSTEM

15.21 In England and Wales, planning controls over minor development have been relaxed. Procedures to streamline the production of local plans and to shorten the time taken to deal with planning appeals will be introduced during 1995. These improvements will reduce uncertainty for developers. The predictability of UK planning systems is already valued by inward investors.

15.22 A consultation paper[7] on the Scottish planning system was published in July 1994. Of those responding, many have expressed concerns about the delays in the planning process, for example, in the preparation, adoption and approval of development plans, and in the appeals system. The Government intends to publish a second consultation document later in 1995 setting out proposals to meet these concerns wherever possible. It will address the scope for the planning system to adopt more effective consultation procedures, improved plan preparation methods, more efficient inquiry procedures, and a more active role in promoting development which is environmentally sustainable.

COMPETITION LAW

15.23 The Government is committed to competition. This protects the interests of UK consumers and enhances the international competitiveness of UK producers.

15.24 Competition is assessed on the basis of the relevant market. What matters is the degree of competition in the actual market in which the goods or services are sold. Increasingly that market is Europe-wide, if not world-wide. Mergers are referred to the

RECENT DEVELOPMENTS IN THE PLANNING SYSTEM

◆ *Additional permitted development rights have been introduced covering flats above shops and extensions or outbuildings on educational and hospital premises*

◆ *Special Industrial-Use Classes have been abolished*

◆ *Planning controls on advertisements have been relaxed*

◆ *Permitted development rights have been introduced for CCTV systems on buildings*

---

[6]*A Framework for Contaminated Land* [Department of the Environment and the Welsh Office] (1994)
[7]*Review of the Town and Country Planning System in Scotland* [Scottish Office Environment Department] (1994)

Monopolies and Mergers Commission (MMC) primarily on competition grounds. The Government is committed to introducing legislation to reform the law on restrictive trade practices and abuse of market power as soon as Parliamentary time permits.

15.25 Since the 1994 White Paper, the Government has taken a number of steps to reduce the burden of competition law on business while maintaining its effectiveness. New thresholds have removed a number of insignificant cases from scrutiny by the Director General of Fair Trading and the MMC. The scope for companies to negotiate undertakings with the Director General as an alternative to a detailed investigation by the MMC was extended in January 1995. Other deregulatory changes include shorter decisions times for handling merger cases. The Office of Fair Trading's Enforcement Code includes targets for responding quickly to complaints and for quick handling of, for example, registrable agreements.

15.26 The Government is encouraging reductions in the cost of complying with EU competition regulation. The Commission raised turnover thresholds from March 1995. The Government will consult business on further possibilities for taking minor agreements outside the scope of the legislation. The UK will encourage the Commission to simplify "block exemptions" as they are reviewed, while providing more comprehensive coverage to ensure that benign agreements are not blocked.

COMMERCIAL LAW

15.27 Arbitration is an important alternative to Court litigation but the legal framework needs improvement. The Government published a consultation document[8] in February 1994 on consolidation and simplification of arbitration law in England and Wales. In the light of responses, it is preparing revised legislation, which goes further than its initial draft in simplifying the law and enabling cost-effective dispute resolution. This will have deregulatory benefits and help to bring more international commercial arbitrations to London. Parallel proposals for Scotland are in preparation.

15.28 The CBI and DTI have encouraged the use of structured mediation and other alternatives to either litigation or arbitration. These can be faster and cheaper. The Lord Chancellor's Department is planning a pilot project in the Patents County Court, to commence in 1995, in which cases suitable for such resolution will be identified by the Court and the parties encouraged to consider its use. More generally, it is for businesses to be alert to the possibility of using an alternative means of dispute resolution and, where appropriate, to write it into their contracts.

15.29 Commercial law should respond to technical developments such as electronic data interchange (EDI). The Law Commission's business law team is reviewing

[8] *A Consultative Paper on Draft Clauses and Schedules of an Arbitration Bill* [DTI] (1994)

legislative impediments to the wider use of EDI. DTI is involved in the preparation by the United Nations Commission on International Trade Law of a model law on the use of EDI. The model law will suggest ways in which legal requirements, for example for a signature or for evidence in writing, might be modified so as to remove inhibitions to the use of EDI.

COMPANY LAW AND CORPORATE GOVERNANCE

Company Law reform

15.30 Since the 1994 White Paper, consultative documents have been issued on a range of priorities including:

- private companies[9];

- registration of charges[10];

- disclosure of interest in shares[11];

- summary financial statements[12]; and

- accounting requirements[13].

15.31 The Government will develop proposals for reform in the light of comments. It intends to bring forward regulations later this year to encourage the use of summary financial statements, simplify statutory accounting requirements and raise the qualifying limits for accounting exemptions for SMEs. The Government is looking at ways to make it easier for companies to be run as groups and has started work on disincorporation. The Law Commission is reviewing shareholder remedies.

Corporate governance

15.32 The Government supports the work of the Cadbury Committee. Standards of disclosure have improved greatly and they indicate a high level of compliance with the Cadbury recommendations[14], especially among larger companies. The City Group for Smaller Companies has published guidance[15] to help smaller companies comply as far as they can. The Government will seek to encourage the growing trend towards institutional shareholders playing a more active role, and it looks forward to the setting up of a successor to the Cadbury Committee.

15.33 Public concern about the remuneration of senior executives in some companies continues. The Government does not support excessive and unjustified pay awards. However, pay is a matter for companies and their shareholders. The

[9]*The Law Applicable to Private Companies* [DTI] (1994)
[10]*Proposals for Reform of Part XII of the Companies Act 1985* [DTI] (1994)
[11]*Proposals for Reform of Part VI of the Companies Act 1985* [DTI] (1995)
[12]*Simpler Procedures for Summary Financial Statements* [DTI] (1995)
[13]*Exemptions from Standards on Grounds of Size or Public Interest* [Institute of Chartered Accountants in England and Wales] (1994). Consultative document on simplification of accounting disclosure to be published later in 1995 by DTI.
[14]*Report of the Committee on the Financial Aspects of Corporate Governance* [Gee and Co Limited] (1992)
[15]*The Financial Aspects of Corporate Governance: Guidance for Smaller Companies* [City Group for Smaller Companies] (1994)

establishment of Sir Richard Greenbury's committee, to review the structure within which pay and conditions for directors are determined and disclosed, and to propose a code of good practice, demonstrates the private sector's concern to regain public confidence. When the Committee's recommendations are available, the Government will be ready to consider any proposals that may require legislative back-up.

Financial reporting

15.34 The Government welcomes the work of the Accounting Standards Board to make accounts more reliable and useful, including:

- publication of standards on accounting for acquisitions and mergers, and on fair values in acquisition accounting; and

> **FINANCIAL REPORTING: ACTION TO HELP SMALL COMPANIES**
>
> - *The statutory audit requirement for many companies was abolished in August 1994. The Auditing Practices Board has issued guidance on audit exemption reports*
>
> - *A working party of accountants has proposed exempting small companies from most accounting standards*
>
> - *APB is reviewing audit methods for small companies*
>
> - *Government is reviewing thresholds for SME exemption from statutory disclosure requirements*

- proposals on group accounts, accounting for deferred tax and related-party transactions.

15.35 The Government welcomes the Auditing Practices Board's (APB) work to update audit standards. A strategy paper, "The Audit Agenda" has been published,[16] guidance on "going concern" and on dealing with fraud has been issued, and guidance is being developed on internal financial control.

INSOLVENCY LAW

15.36 Revised proposals[17] for a new Company Voluntary Arrangement procedure are out to consultation. The new procedure includes a 28 day moratorium, binding on all parties, to give companies in financial difficulty an opportunity to put together a rescue plan for agreement by creditors. The Government is considering issues relating to the proposal for a debt to equity mechanism and whether any other measures should be taken to facilitate Administration.

INTELLECTUAL PROPERTY RIGHTS

15.37 The international provision of adequate intellectual property protection is extremely important to competitiveness, but difficult to enforce. The UK will seek to ensure effective application of international arrangements, including:

- the agreement on Trade Related Aspects of Intellectual Property Rights (TRIPS), which should lead to a global improvement in intellectual property rights and

---

[16]*The Audit Agenda* [Accountancy Books] (1994)
[17]*Revised Proposals for a New Company Voluntary Arrangement Procedure: A Consultative Document* [The Insolvency Service] (1995)

enforcement. The UK will seek to persuade countries to implement early at least the important TRIPS provisions. These include patent protection for pharmaceutical products and comprehensive measures to counter the growing trade in counterfeit and pirated goods, which is particularly affecting sectors like the recorded music industry;

- the new Community Regulation on counterfeit and pirated goods which comes into force on 1 July and strengthens powers at all the EU's external borders to detain these goods;

- the Madrid Protocol, an international system which simplifies registration of trade marks. The new Trade Marks Act provides for UK membership; and

- the Community Patent Convention which the UK has recently ratified. Once the Convention comes into force, standards of enforcement will become more uniform in the European Community.

Members of the public examining counterfeit goods on display at the Patent Office.

15.38 In the UK, the 1994 Trade Marks Act streamlines the UK registration process, eases requirements for appointing licensees and for the transfer of marks, widens rights against infringement, and strengthens the criminal provisions to deal with counterfeiting. A provision in the new Criminal Justice and Public Order Act will allow trading standards officers to act against copyright piracy.

15.39 Intellectual property issues associated with the development of the information superhighway, multimedia systems and biotechnology are a major concern. The Government will seek to ensure that EU legislation on these aspects promotes the competitiveness of UK industry.

15.40 Targets for the Patent Office will encourage it to develop private sector partnerships to make its information and expertise more widely available. It will also extend its search and advisory services to assist SMEs through Business Links. The Patent Office has issued a discussion document on behalf of Government Departments and Research Councils which examines the awareness and use of intellectual property by small firms and suggests possible solutions to problems identified.

LEGISLATION

15.41 Good clear legislation is an essential part of the infrastructure for a competitive business environment. Both the underlying policy and the detail of such legislation therefore need to be subject to thorough, timely and effective consultation, with business groups, practitioners and other interested parties. Much has already been done to make the drafting of legislation more user friendly: business inputs at an early stage should help to take the process further.

15.42 Publication of draft bills, in advance of introduction in Parliament, allows consultation to take place on clarity of structure and presentation, and on drafting detail, as well as on policy. In recent months the Government has done this with provisions on environment agencies and on reserve forces. It hopes to move further in this direction and to increase the number of bills published in draft in advance.

15.43 The Government is concerned that the implementation of new EU legislation should not leave an awkward rump of domestic legislation, either overlapping with the new provisions or maintaining inappropriate or inconsistent provisions with much reduced coverage. In many cases, the Deregulation and Contracting Out Act, along with maximum use of the European Communities Act, should provide the means for a more satisfactory implementation of EU legislation; the Government will consult on how best to achieve this in particular cases.

NEXT STEPS

16.1 The Government said in last year's White Paper that it would keep competitiveness at the top of the agenda. This White Paper demonstrates that commitment. It seeks to be objective, identifying where we need to make improvements as well as existing strengths. It is a report on progress over the past year. It provides a snapshot of the UK's competitiveness. It sets out new policies and initiatives which will assist future competitiveness.

16.2 The past year has been one of strong growth, with few signs of the inflation which has damaged periods of growth over the past 25 years. Productivity is up. Exports are up. Unemployment is down.

16.3 We have made good progress in the factors that determine competitiveness. We continue to close the gap on our major competitors especially in key measures like manufacturing productivity.

16.4 As we improve, more companies and more people realise that over time, as a nation, we can match or exceed the performance of the best. More firms have the determination and ability to direct their resources, and especially people, to winning. The task and the opportunity for all of us is to seek out and apply best practice in all we do, and then to improve on that. It is a task for Government as well as for industry.

16.5 Competitiveness must remain a priority for all of us. Success will give us the higher standard of living we all seek. The Government looks forward to publishing next year a further survey of national competitiveness.

INDEX OF CHARTS

ANNEX

This table records progress made on the commitments and plans undertaken by the Government in the 1994 Competitiveness White Paper. It also shows new initiatives or actions announced in this White Paper. The left hand column lists the initiatives from the 1994 White Paper, including paragraph references. The right hand column indicates progress. New initiatives are shown in bold, with references to the paragraphs in this White Paper where they are discussed. Owing to limited space, many abbreviations are used in this table. Readers will find these explained in the glossary.

SECTORAL OVERVIEW

COMMITMENTS AND PLANS IN CWP1	PROGRESS/NEW INITIATIVES/ FURTHER ACTION
	The Government will invite private sector bodies representing small business to organise a conference on small firms [Box below Para 3.9]

SPONSORSHIP

COMMITMENTS AND PLANS IN CWP1	PROGRESS/NEW INITIATIVES/ FURTHER ACTION
	The DTI intends to attract over 25 new secondees from companies [Para 4.4].

EDUCATION AND TRAINING

COMMITMENTS AND PLANS IN CWP1	PROGRESS/NEW INITIATIVES/ FURTHER ACTION
	The Government will continue to monitor progress against our competitors by participating in the Third International Mathematics and Science Study, participating in the International Literacy Survey, seeking agreement through OECD on further comparisons of pupils' achievements, and examining other ways to benchmark ourselves [Para 7.5].
Para 4.8 – NACETT to review National Education and Training Targets.	**The Government has endorsed NACETT's revised Targets and will work closely with NACETT to promote them, encourage local targets to underpin national ones, work with ITOs developing sector - specific targets and encourage schools, colleges and universities to set their own targets [Para 7.9].**
Para 4.12 - Major reforms to upper secondary education to be introduced in Scotland.	Guidance on development programme plan and interim arrangements issued January 1995. New system to be introduced in 1997/98. Consultation Papers on curriculum guidelines and core skills have also recently been published.
Para 4.12 - Review of curriculum for 14 - 16 year olds in Northern Ireland.	Completed in June 1994. Greater flexibility including development of vocational options will result.
Para 4.13 - The value added by each school and college to be reported as soon as reliable measures are available.	SCAA reported in December 1994. SCAA to develop and pilot national measures.
Para 4.13 - A copy of the updated Parents' Charter to be sent to every household in England and Wales, and to every household in Scotland on request.	Distribution completed. Research into parents' information needs continues.
	Pilot "Schools on Line" initiative connecting about 50 schools to the Internet launched in March 1995 [Box below Para 7.48].
	Consultation paper issued in April 1995 seeking views on the value of the Information Superhighway in education [Box below Para 7.48].

COMMITMENTS AND PLANS IN CWP1	PROGRESS/NEW INITIATIVES/ FURTHER ACTION
Para 4.18 - The remainder of the Careers Service to be contracted out in England, Scotland and Wales.	All areas in Wales under contract from April 1995. All areas in Scotland and England will be contracted out by 1996.
Box after 4.24 - NCVQ working with others to ensure vocational qualifications count in HE and vice versa.	NCVQ/UCAS/GATE project in progress. 55 per cent of GNVQ candidates for HE in 1994 were accepted.
Advanced Highers to be available in Scotland.	To be introduced in 1997.
Para 4.25 - Colleges and business links to be strengthened by involvement of TECs.	TECs and FEFC now involved in regional and sub-regional groupings to advise on applications to new TEC-held FE Competitiveness Fund.
Para 4.27 - Funding for FE sector to be output related.	A proportion of FEFC funding is now output related. Similar measures being developed in Scotland.
Para 4.27 - Regular reports to be issued on the performance of each college.	Reports on 113 colleges in England issued by end March 1995. Five quality assessment reports issued in Wales in 1994/5. Performance indicators published annually in Scotland.
Para 4.28 - New national Charter for FE to be issued. Each FE college to publish its own Charter.	All FE colleges in England and Wales have issued individual local charters. All colleges in Scotland will have published charters by the end of 1995/96. The new National Charter will be issued in England in autumn 1996.
Para 4.30 - Government, employers, TECs and ITOs progressing the introduction of Modern Apprenticeships.	1400 apprentices were in training in England in 17 sectors by April 1995. More sectors to introduce Modern Apprenticeships by September 1995. Nearly 500 people started Modern Apprenticeships in Wales in 1994/95. **Modern Apprenticeships to be introduced in Scotland and Northern Ireland in 1995/96 [Boxes below Para 7.50].**
Para 4.31 - Training Credits to be offered to all 16 and 17 year old school leavers in England and mainland Scotland.	To be offered from April 1995 (except in Argyll) to all eligible school leavers. Also to be offered to all eligible 16 to 17 year old school leavers in Wales.
Para 4.34 - A new Charter for HE will be issued in 1995/6.	Action in hand on Charter for England.
	Charter for Wales to be published autumn 1995.
	Revised Scottish Charter expected after research completed.
	The Government will encourage higher education institutions to make available information about the employment of new graduates, by subject [Para 7.31].
Box after 4.38 A new curriculum and assessment programme for pupils aged 5-14 to be introduced in Scotland.	Full implementation expected by mid-1999.
Box after 4.38 Secretary of State for Wales to publish strategy document on education, training and enterprise in Wales.	"People and Prosperity: an Agenda for Action in Wales" published March 1995.
	"A Bright Future: Getting the Best for Every Pupil at School in Wales" sets out a programme to help performance, and consults on a target to raise GCSE results in Wales in literacy, numeracy and scientific understanding. Targets will be published in Autumn 1995 [Box below Para 7.50].
Box after 4.38 The Northern Ireland Curriculum is being introduced	Amended Curriculum to be introduced September 1996.
Box after 4.38 In Northern Ireland training schemes are being restructured into a new Jobskills programme.	New programme launched in October 1994.
Para 4.40 - The National Curriculum is being streamlined.	Revised National Curriculum distributed to schools in January 1995.
Para 4.40 - Testing is being focused more closely on key skills	Revised arrangements for 1995 announced in September 1994.
Para 4.41 - Development of new vocational qualifications for 14-16 year olds.	117 schools to pilot Part one GNVQs from September 1995. More pilots to start in September 1996.
	The GNVQ Key Stage 4 Development Scheme in Wales offers young people in pilot schools the opportunity to take either Part one GNVQs or full GNVQs at age 14-16.
Para 4.42 - Introduction of General Diploma.	Introduction not to go ahead for the time being. Priority given to securing standards in National Curriculum core subjects and piloting of Part One GNVQs.
Para 4.43 - New training scheme for new head teachers.	"Headlamp" Scheme to begin in September 1995.

COMMITMENTS AND PLANS IN CWP1	PROGRESS/NEW INITIATIVES/ FURTHER ACTION
Para 4.44 - Increase in-service teaching for careers teachers	GEST programme commenced April 1995. NICEC Guide to training issued February 1995. Revised Open College distance learning pack available May 1995.
Para 4.44 - Policy statement and publication of revised "Working Together" good practice guide for careers education and guidance.	Revised document issued as "Better Choices" in November 1994. Further Guidance to be issued in June 1995 and regional seminars to be held in winter 1995.
Para 4.45 - All schools to provide policy statements on careers education.	Schools now required to include careers education and guidance provision in school prospectus.
Para 4.45 - All schools to enter into agreements with local career service.	Many schools now have service level agreements. Nearly all schools to have arrangements by April 1996.
Para 4.45 - Inspection programme to monitor schools' performance in careers education.	Independent inspectors required to look at careers education and guidance provision and report on its effectiveness.
Para 4.46 - Government to provide £87 million to improve careers guidance.	Enhanced levels of guidance for 13,15 and 17 year olds will be fully in place by 1997/98. 13 year olds already benefiting from these improvements.
Para 4.47 - Comparable steps in Scotland.	All career services reaching service level agreements with their schools and colleges. An additional 8,500 action plans agreed for 1995/6. **By Summer 1995, 15 out of 17 areas of Scotland will have new careers service companies. The Scottish Office expects to spend an extra £8.5 million over the next three years on enhanced careers guidance and training [Box below Para 7.50].**
Para 4.48 - Increase resources for spreading best practice identified through TVEI.	Funding of £3 million available for 1995/6 in England. Extra resources also provided in Scotland. Welsh TECs are building on the work of TVEI using their education - business funds.
Para 4.48 - TECs to ensure school leavers could have had a week's work experience; Government to provide £23 million in period to 1997/8.	£5 million allocated to TECs in 1995/96 and over 300,00 pupils to benefit in 1995/96 under new arrangements. Revised booklets on work experience issued March 1995. Guidance issued to TECs, GOs and others on planning and organisation of work experience. Further examples of good practice under consideration. In Wales, TECs have to support two weeks work experience pre 16.
Para 4.48 - New objectives to improve the focus and quality of school/business links.	ED/DFE/ESSO guide for employers on good practice in education/business links "Making Education our Business" published March 1995. "A Framework for Action" launched March 1995 by the Scottish Consultative Council on the Curriculum. "People and Prosperity" defines objectives in Wales.
Para 4.49 - Introduction of a code of practice to ensure consistent GCE assessment.	SCAA and the exam boards have agreed near full implementation by 1996.
Para 4.49 - Recognition of exceptional achievement by pupils.	SCAA advice currently under consideration.
Para 4.49 - Action to make AS levels more attractive to young people.	Leaflet on usage of AS examination has been issued.
Para 4.49 - Greater emphasis on the practical in GCE syllabuses.	Options being considered.
Para 4.50 - Review of GNVQ assessment and grading.	Major changes in arrangements will be in place by September 1995. A small group will suggest next steps.
Para 4.50 - Clarification of GNVQ knowledge requirements.	New format specifications are being phased in. The first five will be in place in September 1995.
Para 4.50 - NCVQ to act with SCAA on GNVQs.	Part one pilot schemes proceeding as planned. **The pilot will be evaluated to ensure that these qualifications are of high quality, manageable for teachers and rewarding for pupils, with clear routes to further education and work-based training opportunities beyond 16 [Para 7.26].**
Para 4.50 - Improved links between general and vocational qualifications.	SCAA and NCVQ working to develop the Part One GNVQ for pilot in September 1995.
Para 4.51 - Continued introduction of GNVQs in schools and colleges.	GNVQ Quality framework was launched in March 1995.
Para 4.51 - Teacher training to aid the continued introduction of GNVQs in schools and colleges.	£14 million GEST funding was provided for 1995/6, an increase of £9 million on 1994/5.
Para 4.52 - Review of structure of existing NVQs and SVQs.	**A survey of the top 100 NVQs and SVQs will be carried out this year, and all NVQs and SVQs will be reviewed by March 1998 [Para 7.17].**

COMMITMENTS AND PLANS IN CWP1	PROGRESS/NEW INITIATIVES/ FURTHER ACTION
Para 4.52 - Improved marketing of NVQs and SVQs to employers.	NCVQ has prepared a marketing strategy for the next three years. It has published a document "Establishing the Benchmark" based on the key themes of the strategy. Implementation work has started. SCOTVEC plans are being finalised with a view to contracting in May 1995.
Para 4.52 - Local quality assurance schemes for NVQs and SVQs.	Field force of quality auditors now being recruited. Operations will start in May-July 1995.
Para 4.53 - TECs to assist FE colleges to prepare strategic plans.	A guide on good practice published May 1995. Guidance agreed between the Secretaries of State for Education and Employment on meeting the needs of the economy and competitiveness. FE colleges in Scotland are required to consult their local LEC when preparing development plans. Guidance on closer co-operation between FEFCW, colleges and TECs in Wales was published in April 1995.
Para 4.53 - TECs to approve FE college plans.	Early feedback on new arrangements is positive.
Para 4.53 - TEC Competitiveness Fund to be established.	New arrangements started in England in spring 1995. Arrangements introduced in Wales in April 1995. LEC Competitiveness Fund to be introduced in Scotland 1995/96
Para 4.53 - Closer co-operation between FEFC, colleges and TECs.	Funding Council budgets in England and Wales for 1995/6 reflects commitment.
Para 4.54 - New body to be established to promote quality in FE.	The Further Education Development Agency (FEDA) for England and Wales became operational on 7 April 1995.
Para 4.55 - Industry to develop accelerated Modern Apprenticeships for 18-19 year olds.	ITOs and TECs have been working together and accelerated Modern Apprenticeships will be launched in England in conjunction with Modern Apprenticeships from September 1995 (for Scotland, see entry under Para 4.65).
Para 4.58 - Consultation on the practicalities of learning credits, and consideration of establishing pilot schemes for learning credits to be based on local partnerships.	Ministers are considering next steps in the light of the consultants' report [Para 7.33].
	The Government has commissioned Sir Ron Dearing to undertake a review of 16-19 qualifications. It will take about one year, with an initial report in July 1995 [Para 7.28].
	The Government will legislate at an early opportunity (following consultation) to improve careers education and guidance in maintained schools and colleges [Para 7.36]
	The Government will work with the School Curriculum and Assessment Authority to develop guidance on coaching, case studies and project work, to improve pupils' negotiating and decision making skills [Para 7.36]
	The Government will develop and publish data on achievement and career routes from schools, colleges and work-based learning options, to provide pupils with more informed choices at age 16 [Para 7.36]
	The Government will improve the links between the various bodies responsible for quality assurance (OFSTED, the Further Education Inspectorate and the Employment Department's Quality Assurance operation) [Para 7.37].
	The Government will require schools to demonstrate their awareness of the needs of labour markets and higher education through school development plans [Para 7.37]
	The Government will strengthen the OFSTED Framework of Inspection to ensure that inspectors seek evidence that schools have provided good careers education and impartial guidance [Para 7.37].
	The Government will develop closer team working on careers education inspections, between the three inspectorates responsible, once the current round of OFSTED primary school inspections is largely complete [Para 7.37].
	The Government will investigate whether there is a case for encouraging a more consistent approach to funding methodologies across the sectors and to funding levels for similar qualifications in different sectors [Para 7.38].

COMMITMENTS AND PLANS IN CWP1	PROGRESS/NEW INITIATIVES/ FURTHER ACTION
	The Government will legislate to remove the requirement that potential new further education providers must gain the sponsorship of an existing college before being able to receive FEFC funding [Para 7.38].
	The Government will consider relaxing the detailed central Government controls over the opening and closing of sixth forms [Para 7.38].
	The Government will consider further the case for introducing capital charging for schools and further education sector colleges, to put them on the same financial basis [Para 7.38].
	The Government will legislate to remove borrowing restrictions on grant maintained schools, thus placing them on the same basis as further education sector colleges [Para 7.38].
	The Government is committed to providing over time a pre-school place for all four year olds whose parents wish to take it up. Details of the new programme will be announced soon [Para 7.24].
Para 4.59 - Government funding to train 24,000 key staff in firms with less than 50 employees.	Skills for small businesses initiative started in April 1995.
Para 4.59 - TECs to work with BLs and other networks serving small firms to provide companies with means of sharing ways to meet training needs.	Tenders invited in April/May 1995. Details of individual projects to be available in June 1995.
Para 4.59 - TECs to be encouraged to ask large firms who are Investors in People to offer training advisers to small suppliers.	Tenders invited in April/May 1995. Details of individual projects to be available in June 1995.
Para 4.60 - Investors in People promotion to be given more resources.	Investors in People (UK) have produced proposals and are working up details.
Para 4.60 - All Government Departments to proceed towards attaining Investors in People status, if they have not already.	At April 1995, 16 Central Government organisations, or parts of organisations, had Investors in People standard, representing 10 per cent of the Civil Service. A further 41 had made a commitment.
Para 4.61 - Government to encourage improved vocational information and advice at local level by TECs and others.	For 1995/6, TECs may spend up to 2.7 per cent of Training for Work Budgets on vocational information and guidance, subject to TECs' matching contributions.
Para 4.62 - Career Development Loan Scheme to be made more accessible.	From September 1995 the Government will pilot in one region a scheme to allow borrowers who have completed training funded through Career Development Loans to delay the start of their repayments by up to 18 months in certain circumstances. The Government will also seek ways of increasing the use of CDLs in further and higher education for students who are not eligible for mandatory awards [Para 7.17].
	The Government will examine the UK's performance at the level of basic qualifications for employment and compare it with those of our leading competitors. The Government will work with ITOs and NACETT to benchmark companies' training effort and output for the workforce in work. The Government will report the outcome of this work in its next national survey of the UK's competitiveness [Para 7.16]
	The Government will hold a new Small Firm Training Challenge with a fund of £5 million [Para 7.14].
	The Government, with NACETT, will introduce a Sector Targets Challenge for ITOs later in 1995 [Para 7.15].
	Government is supporting around 30 TECs and up to five ITOs to develop and implement local and sectoral strategies for lifetime learning [Para 7.17].
	The Government is continuing to provide training for unemployed people through Training for Work, and maintaining at 1994/95 levels the number of places for people with disabilities, those needing literacy or numeracy training, those for whom English is a second language, and those under 25 unemployed for over two years [Para 7.17].
	The Government will maintain the number of unemployed people allowed to study part-time while on benefit, provided that they remain available for work and continue to seek it actively [Para 7.17].

COMMITMENTS AND PLANS IN CWP1	PROGRESS/NEW INITIATIVES/ FURTHER ACTION
Para 4.62 - Government to consult on voluntary training accounts	The Government intends to publish a consultation document on individual responsibility for lifelong vocational learning, seeking views on a wide range of issues [Para 7.18].
	The Government will fund a small number of TECs to investigate how training opportunities can be designed and delivered to best meet the needs of all young people [Para 7.30]
Para 4.63 - Government to promote educational expertise via EU programmes.	SOCRATES proposal adopted by the Council of Ministers in March 1995. Member States currently discussing with the Commission how best to implement SOCRATES in 1995.
Para 4.63 - Government to press that EU educational programmes be geared to competitiveness.	Discussions are still at an early stage.
Para 4.65 - Policy on accelerated apprenticeships in Scotland to be considered.	Accelerated apprenticeships to be introduced in Scotland in 1995/96 [Box under Para 7.50].
	Following responses to consultation paper "Training for the Future", the Secretary of State for Scotland has announced plans to spend £25.5 million over the next three years on a range of training initiatives [Box under Para 7.50].

EMPLOYMENT

COMMITMENTS AND PLANS IN CWP1	PROGRESS/NEW INITIATIVES/ FURTHER ACTION
Para 5.15 - Continual review of industrial relations and trade union law.	The Government keeps the law under review and would be prepared to propose changes if necessary and workable.
Para 5.17 - Continual promotion of effective employee involvement.	The Government has run a campaign with the CBI called "Managing for Success" to publicise successful practice.
Para 5.17 - UK to ensure that EU does not impose a transnational framework of employee involvement law on UK.	The Government is committed to the principle of employers informing and where appropriate consulting their employees about matters which affect them. However, it believes that UK companies should be free to develop arrangements appropriate to their circumstances and those of employees. It has therefore continued to oppose Directives which might impose unnecessary burdens on UK employers.
Para 5.18 - Government to monitor the reaction to ED's publication "The Competitive Edge."	Document generally well received. It provides a succinct introduction to a range of employee involvement schemes.
Para 5.19 - Government to ensure that employment rights for individuals strike a proper balance with potential burdens to employers.	Consultation on the Green Paper "Resolving Employment Rights Disputes: Options for Reform" ended March 1995. Government considering responses. The Disabled Discrimination Bill completed its third reading in the Commons in March 1995.
Para 5.21 - Government to strengthen its active labour market policies through the Jobseeker's Allowance.	Jobseekers Bill before Parliament
Para 5.24 & 5.25 - Government to reinforce incentives to work and encourage employers to recruit long-term unemployed people.	The measures announced in the 1994 Budget are being introduced [Box below Para 8.21].
Para 5.26 - Disregarded costs up to £40 a week for childcare in calculation of in-work benefits.	New measure implemented from October 1994.
Para 5.27 - Initiative in Northern Ireland to tackle sexual discrimination.	Various agencies are considering how best to take forward.
Para 5.27 - Consideration of an initiative in Scotland to tackle sexual discrimination.	Scottish Enterprise is developing proposals for a Fair Play Initiative, as well as supporting Training 2000, which works with employers to promote women's training and development.
Para 5.27 - Expansion of the out-of-school child-care initiative.	£45 million allocated to help create up to 50,000 additional places over three years. In 1994/95 the out of school childcare grant helped provide 19,000 additional places.

The initiative is on course to meet targets in Scotland. |
| Para 5.27 - Regional partnerships in England to help women reach their full potential. | There is to be a national seminar of partnerships in June 1995. Most had finalised action plans in spring 1995. |

COMMITMENTS AND PLANS IN CWP1	PROGRESS/NEW INITIATIVES/ FURTHER ACTION
Para 5.28 - Government to provide guidance on the establishment of equal opportunity groups.	Guidance booklet issued on 12 May 1994.
	Right of non-discrimination against disabled people in employment will be supported by a Code of Practice and guidance [Para 8.25].
Para 5.29 - Removal of ceilings on compensation for religious/political discrimination cases in fair employment tribunals in Northern Ireland.	Legislation came into force in May 1995.
Para 5.30 - Introduction of "Access to Work".	Completed. Review of first year of scheme to be undertaken summer 1995.
Para 5.33 - Legislation on pensions to improve security and equality in occupational pension schemes.	Pensions Bill before Parliament.
Para 5.34 - Consultation on access to local authority and housing association housing in Scotland.	Decision expected in 1995.
	The Government will continue to encourage investment in the private housing sector, promote the development of affordable rented homes, and support schemes which make it easier for tenants in social housing to move [Para 8.15].
	The Government will publish a guide for employers showing successful examples of pay flexibility [Para 8.23].
	The Government will continue to introduce greater flexibility in public sector pay through local pay determination and performance pay [Para 8.23].

MANAGEMENT

COMMITMENTS AND PLANS IN CWP1	PROGRESS/NEW INITIATIVES/ FURTHER ACTION
Box 6.10 - Guidance to be issued to help small businesses seeking BS ISO 9000 (formerly BS 5750) certification.	Planned for issue May 1995.
Box 6.10 - Design Council to act at national level and encourage design expertise to be made available through Business Links and Scottish Design Ltd.	Design Counsellors being appointed by Business Links. Design Council re-launched as a strategic body December 1994. Northern Ireland: New Design Directorate established February 1995. Wales: Welsh Design Advisory Service launched in December 1994. Directory of Design Expertise now in preparation. Scotland: Design expertise is available through Scottish Design Ltd.
Para 6.16 - Improve UK competitiveness through better use of engineering by taking action in five areas identified in the White Paper.	Action for Engineering launched in October 1994 [Para 9.21].
Para 6.17 - Government to introduce engineering bursaries to encourage students with good grades in GCE A levels or equivalent qualifications to choose engineering degree courses.	Scheme started September 1994 and is UK wide. 2107 bursaries have been awarded in 1994-5, 1751 for England, 76 for Wales, 188 for Scotland and 92 for Northern Ireland.
Para 6.19 - DTI expects to continue to contribute to the costs of many Business Links Services via its funding of TEC enterprise activities and the provision of DTI services through Business Links.	Funding arrangements for 1995-96 and beyond have been implemented.
Box 6.19 - A network of Business Links which covers all parts of England, building up to about 200 outlets, all accredited as meeting and maintaining high quality service standards.	**200 outlets expected by the end of 1995. Within three years of opening, all Business Links will be assessed against ISO 9000 and Investors in People [Box below Para 5.33].**
Para 6.22 - CBI and DTI to conduct a study of 100 of the best UK companies to identify links between external influences on companies and best practice in management and innovation.	"Winning" report published November 1994. Over 35,000 copies issued.
	The TEC network is extending the "Winning" report approach to over 500 smaller companies. Report is in preparation and will be used to spread best practice [Para 9.9].

COMMITMENTS AND PLANS IN CWP1	PROGRESS/NEW INITIATIVES/ FURTHER ACTION
Para 6.24 - Government to establish a regional network which will promote best practices in supply chain partnerships.	Ten Regional Offices launched April 1995. Offices will help purchasers find competitive suppliers, help suppliers exploit new opportunities, put suppliers in touch with Business Links, and aim for £260 million of contracts to be awarded by purchasers to suppliers introduced by the network in the first three years [Para 5.35].
Para 6.25 - DTI and BSI working with industry to develop BS 5750 and product certification standards further to promote continuous improvement.	BSI programme Advisory Groups established to consider management systems standards and prepare for second revision of ISO 9000. Certification bodies working on sector and product specific certification schemes [Para 9.28].
Para 6.27 - Government to offer funding to ensure management NVQs are up to date and widely used by employers.	ED to revise standards by August 1995.
Box 6.27 - Review of the management content of NVQs, exploring a flexible "core and options" approach.	As above. Management Charter Initiative (MCI) to revise standards by August 1995.
Box 6.27 - TECs to be encouraged to promote improvements in management training amongst smaller companies.	TEC activity commenced in April 1995. Regional strategies being produced. DTI booklet "People make Profit" on management development for small companies published March 1995.
Box 6.27 - Case for targets for management development to be considered.	Proposed new higher level skills target to include management.
Box 6.27 - Identification and publicity of examples of good practice in management training in smaller firms.	Study reported February 1995 on information needed by TECs and others. This will provide a work plan for MCI. Exemplar projects to start in 1995-96.
Box 6.27 - Government to look to business schools and others to contribute to improving the skill base by continued improvement in the relevance of quality of courses.	Development of Innovation Masters degrees. Introduction of Innovation modules to Masters Degrees.

Support of modular Masters programme in Technology Management. Provision of bursaries to high quality applicants from April 1995.

Encourage dialogue between industry and business schools to ensure courses maximise benefit to UK industry.

Continued support for the modular Masters programme, including sponsorship of a conference for employers and academics (October 1995) and press publicity. |
| Para 6.28 - Five previous actions to be taken into account in the Welsh Strategy on Skills and Enterprise and in the current review of Scottish training policy. | "People and Prosperity" action plan for Wales published March 1995.

Scotland: Guidance to Enterprise Agencies emphasises management training in smaller companies. |
| Para 6.28 - In Northern Ireland a high priority to continue to be placed on management development and training. | Northern Ireland Training and Employment Agency to revise which targets will be included in the Training and Employment Agency's Corporate Plan 1995-98 and Operational Plan 1995-96. |
| Para 6.29 - A new structure of the engineering institutions to provide a single voice at national level and enhance co-operation at a regional and local level. | New structures to be in place by January 1996. DTI have provided some funding for legal and administrative work to establish new body. |
| Para 6.31 - Rolling three year funding to be offered to TECs which have established strong partnerships in their area, are making satisfactory progress in setting up Business Links, and have obtained a three year licence from their Government Regional Office. | The first three-year contracts awarded in February/March 1995.

The second round of licensing criteria includes updated clauses on Business Links. TECs now have to have a Business Link open before they can receive a licence. |
	The Government will continue to support the training of key staff within TECs to enable them to provide effective advice on management development [Para 9.17].
	The Government will encourage all TECs to develop strategies for improving the skills of local management [Para 9.25].
Para 6.31 - Review of experience of the Personal Business Adviser in early Business Links so as to maximise their effectiveness.	Review completed. Continuous development programme being developed.
Para 6.31 - DTI to extend its funding to help meet costs of Personal Business Advisers after a three year pump-priming period.	Beyond the pump-priming period, the Government will continue to contribute to Business Link services [Box below Para 5.33].

COMMITMENTS AND PLANS IN CWP1	PROGRESS/NEW INITIATIVES/ FURTHER ACTION
	Specialist Business Counsellors on Export, Design, and Innovation and Technology may be needed beyond the three years for which Government funding is currently agreed. DTI will review their performance. Subject to this review, it will extend funding to help meet the continuing costs of their services [Para 9.17].
Para 6.32 - Business Links to become normal point of entry for DTI services.	Current services are available through Business Links. Service Review under way. All DTI funded business support services for SMEs will normally be delivered through Business Links by April 1996.
Para 6.32 - In England, other Government Departments will increasingly make their services available through Business Links.	Work continuing. Local level work facilitated by DTI.

Seminar on MOD Procurement Policy with Business Links in the Northern Region in May/June 1995. If useful, this will be extended to all Business Links. |
Para 6.33 - A prospectus will soon be published inviting proposals for the improvement and the delivery of business services in Wales.	Completed: eight Business Development Consortia covering the whole of Wales have been approved and will be established during 1995.
Para 6.33 - Scottish business shops will provide a local first point of access to these and other services.	Forty Business Shops to be established by end of 1995.
	The Government will make available £100 million over four years from 1995-96 to support bids from Business Links and regional consortia to deliver business development programmes [Para 9.17].
	DTI's Managing in the '90s programme will be relaunched in summer 1995. It aims to involve more than 200,000 people over the next three years [Para 9.18] and to increase by 25 percent per year the number of companies participating in inter-company visits (5,000 in 1995-96).
	Working with CBI and others, DTI is introducing a national benchmarking service. From autumn 1996, firms will be able to obtain performance comparisons against national and sectoral benchmarks [Para 9.19].
	DTI will encourage companies to use advertising successfully by publishing a best practice guide in summer 1995, holding regional seminars, and supporting a pilot Business Link event in the autumn of 1995 [Box below Para 9.22].
	The Government is encouraging other EU states to adopt a regulatory environment towards advertising that minimises restrictions on freedom to advertise [Box below Para 9.22].
	The Government is working with industry on a response this summer to the EU Green Paper on Commercial Communication [Box below Para 9.22].
	MCI members will market standards for senior managers, including leadership [Para 9.24].
	ED will encourage the IoD to adapt for public sector boards such as those within the NHS their standards of good practice for Boards of Directors [Para 9.24].
	ED is promoting wider adoption of competence-based qualifications in business schools, with the aim that 50 per cent will offer them within two years [Para 9.25].
	The Government will ask MCI to generate learning materials to support Business Link activities, develop standards for management consultants, and explore competence-based approaches to the continuing professional development of managers [Para 9.25].
	The Government will continue to encourage institutions of higher education to develop courses which meet industry's needs [Para 9.25].
	DTI is working to ensure that the merger of the National Measurement Accreditation Service and the National Accreditation Council for Certification Bodies enhances the benefits of accredited certification under ISO 9000 [Para 9.28].

COMMITMENTS AND PLANS IN CWP1	PROGRESS/NEW INITIATIVES/ FURTHER ACTION
	Through Business Links, DTI will promote a more coherent approach to quality by encouraging industry to use a combination of ISO 9000, benchmarking, Investors in People, Quality Awards and quality-related NVQs and SVQs to improve business performance [Para 9.28].

INNOVATION

COMMITMENTS AND PLANS IN CWP1	PROGRESS/NEW INITIATIVES/ FURTHER ACTION
Para 7.10 - Technology Foresight Programme will help to identify opportunities by examining both market developments and technological capabilities within the UK over the next two decades.	Reports of the 15 sector panels were published in March and April 1995. The main Technology Foresight report was published on 22 May 1995.
	The Government will disseminate Foresight findings widely [Para 11.14]
	The Government intends to develop new LINK programmes in areas of promise identified by Foresight [Para 11.15]
	The Government intends to launch a competitive Foresight Challenge, providing £40 million over the next three years, to be matched by industry [Para 11.5]
	Departments will take the results of Foresight into account in developing their science and technology (S&T) programmes [Box below Para 11.14].
	The Government will use Foresight reports to identify areas where European collaboration would be fruitful [Para 11.28].
Para 7.11 - Departments with significant S&T expenditure to take account of wealth creation in pursuit of their objectives.	The 1995 Forward Look Overview will describe the performance by Departments and Research Councils against key Science Engineering and Technology White Paper objectives. Departments and Research Councils will include examples of performance in their individual 1995 Forward Look Statements. Further progress will be monitored by the Cabinet Official Committee on Science and Technology and reported in succeeding Forward Looks.
Para 7.13 - Research Councils and Higher Education Funding Councils to give appropriate recognition to the relevance as well as the excellence of proposed research when setting priorities and allocating resources	Specific research funds are being allocated to Northern Ireland Universities. The Scottish Higher Education Funding Council allocates 5 per cent of its research funds by reference to contract income. Research Councils have established machinery for improving their contacts with users in order to improve their assessment of relevance. Higher Education Funding Councils to take account of user-related research in next Research Assessment Exercise. Suggestions made will feed into guidance to panel chairmen later in 1995. All Funding Councils to ask institutions for their response to Technology Foresight and the Forward Look in their strategic plans.
Para 7.14 - Government to contribute on average £360 million a year to the EU R&D Framework Programme.	The 18 specific R&D programmes making up the Framework Programme were agreed by the Council of Ministers before the end of 1994 and are now being implemented.
Para 7.19 - Government Departments are promoting the public understanding of science, engineering and technology (SET).	Co-ordinated campaign began 1993-94. Projects include the annual National Week of Science, Engineering and Technology. New initiatives will include the OST Awards for Best Science Schools (Primary and Secondary), and a Student Placement Scheme. Committee under Professor Sir Arnold Wolfendale to advise Chancellor of the Duchy of Lancaster on measures to equip scientists and engineers to contribute to public understanding in their fields. The Scottish Office published a consultation document "Turning the Light on Science" on 26 September 1994. The document reviewed public understanding on science activities in Scotland and the final report will be published in December 1995.

COMMITMENTS AND PLANS IN CWP1	PROGRESS/NEW INITIATIVES/ FURTHER ACTION
Para 7.22 - Government and Research Councils to promote a greater interchange between industry and universities.	The research Masters pilot to be launched in October 1995 to test the effectiveness of a one-year research Masters as a direct route into employment and as a preparation for a PhD. The number of industrial CASE awards funded by the Research Councils is expected to increase to around 300 in 1995-96; additional funding is also being provided to ESRC to fund an extra 50 studentships. The Royal Academy of Engineering plans to fund new schemes for seconding academic engineers into industry, and will fund new visiting industrial chairs of engineering design in universities.
Para 7.27 - Business Links to be a unifying access point in England for all the available support on innovation, particularly for smaller firms.	Twenty-two Business Links have appointed a total of 30 Innovation and Technology Counsellors. Support mechanisms now accessed through Business Links. By the end of 1995, the services of Counsellors will cover all 200 Business Links.
Para 7.27 - Equivalent arrangements to previous item to be developed in Scotland through the network of Business Shops.	Scottish Office has introduced a Diagnostic and Consultancy Service and a Technical Advice Service which includes regionally based Innovation Technology Counsellors and Innovation Credits. These services can be accessed through the Business Shop network.
Para 7.27 - As immediately preceding item through the Industrial Research and Technology Unit (IRTU) in Northern Ireland.	IRTU offers wide range of support services and access to consultancy; new initiatives include Environmental and Technology Audit Schemes; Design Directorate; Waste Exchange Bureau; technology transfer agreement with US.
Para 7.27 - Similar business centres are under consideration in Wales.	Eight Business Development Consortia covering the whole of Wales have been approved and will be established during 1995.
Para 7.28 - Promoting technology use and adaptation, including Research and Technology Organisation (RTO) work.	Consultations with the Association of Independent Research and Technology Organisations continuing. Pilot projects created, and study conducted on transfer of technology from RTOs to SMEs. £15 million national programme by the Welding Institute announced on 1 November 1994 on technology transfer in materials joining.
Para 7.28 - Access to EU programmes.	A series of promotional events, aimed particularly at SMEs, to improve awareness of the EU R&D Fourth Framework Programme and to encourage UK participation. Guide to EU R&D published in December 1994.
Para 7.29 - Six sectoral working groups to produce practical guidelines and develop a common understanding of the nature of risks and reward involved in innovation amongst company managers, analysts and investors.	Myners Group of senior industry figures, investing institutions and their professional advisors reported February 1995. "Money and Machines" Report published February 1995. Biopharmaceutical group, facilitated by Sciteb, completed dialogue and produced report 1994. Follow-up for the above three will fall primarily to private sector.
Para 7.29 - Stimulation of the free exchange of information between Government, industry and regulators, including the large amount of information on best available technologies held by Her Majesty's Inspectorate of Pollution.	DOE and DTI have commissioned pilot sector opportunity briefs on the best available technologies based on HMIP's material. Pilot brief on non-ferrous metals industry was completed April 1995. Review pilot study and consider producing similar briefs in ten other industries. The chemicals sector group held meetings in January and March 1995 and a further meeting is planned. Preparations are also under way for construction and textile industry dialogues.
Para 7.30 - Extension of the Teaching Company Scheme (TCS).	DTI and other sponsors have agreed a five year strategic plan for TCS, targeting new fields of activity.
Para 7.30 - New Teaching Company Centres to be developed to help smaller firms benefit from the skills of graduates.	Eleven Centres opened. By the end of 1995, this will increase to 17 and cover the whole of the UK [Para 11.21].
Para 7.30 - Government to consider options for a scheme, similar to the TCS, to promote the transfer of people of technician level from Further Education Institutions to local companies.	Consultative document in circulation to potential participant organisations. If accepted, scheme intended to commence in academic year 1995/96.
Para 7.31 - "Innovation Credits" to be introduced and made available through Business Links.	Pilot phase of Innovation Credits has been operating since 1 December 1994. Use of credits to be reviewed in June 1995.

COMMITMENTS AND PLANS IN CWP1	PROGRESS/NEW INITIATIVES/ FURTHER ACTION
Para 7.31 - Networks of local contacts (NEARNET) established across the UK to enable local providers of innovation support to be brought together in a coherent way.	Technology Counsellors are now using local providers of innovation support to satisfy the majority of client needs.
Para 7.31 - National centres of expertise linked through an actively managed network (SUPERNET).	SUPERNET launched on 5 November 1994. Forty-five business support organisations are now accredited members: expected to increase to about 80 members by end of 1995.
Para 7.31 - Overseas Technology Services (OTS) to be expanded to cover a wider range of sectors, professional disciplines and countries.	The Government plans to create a pilot network of technology promoters to cover Japan, the US, Germany, France, and later, South East Asia [Para 11.24]. The Government plans to develop the Engineers to Japan scheme, applying it to other markets and disciplines, involving secondments to and from the UK [Para 11.24]. The Government plans to offer technical information from overseas to UK firms over the Internet [Para 11.24].
Para 7.31 - OTS to be more accessible through Business Links in England, and other suitable bodies in Scotland and Wales.	New services in design stage take full account of delivery through Business Links.
Para 7.31 - Pilot schemes to be established to enable firms to have prompt and more direct access to the latest ideas and developments overseas.	Inter-departmental review of overseas science and technology representation undertaken by DTI, OST, FCO and British Council. Report published in December 1994. OTIS extended in second half of 1994 to cover Seoul, Osaka, Hong Kong, Taipei, and Austria. **Extension to follow throughout 1995.**
	Technology-based business support organisations will be developed into a network directing innovation and technology services to smaller firms [Para 11.20].
	A programme is planned to bring new technologies to the attention of small firms around the country through Business Links [Para 11.21].
	The Postgraduate Training Partnership scheme for collaborative partnerships between universities and RTOs will be extended to about 200 industrially relevant projects [Para 11.21].
	The Shell Technology Enterprise Programme will be extended for three more years to enable it to cover the whole country [Para 11.21].
	The Government is improving its SMART and SPUR schemes by combining them, and providing a budget of £76 million over the next three years [Para 11.30].
Para 7.32 - Smaller companies receiving Government support for innovation also to receive help to find sources of private finance and sources of assistance in developing business skills.	New applicants for DTI schemes to be referred to Business Links to receive business counselling and help including help with finding sources of finance. **The Government is piloting a pre-finance evaluation service to help smaller firms with problems in raising medium and long-term finance for innovative and high technology projects [Para 11.30].**
Para 7.33 - Higher Education Institutions increasingly to receive financial recognition from the HEFCs for research conducted in partnership with industry. This will amount to a significant proportion of the relevant income from industry.	England: About 2.5 per cent of the total level of annual contract income from the private sector in 1994-5 was allocated in this way. This will rise to 5 per cent in 1995-6. Scotland: 5 per cent of SHEFC research funds allocated by this method for 1994-95. SHEFC decided to make allocations on basis of external funds for 1995-96 and 1996-97. Wales: 3 per cent of HEFCW research fund allocated in this way in 1994-95. In addition, 9 per cent is aimed at raising quality of research, with priority given to research which supports economic development.
Para 7.33 - The proportion of the HEFCs' agreed total budgets used for the purpose outlined above to increase.	In England funding to reward collaborative research to be doubled in 1995-96 to £20 million.
Para 7.33 - Individual academics will be rewarded for undertaking collaborative work with industry through "Realising Our Potential" Awards.	"Realising our Potential" Award Scheme was launched February 1994. In 1995-96 it is expected that some £22 million will be spent on ROPA awards.
Para 7.33 - HEFCs to take full account of results of Technology Foresight Programme in allocating funds between subjects.	Technology Foresight Programme outcomes in May 1995 will be taken into account for funding for 1996/97.

COMMITMENTS AND PLANS IN CWP1	PROGRESS/NEW INITIATIVES/ FURTHER ACTION
Para 7.33 - The next Research Assessment Exercise (RAE) by the HEFCs to include full recognition of high quality research undertaken in partnership with industry.	Decision announced in HEFCs' June 1994 circular. Details now being worked up by RAE panels. Next RAE due 1996.
	The MOD will later in 1995 present its longer term technology strategy to industry to encourage further collaboration in research [Para 11.35].
	The Government will set up a new working forum between MOD, OPSS, DTI and the Research Councils to improve coordinated planning of civil and defence science and technology [Para 11.35].
	DTI plans to launch a major Information Society initiative in autumn 1995 [Para 11.17].

FAIR AND OPEN MARKETS

COMMITMENTS AND PLANS IN CWP1	PROGRESS/NEW INITIATIVES/ FURTHER ACTION
Para 8.10 - Government to ensure that Single Market Rules are enforced throughout the EU.	Resolution on administrative cooperation passed 16 June 1994. Informal UK paper sent to Commission on how to improve complaints procedure. Contributing to Community 'directory' of enforcement officers. Working on studies of: - implementation and enforcement of selected directives - operation of the Single Market in sectors where no EU harmonising laws apply - chemicals sector.
Para 8.10 - DTI to launch a new guide for UK firms on how to get Single Market problems sorted out.	Completed. Guide and publicity pamphlet published in September 1994.
Para 8.10 - Government to work for genuine free trade under EU Association Agreements.	Agreements in place with countries of Central and Eastern Europe. White Paper on approximation of Central and East European laws to Single Market legislation to be agreed by June 1995.
Para 8.11 - Government to press for further reductions in support for agriculture in the EU and more widely.	Agrimonetary switchover mechanism abolished January 1995.
Para 8.12 - UK to pursue further negotiations on removing legitimate barriers to trade in areas such as financial services, telecommunications, maritime services, aerospace and steel.	The Government continues to press for further market opening on trade in services and to explore prospects for securing agreement between the chief negotiators for a Multilateral Steel Arrangement and new GATT Civil Aircraft Agreement.
Para 8.12 - Government to require delivery of real market opening by new countries joining GATT/WTO.	Applications from several countries well advanced (for example China), others pending (for example Russia). Ensuring the 25 or so new applicants meet WTO requirements [Box below Para 12.4].
Para 8.12 - Government to ensure vigorous EU use of new GATT/WTO provisions for arbitration and retaliation against barriers which breach GATT/WTO obligations.	Commission pursuing WTO action against taxation of whisky in Chile and Japan at urging of UK.
Para 8.12 - Government to work in the WTO on new trade issues to promote open markets and discourage trade restrictions.	The Government is pressing in international fora (G7 and OECD) for further trade liberalisation covering deregulation, subsidies, investments, standards, intellectual property, government procurement and competition. WTO Trade and Environment Committee to report to first biennial meeting of Ministerial Conference, late 1996. **The Government to develop the international taxation framework [Box below Para 12.4].**
	The Government plans to set up by summer 1995 a trade policy consultation forum [Para 12.5].
	The Government is taking a systematic approach through its Trade Barriers Initiative. It will issue regular reports on the Initiative [Para 12.9].
	The Government is reviewing how the DTI's Single Market Compliance Unit's activity could be boosted [Para 12.13].
Para 8.12 - Government to support cases for use of commercial defence instruments where there is justification on economic grounds for doing so, taking full account of UK producer, consumer and industrial user interests.	The Government has initiated discussions on the approach the Commission should take in its review this year of the quotas against non-textile goods from China, to ensure they are fully justified.

COMMITMENTS AND PLANS IN CWP1	PROGRESS/NEW INITIATIVES/ FURTHER ACTION
Para 8.17 - Government to press for full implementation of the GATT subsidies agreement.	EU has implemented agreement. Government is monitoring notifications from third countries. UK will continue a pragmatic approach to achieve transparency and ensure the agreement works.
	The Government is pressing for rapid action to extend liberalisation in the EU to electricity, gas and telecommunications markets [Para 12.14].
Para 8.19 - Government to press the Commission to adopt its proposals to limit aid for capital intensive projects.	DTI launched UK proposals on priorities for Commission's new efforts to control state aid in April 1995.
Para 8.19 - Clearer Commission guidelines for acceptable boundaries of "grey" areas of state aids.	Discussions with all Member States and Commission on employment aids in December 1994.
Para 8.19 - Tighter and more effective control of state aids to specific industry sectors, such as steel and shipbuilding.	OECD agreement to curtail shipbuilding state aids. Commission now monitoring state aids in December 1994.
Para 8.19 - The extension of Commission monitoring of aid for publicly owned manufacturing companies to cover publicly owned utilities.	DTI launched UK proposals on priorities for Commission's new efforts to control state aid in April 1995
Para 8.19 - Stricter control of subsidies to prevent liberalisation of air transport and shipping being undermined.	The Government has challenged Commission decision on Air France.
Para 8.19 - Uniform application of state aid rules throughout the European Economic Area.	EFTA Surveillance Authority set up.
Para 8.19 - Progressive adoption of state aid disciplines by Central and Eastern European countries.	Key milestones confirmed by the European Council at Essen, December 1994.
Para 8.19 - More prompt and determined action by the Commission on agricultural state aids, in particular those that had not been notified.	Commission declared French aid for pig meat and Irish aid for mushrooms illegal and required repayment.
Para 8.19 - Greater transparency and swifter handling of complaints by the Commission.	Commission handbook on state aids procedures to be published shortly. UK proposals taken up at official and ministerial level. Encouragement of parallel CBI proposals.
Para 8.19 - More effective action to secure repayment of aid judged to be illegal, including use of Article 171 of the Maastricht Treaty.	DTI launched UK proposals on priorities for new Commission's efforts to control state aid in April 1995.
Para 8.20 - Tighter, or new, rules where necessary on state aids to protect particular sectors from unfair competition.	DTI launched UK proposals on priorities for new Commission's efforts to control state aid in April 1995.
Para 8.23 - Continuation of the reduction in CAP support prices to bring supply and demand into balance.	3 per cent reduction in butter intervention price; substantial reduction in support for dried fodder in July 1994.
Para 8.23 - Removal of supply controls on agricultural and food processing industries.	Little progress expected in short term.
Box 8.29 - Strengthening of Scottish Trade International.	First Director appointed April 1994. Management further strengthened October 1994. **Scotland-wide Export Development Strategy in preparation [Para 12.20].**
Box 8.32 - Series of sector based events as part of the Indo-British partnership.	Ten missions to India; 15 UK roadshows. 15 per cent more exports in 1994. Further events planned.
	Pilot video-conferencing and electronic mail systems to link Posts with Business Links and their clients [Para 12.30].
Para 8.33 - Export Promoter scheme being extended.	100th Export Promoter secured July 1994. Companies still offering good secondees.
Para 8.35 - Trade associations, chambers of commerce and other business support groups should give priority to the development of high quality export advice and support.	Being achieved through Business Links. **Government to introduce "Export Challenge" to part-fund innovative projects with Trade Associations [Box below Para 12.30].** **The Government will examine ways in which Business Links could assist SMEs in applying for export credit insurance [Para 12.27]**
Para 8.36 - A package of promotional services, training and support for exporters to encourage and help many more companies to become exporters.	Training of Business Links' Personal Business Advisers in export services.
	The Government will aim, together with Business Links, to introduce at least 30,000 new exporters to foreign markets by the year 2000 [Para 12.24]
	The Government will raise the level of professionalism of civil servants doing trade promotion work [Para 12.25]

COMMITMENTS AND PLANS IN CWP1	PROGRESS/NEW INITIATIVES/ FURTHER ACTION
	The Government will increase the provision of export services and training through Business Links, and by the end of 1995 bring in a package of financial and other incentives to help SMEs [Para 12.27].
	The Government will increase support for Trade Fairs and for Inward and Outward Missions by nearly £30 million over the next four years [Para 12.28].
	The Government will mount a rolling programme of major all-British exhibitions on the lines of the recent Partners in Progress fair in Jeddah [Para 12.29].
	The FCO will strengthen its support for exporters during 1995, creating new posts, increasing staff and deploying staff swiftly to meet temporary surges in demand [Para 12.30].
Para 8.36 - Export development counsellors in about 70 of the larger Business Links.	All 70 should be in place by end 1995 [Para 12.20].
Para 8.36 - Sectoral and locally based export promotion initiatives as part of the "Celebration of Industry" programmes being piloted in the West Midlands, Kent and elsewhere.	North Wiltshire launched March 1994. Kent in preparation. Birmingham initiative will form part of West Midlands "Industry '96" campaign. Other regions to consider similar measures.
Para 8.36 - Pilot system for referring companies from the banks to Overseas Trade Services.	First referral system between OTS and bank piloted in summer 1994. Other pilots following. Developing banks' relations with Business Links.
Para 8.36 - The Language for Export Initiative will be followed up by developing a strategy to encourage businesses to take into account foreign languages and cultural issues in their export plans	DTI subsidised pilot "Languages in Export Advisory Scheme" being developed. Promoted to companies from April 1995. Language for Export Initiative to be extended for a further 2 years.
	An enhanced export promotion programme for the construction and water industries is planned for 1995-96 [Box below Para 12.21].
	The Treasury will promote exports of UK expertise in privatisation through a new dedicated unit [Box below Para 12.21].
	The Welsh Office will extend until 1999 a programme of taking SMEs to new markets [Box below Para 12.21].
Para 8.59 - Additional emphasis to upgrading skills and technology when allocating Regional Selective Assistance (RSA) funds.	DTI running a pilot exercise.
Para 8.59 - RSA negotiations with companies will be conducted in a user friendly way.	Administrative procedures and language of offer letters and brochures have been reviewed and simplified. Procedures will be reviewed in a further year.
Para 8.59 - Identification of overseas companies with potential to invest in the UK	The US, Japan, Korea and Taiwan identified as key sources of inward investment. **Additional IBB and FCO resources to be allocated to these markets [Para 12.44]. The Government will examine with existing companies the prospects for an action plan to encourage inward investments in the food industry [Para 12.45].**
Para 8.59 - More effective help to investors to find sources of components.	Enhanced Aftercare Programme for investors to be established during 1995 [Para 12.44]. Regional Supply Network in place Spring 1995 [Para 5.35].
Para 8.59 - New investor category in the Immigration Rules.	Rules implemented on 1 October 1994.
Para 8.59 - Private sector secondees being recruited and greater interchange between IBB and FCO staff.	Director Asia Pacific appointed January 1995. Further appointments during 1995. Discussions on IBB/FCO interchange to continue.
Para 8.59 - Encouragement to RDOs to benchmark the 'product' they offer the investor.	RDOs now benchmarking through performance measures. Innovation Unit working on further proposals.
Para 8.59 - Government will concentrate on the needs of investors, including infrastructure provision and overcoming planning delays. This will include encouraging and assisting all regional interests to work together to ensure that the investor is presented with a single approach.	September 1994 revision of Memorandum of Understanding between GOs and IBB emphasises need for wider investor support. Number of RDOs has increased. **A further £400,000 set aside to improve investor service by Government in East and South East [Para 12.41].**
Para 8.59 - Establishment of a national regional strategic site bank with English Partnerships.	Design study in place. Subject to results expect to move to Pilot Phase July 1995.
	The Government will increase the IBB's staff by over 20 per cent [Para 12.44].

COMMITMENTS AND PLANS IN CWP1	PROGRESS/NEW INITIATIVES/ FURTHER ACTION
Para 8.60 - Export promoters to look for investment opportunities in the markets for which they are responsible.	Instructions issued to all Export Promoters and Heads of DTI Markets Branches.
Para 8.60 - OTS Country Market Plans to highlight the potential for investment, and draw relevant opportunities (and risks) to the attention of potential investors.	Dealt with as appropriate for each market.
	Government seeking rapid progress on Multilateral Agreement on Investment [Para 12.48].
	The Government will expand the network of bilateral Investment Promotion and Protection Agreements [Para 12.47].
Para 8.60 - The network of double taxation treaties to be expanded, and existing ones modernised.	Nearly 100 Double Taxation treaties now in force. Fourteen new or revised treaties completed Parliamentary passage in 1994-95. About 20 more in progress [Para 12.47].
Para 8.60 - Review of ECGD's overseas investment insurance scheme.	Review led to a 30 per cent cut in average premium rates. Levels of control now more linked to risk.
Para 8.60 - Evaluation of the Overseas Investment Enquiries Service and Strategic Alliance Service, to see if there are lessons for other markets.	Reviews complete. Strategic Alliance Service scheme for North America modified and extended to cover Latin America. **Will increase promotion of Investment Enquiries Service.**
Para 8.60 - Study of outward investment to consider what further support the Government might offer UK overseas investors.	Study nearing completion. **Government considering practical steps to assist overseas investors during 1995. The Government will by September 1995 improve collection and dissemination of information on investment opportunities overseas.**
	The Government will by September 1995 launch a pilot initiative to promote networking and joint marketing between UK companies overseas [Para 12.48].

FINANCE FOR BUSINESS

COMMITMENTS AND PLANS IN CWP1	PROGRESS/NEW INITIATIVES/ FURTHER ACTION
Box 9.17 - New powers in force during 1995 on Open Ended Investment Companies.	Draft regulations being prepared. Tax aspects contained in the current Finance Act 1995.
Para 9.18 - Treasury to look at the whole area of the supply of finance to industry under its Industrial Finance Initiative.	IFI concluded with package of smaller firms measures announced in 1994 Budget. The analysis will continue to inform policy.
Para 9.22 - The question of full and clear disclosure of directors' remuneration to be on the agenda of the successor to the Cadbury Committee.	Committee under Sir Richard Greenbury has been set up to identify good practice in determining directors' renumeration.
	The Government will seek to encourage the growing trend towards institutional shareholders playing a more active role [Para 15.32].
Para 9.24 - Government to act as facilitator for the private sector led working group on cooperation between corporate management and institutional shareholders.	Myners report published in February 1995
Para 9.25 - Government to work with others to raise awareness of informal investment.	Five pilots schemes to introduce business angels to companies have been successfully concluded. **The lessons learned will be disseminated later this year [Para 13.17].**
Para 9.26 - Re-examine the regulatory requirements for insurance companies for the valuation of non-listed securities.	DTI has agreed to relax these requirements [Para 13.16].
Para 9.27 - Government to identify whether and how the provision of appropriate advice and counselling can improve the survival rate of Small Firms Loan Guarantee Scheme Borrowers.	Ten pilots launched in September 1994 for period of three years. First stage evaluation to start late 1995.
	SFLGS is being reviewed. Any changes will be implemented this year [Para 13.23].
Para 9.27 - Government recognises that Business Links have a role to play in helping SMEs identify and access appropriate forms of finance.	**Business Links will deliver a new service to help growing businesses get access to the most appropriate finance package [Para 13.22].**

COMMITMENTS AND PLANS IN CWP1	PROGRESS/NEW INITIATIVES/ FURTHER ACTION
Para 9.27 - Consideration of ways of encouraging the trading of shares in smaller companies.	The Stock Exchange's Alternative Investment Market goes live in June 1995. Other Exchanges are developing (Tradepoint, EASDAQ, ESI)
Para 9.29 - Government Departments to comply with the CBI prompt payers code; to set out payment policies in their annual reports and state whether CBI code has been observed, and to publicise their arrangements for handling complaints of late payment.	**Two-thirds of Departments improved their performance in 1994-95 [Box below Para 13.25].**
Para 9.30 - Work with the business community to develop further proposals for a British standard for prompt payment.	A working group of business representatives chaired by the CBI has been established and is developing a draft standard.
Para 9.30 - Public companies to be required to state their payment policies in their director's reports.	Consultative document issued in February 1995 seeking comments on draft regulations.
Para 9.30 - Streamlining of court procedures and a review of the small claims limit.	Changes being considered to court procedures. Small claims limit being examined as part of Lord Woolf's review of civil proceedings.
Para 9.30 - Work through trade associations, Business Links and others to improve credit management in small firms.	New guide to credit management "Make the Cash Flow" published in November 1995. Credit and cashflow management incorporated into guidance to Business Links and Personal Business Advisers.
Para 9.31 - Government to keep the position on late payment under review.	Government will take stock of position in May 1996.
	The Government will loosen restrictions on the corporate bond market this year [Para 13.6].
	The Government will allow preference shares and bonds of non-financial companies into Personal Equity Plans [Para 13.6].
	The Government is examining the scope for relaxing the Financial Services Act to improve the supply of information on smaller investment opportunities [Para 13.17].
	The Government will participate in a panel to encourage the development of a UK business incubator movement [Para 13.18].
	The Government will encourage greater competition in the provision of finance to SMEs [Para 13.21].
	The Government is consulting on the idea of a Financial Management Certificate [Para 13.27].

COMMUNICATIONS AND INFRASTRUCTURE

COMMITMENTS AND PLANS IN CWP1	PROGRESS/NEW INITIATIVES/ FURTHER ACTION
Para 10.5 - Government to improve access to the international telecommunications market in order to lower prices.	Liberalisation of UK/US international simple resale of voice telephony agreed in October 1994. Pursuing wider liberalisation in WTO negotiations.
Para 10.7 - Government to secure a competitive telecommunications infrastructure which can meet new commercial demands.	Commitment reaffirmed in Broadband Command Paper published in November 1994.
Para 10.10 - Initiatives in conjunction with industry, to improve the performance of telecommunication manufacturers and suppliers.	DTI and industry initiative launched to address shortage of skilled radio frequency engineers. Telecoms 2000, a continuous improvement initiative for SMEs in the supply chain completed in April 1995. A competitiveness study into the telecoms software industry was published in May 1995. **A study examining the feasibility of a market developing in the trading of Telecoms software objects, and a joint DTI/Cable Communications Association study into the software requirements of the cable industry, are to be published shortly.**
Para 10.11 - To press for faster progression of EU liberalisation of voice telephony services.	Telecommunications infrastructure and voice telephony services will be liberalised in at least eight EU states by 1 January 1998 [Para 14.4].
Para 10.14 - White Paper on the future of the BBC.	Published in July 1994.

COMMITMENTS AND PLANS IN CWP1	PROGRESS/NEW INITIATIVES/ FURTHER ACTION
Para 10.14 - Review of the restrictions on ownership of broadcasting and newspaper companies.	Proposals will be published soon.
	DNH intends to produce a consultation document within the next few months on a regulatory framework for digital broadcasting [Para 14.14].
Para 10.16 - Rolling review of Government Departments' use of radio spectrum.	Reviews have covered three ranges of radio spectrum. A National Spectrum Management Committee is being established.
Para 10.16 - The release of spectrum for use by the emergency services to be pursued in consultation with Nato allies.	Agreement reached. Discussions on further access for civil users to military spectrum continuing.
Para 10.17 - Consultation options for more efficient management of the spectrum.	Long-term spectrum strategy published in March 1995. **Decisions on the future management of the radio spectrum following consultation will be announced shortly [Para 14.13]. Spectrum is to be made available to improve and extend access to advanced digital services [Para 14.12]**
Para 10.19 - Response to Trade and Industry Select Committee on its Post Office Review.	The Government announced in May 1995 the outline of a revised control regime to help the Post Office succeed in a more competitive environment [Para 14.22].
Para 10.23 - Further work to improve understanding of wider costs and benefits of transport.	**Initial work identified need for detailed case studies. Further research, based on case studies of the impact of the transport infrastructure on business costs and location decisions will begin later in 1995.**
Box after Para 10.25 - Consultation on privatisation of CAA's air traffic control operations.	Following public consultation, Government announced in November 1994 that it favoured privatisation in principle.
Box after Para 10.25 - Privatisation under consideration of more Trust ports.	Dundee decision to privatise announced November 1994.
Box after Para 10.25 - Privatisation of Belfast airport.	Privatised in July 1994 through management and employee buyout.
Box after Para 10.25 - Privatisation of local authority airports.	Sale of Cardiff and Bournemouth Airports completed. Local authorities are now able to spend 75 per cent of income from the sale of shares in public airport companies on capital investment projects. [Para 14.69].
Para 10.25 - Privatisation of local authority owned bus companies.	Privatisation of London Buses completed January 1995. Twenty-eight local authority bus companies (including the seven largest) already sold. Local authorities outside London are now able to spend 75 per cent of the income from sale of bus companies on capital investment projects.
Para 10.29 - Development of motorway tolling.	Working with industry to assess technology for tolling. **If assessment justified it, the Government would consider legislation to provide for motorway tolling [Para 14.59].**
Para 10.29 - Research into congestion charging in urban areas.	Research on London nearing completion. Other research in progress elsewhere.
Para 10.30 - Introducing PFI into the current road building programme, through Design Build Finance and Operate contracts.	Full invitations to tender for the first four DBFO schemes were issued in January 1995. Bids to pre-qualify for the competitions for a further four DBFO projects were received in March 1995. Scottish Office has developed a new contract form where payment is linked to performance of completed roads.
	The Scottish Office will publish a document on better management and maintenance of the trunk road network [Para 14.49].
	£79 million has been set aside in 1995-96 for measures outside London to encourage public transport and offer attractive alternatives to car users [Para 14.55]
	£15 million is to be provided for innovative schemes proposed by London boroughs covering both road and rail transport [Para 14.55].
	The Government will publish the series of speeches by the Secretary of State for Transport initiating the national debate on transport priorities and inviting comments from interested parties [Para 14.53]
Para 10.31 - Changes in Highway Inquiry Procedural Rules.	New rules introduced January 1995.

COMMITMENTS AND PLANS IN CWP1	PROGRESS/NEW INITIATIVES/ FURTHER ACTION
Para 10.31 - Trial of pre-inquiry planning conference.	The use of planning conferences on selected road schemes was announced in August 1994.
Para 10.37 - First six passenger train operating companies to be franchised.	Pre-qualification documents for the first eight franchises issued December 1994. 51 per cent of services to be franchised by 1996.
Para 10.37 - Railtrack to have major incentives to bear down on costs.	Tough price regime set by Regulator for Railtrack's charges for network access for 1995-96 to 2000-01. Privatisation will also increase efficiency.
Para 10.39 - Competition for new privately financed trains for London Underground Northern Line.	Contract signed with GEC-Alsthom April 1995. First new trains expected in mid-1996.
	The Government intends to select the consortium to design, build, finance and operate the Channel Tunnel Rail Link before the end of 1995 [Box by Para 14.60].
Para 10.40 – Local authorities to be encouraged to give greater priority for buses in traffic management schemes.	Bus priorities being encouraged through "package approach" to local authority funding.
Para 10.44 - To press for full implementation of the single market in air transport and its extension to other European countries.	Single market extended to European Economic Area in July 1994. EU/Swiss Mandate agreed. Mandate with Central and Eastern European states under discussion.
Para 10.44 - Government to seek liberalisation of air service arrangements.	Liberal air service agreements concluded with all former Soviet Union states and with the Czech Republic, Slovakia and Croatia. Unilateral liberalisation of services between UK and all US airports except Heathrow and Gatwick for US and UK airlines.
Para 10.45 - Consult on the scope for developing civil aviation at RAF Northolt.	The Government has concluded that high capital costs and physical constraints would make a civil enclave unviable. **Scope for more shared use of facilities under examination [Para 14.70].**
Para 10.49 - Press for liberalisation of shipping services.	Practical implementation of single EU market proceeding. UK operator Cenargo International commenced ferry service between Spain and Morocco. Work under way in the GATS Negotiating Group to liberalise shipping worldwide. Group due to report by June 1996. UK-led European maritime nations, Japan and the Commission in talks in April 1995 to press for the US to maintain and extend opportunities for non-US lines in US shipping markets.
Para 10.49 - Press for the control and elimination of state aid to the shipping industry.	Commission's proposals awaited. UK supported Commission in action against Italian Government over recapitalisation of two state-owned shipping companies.
Para 10.50 - Press for arrangements for maritime competition rules which ensure efficient and competitive services.	Commission has issued a report. Implementation awaits legal clarification.
Para 10.58 - More customers to be able to choose supplier of electricity.	OFFER consultation document issued January 1995. OFFER propose to hold trials for new trading arrangements in 1996. All customers will have that choice from 1998 [Para 14.31].
Para 10.61 - Consultation on changes to the electricity pool.	Director General for Electricity Supply considers that there is no case for trading outside the pool at present. Changes are being prepared within the pool and further developments are likely to result from the introduction of full competition in 1998.
Para 10.62 - Review of price controls on electricity distribution throughout Great Britain.	Review completed and recommendations accepted in England and Wales. Possible tightening of controls from April 1996 [Para 14.30]. Scottish Power plc has accepted price controls, but Scottish Hydro-Electric has not. Latter company has been referred by OFFER to the MMC, which will report in May 1995. Northern Ireland – 1995-96 tariffs approved in February 1995. Work on a price review will begin in mid-1995 [Para 14.30]. Introduction of wholesale electricity trading system by November 1996.
Para 10.63 - Support the European Commission's efforts to increase competition in electricity supply throughout the EU.	Negotiations continue on Commission's proposal to liberalise EU electricity markets.
Para 10.63 - Support European Commission in addressing anti-competitive practices in electricity supply.	In March 1995, the UK intervened in cases brought by the Commission against five Member States in respect of import and export monopolies.

COMMITMENTS AND PLANS IN CWP1	PROGRESS/NEW INITIATIVES/ FURTHER ACTION
	The Government intends to privatise parts of the nuclear industry in 1996 [Para 14.33]
	The Government is committed to opening up the domestic market for dealing with nuclear liabilities [Para 14.34].
Para 10.67 - Consultation document on implementing the MMC Report on Gas.	Legislation to end monopoly of supply of gas to small businesses and domestic consumers introduced in February 1995. Competition to be phased in between 1996 and 1998 [Para 14.24].
Para 10.68 - Gas pipeline from mainland to Northern Ireland.	Premier Transco Ltd to build pipeline. Due for completion in 1996. DTI has asked an industry-wide steering group to report on access to offshore infrastructure. DTI will consider whether the current regime needs to be amended [Box below Para 14.25].
	In Northern Ireland, a Next Steps Agency will become responsible for water and sewerage services from April 1996 [Para 14.41].
	The Government will explore with interested parties whether revised Building Regulations could benefit the non-domestic sector through greater energy efficiency [Para 14.39]

LONDON

COMMITMENTS AND PLANS IN CWP1	PROGRESS/NEW INITIATIVES/ FURTHER ACTION
Para 11.3 - Vigorous promotion of inward investment opportunities in London.	London First Centre open April 1994. In receipt of £0.68 million DTI funding 1994-95.
Para 11.3 - Substantial improvements to London's transport infrastructure.	Red Routes in progress. Rail Franchising ongoing. Private finance instrumental in Heathrow Express, CTRL, JLE, Northern Line trains and Docklands Light Railway extension [Box below Para 5.35].
Para 11.3 - Promotion of investment in London's skill-base.	Pan-London credit system – NETWORK – supported by London TECs, launched April 1995. Provides young people with access to training options including Apprenticeships and Accelerated Modern Apprenticeships.
Para 11.3 - Development of plans for a pan-London Business Link.	Opening of Business Link London network is expected to be phased over the second half of 1995.
Para 11.3 - Encouragement of the re-use of urban land and buildings in London.	Forty-nine successful Single Regeneration Budget bids announced December 1994. Draft Strategic Guidance for London Planning Authorities was issued for consultation in March 1995. Further round of SRB bidding to be held in 1995.
Para 11.3 - Initiation of a wide range of measures to improve the quality of life in London.	Package of measures designed to improve air quality in the capital announced January 1995.
Para 11.3 - Publication of a London Pride Prospectus.	Prospectus launched January 1995. Government Office for London will work with London Pride Partnership as it takes its agenda forward.
	The Government Office for London will work with the Sports Council, local authorities and others to support and enhance London's international reputation as a sports venue [Box below Para 5.35].
	Action plan on manufacturing will be taken forward by manufacturers in partnership with Government and local business organisations [Box below Para 5.35].

REGENERATION

COMMITMENTS AND PLANS IN CWP1	PROGRESS/NEW INITIATIVES/ FURTHER ACTION
Para 12.12 - Regional Challenge to be introduced in parts of England and Wales.	Launched February 1995.
Para 12.12 - Simpler, and more effective, administration of the European Structural Funds.	Single Programmes agreed for Objective 1, 2, 3 and 5b operations. The Single Programming Documents will last until 1999 for Objective 1 and 5b, and 1996 for Objective 2.

COMMITMENTS AND PLANS IN CWP1	PROGRESS/NEW INITIATIVES/ FURTHER ACTION
Para 12.12 - Regional priorities and criteria for the Structural Funds to favour proposals aimed at improving competitiveness.	Taken into account in the Single Programmes (see above).
Para 12.12 - Consideration of how to extend the "challenge approach" to further domestic programmes.	Single Regeneration Budget uses the challenge approach, providing total resources of around £1.3 billion annually, with over £800 million available over the next three years for new schemes following competitive tendering. The SRB aims to attract matching private sector and European Structural Funds funding [Para 5.25].
	Government Offices will encourage future SRB bids aimed at raising levels of educational attainment [Para 5.26}
	Rural White Paper to be published in Autumn 1995 [Para 5.27].
	Scottish Enterprise Networks expect to assist over 15,500 businesses, provide 38,000 square metres of premises, encourage £60 million private sector property investment, bring 700 hectares of land back into use, train 37,000 young people, provide training to 30,000 adults, pilot a Small Business Loan scheme, and work on the Scottish launch of the Alternative Investment Market [Box below Para 5.27].
	Scottish Enterprise Business Birth Rate Strategy aims to help create an additional 25,000 businesses in Scotland by 2000 [Box below Para 5.27].

COMMERCIAL FRAMEWORK

COMMITMENTS AND PLANS IN CWP1	PROGRESS/NEW INITIATIVES/ FURTHER ACTION
Box 13.8 - Government to consider with the Health and Safety Commission and others, how best to carry into effect the recommendations of the Commission's review of health and safety legislation.	HSC have agreed an action plan following consultation. Full implementation within three to five years.
	A major initiative to simplify health and safety guidance and reduce paperwork is planned [Box below Para 8.10].
	Implementation of six key EU directives on health and safety is to be evaluated [Box below Para 8.10].
	A discussion document on health and safety for small firms and the self employed will be published [Box below Para 8.10].
Para 13.9 - Proposals for a simple, consistent and safe regime for food temperature controls.	Draft Regulations were sent to the European Commission in September 1994, and are expected to be approved and brought into force by September 1998.
Para 13.10 - New Deregulation Task Force to follow up the reviews, and ensure the views of business are heard in discussions on regulations.	Final response to Lord Sainsbury on outstanding recommendations - March 1995. New task force report expected in Summer 1995.
Para 13.11 - Deregulation and Contracting Out Act to provide a mechanism for removing unnecessary burdens in existing primary legislation.	Received Royal Assent November 1994. First orders laid April 1995 with others at regular intervals thereafter.
Para 13.12 - Before new regulations are introduced, business will be consulted, and the costs and benefits fully assessed.	First six monthly Command Paper produced December 1994. DTI will issue revised guidance to Departments summer 1995.
Para 13.14 - Reviews to remove duplication in enforcement at national and local levels.	Both reviews published and public consultation complete. Inter-departmental discussions on-going.
	The Government is consulting on the development of a new model appeals procedure [Para 15.8].
	A new Cabinet sub-committee on deregulation will be set up [Para 15.6]
Para 13.15 - Government to continue to press the relevant authorities to ensure that international regulations are properly enforced.	EU has put forward resolutions to help ensure that Single Market regulations are properly enforced. Quadrilateral officials group established.
Para 13.16 - Government to form strategic alliances to place deregulation at the top of the Community agenda.	Anglo-German business group's final report discussed at Anglo-German summit in May 1995. Strategic alliances with other Member States strengthened through bilateral meetings at Ministerial and official level during 1995.

COMMITMENTS AND PLANS IN CWP1	PROGRESS/NEW INITIATIVES/ FURTHER ACTION
Para 13.16 - Government to promote a burden-minimising approach to EU legislation.	See above. Also, all EU Explanatory Memoranda which will affect British business to contain Compliance Cost Assessments.
Para 13.19 - Government to consult local authorities on enabling them to agree with applicants seeking planning permission timetable for decision, with the applicant meeting the cost of the extra resources required.	Business did not support proposal. Proposal dropped.
	In England and Wales, procedures to streamline production of local plans and to shorten the time taken to deal with planning appeals will be introduced during 1995 [Para 15.21].
	The Government intends to publish a second consultation document in 1995 on the planning system in Scotland [Para 15.22].
Para 13.20 - Government to review the procedures for alerting small businesses to new environmental regulations, and for explaining them.	A review of current practice completed in January 1995. Consultation with industry is now nearing completion and work has begun on a draft report.
Para 13.20 - Consideration of whether charges for Integrated Pollution Control can be discounted for companies with independently verified environmental management systems.	HMIP will consider whether IPC charges should be discounted as part of a fundamental review of its charging scheme. This will commence in the financial year 1995-96.
Para 13.20 - Government to fund evaluation of the environmental and economic effects of Integrated Pollution Control.	A pilot study of IPC authorizations was completed in April 1995. A twelve month evaluation is now taking place.
Para 13.24 - Greater weight to be given to business priorities in Government support for the British Standards Institution.	Reflected in grant-in-aid conditions. Testable objectives to be set for BSI. BSI bidding against priorities determined by its consultative committees.
Para 13.24 - Government to support efforts to secure the adoption of UK standards in other countries, particularly in the developing world, on a bilateral basis.	Reflected in funding arrangements for RESOURCE Ltd and survey conducted on behalf of National Measurement System Policy Unit.
Para 13.25 - Abolition of the statutory marketing arrangements for milk and potatoes.	Achieved November 1994 (Milk). Announced (Potatoes) for 1997; deregulatory measures in interim.
Para 13.25 - Removal of restrictions on letting land as part of reforms of agricultural tenancy law.	Agricultural Tenancies Act received Royal Assent
Para 13.29 - Introduction of legislation to reform the law on restrictive trade practices and abuse of market power.	The Government is committed to introducing legislation as soon as Parliamentary time permits.
Para 13.30 - Extension of the scope of companies' ability to offer undertakings as an alternative to a detailed investigation by Monopolies and Mergers Commission.	Completed. Came into force 3 January 1995.
Para 13.30 - Insignificant cases to be removed from competition scrutiny.	Completed.
Para 13.30 - Target times for decisions on competition cases will be shortened.	Completed.
Para 13.31 - European Commission to be encouraged to reduce delays in handling cases under Articles 85 and 86 of the Treaty of Rome.	UK pressing Commission to set internal time limits. Commission considering alternative guidance on agreements with minor effect on competition. De minimis threshold has been raised.
Para 13.31 - European Commission to be encouraged to continue to demonstrate that business is treated fairly in competition matters.	Commission has extended role of Hearing Officer to ensure increased access to relevant information for parties under investigation and ensure the right of parties to be heard as appropriate.
	The Government will consult business on further possibilities for taking minor agreements out of the scope of competition legislation [Para 15.26].
	The UK will encourage the Commission to simplify "block exemptions" as they are reviewed [Para 15.26].
Para 13.31 - European Commission to be encouraged to ensure transparency and consistency in its policies on fines.	In recent cases, the Commission has explained its fining policy more fully.
Para 13.34 - Consultation on consolidation and simplification of arbitration law in England and Wales.	A revised draft, taking account of responses to consultation, will shortly be issued.
Para 13.34 - Proposals for the development and reform of arbitration in Scotland.	Report being prepared for submission to Lord Advocate who will decide upon further action.
Para 13.35 - Government keen to encourage the use in appropriate cases of other forms of alternative dispute resolution (ADR).	Lord Chancellor evaluating potential of ADR and the various research options which may assist him.

COMMITMENTS AND PLANS IN CWP1	PROGRESS/NEW INITIATIVES/ FURTHER ACTION
	The Lord Chancellor's Department is planning a pilot project in the Patent County Court to encourage parties to use alternatives to litigation [Para 15.28].
Para 13.36 - Study of the role of trust law in the commercial field.	The Law Commission's business law team, set up in February 1994, now working on various topics including Electronic Data Interchange.
Para 13.37 - Review of company law so as to make it easier for companies to be run as groups without undermining the legitimate interests of creditors.	Informal consultation completed and alternative approaches being developed in the light of responses.
Para 13.37 - Review of law to clarify directors' duties.	Publication of consultative document suspended following setting up of Greenbury Committee.
Box 13.37 - Regulations to enable up to half a million small companies to dispense with statutory audit requirements.	Regulations came into effect August 1994.
Box 13.37 - Consultation on implementation of EU option to classify more companies as small for accounting purposes	Consultation document issued in May 1995.
Box 13.37 - Consultation on the application of accounting standards to small companies.	Responses received February 1995; now being considered by working group of the Consultative Committee of Accountancy Bodies.
Box 13.37 - Feasibility study on the best way forward for reform of the law for small private companies.	A consultative document on the results of the feasibility study was issued. DTI is now considering the responses.
Para 13.38 - The Government will keep the Financial Reporting Council informed over the timing of its own consultation on company law.	Taking place on a continuing basis.
Para 13.40 - Discussion on issues arising from recent consultation of company rescues.	Further consultative document setting out a revised proposal for a new Company Voluntary Arrangement issued April 1995. The Government is considering the proposal for a debt to equity mechanism and whether any other measures should be taken to facilitate administration.
Para 13.45 - Trade Marks Bill.	Enacted.
	The Government will seek to ensure effective application of a range of international intellectual property rights arrangements [Para 15.37].
	The Government will seek to ensure that EU legislation on the development of the information superhighway, multimedia systems and biotechnology promotes the competitiveness of UK industry [Para 15.39].
	The Patent Office will extend its search and advisory services to assist SMEs through Business Links [Para 15.40].
Para 13.59 - Consultation on the closer alignment of definitions used in assessing national insurance contributions and income tax.	The 1994 Budget announced various measures and programmes of closer working. Further informal consultation with business planned for mid-late 1995.
Para 13.61 - Review of how the work of the Inland Revenue, Customs and Excise, and the Contributions Agency can best be co-ordinated to minimise costs on business arising from tax collection and compliance.	The Chancellor has announced closer working between the Revenue and Customs; and the Revenue and Contributions Agency. Action plans being drawn up and implemented.
	A pilot scheme to give rulings on the tax treatment of transactions undertaken before tax returns are completed was introduced from 1 December 1994 [Box below Para 2.24]
	A single point of registration for new businesses for tax, national insurance and, where appropriate, VAT will be piloted in the next two years [Box below Para 2.24].
	Proposed annual rather than quarterly VAT payments for firms with a turnover of less than £100,000. If agreed, will be phased in between December 1995 and 1996, saving £85 million a year [Box below Para 2.24].
	The Inland Revenue is reviewing ways to reduce the complexity of tax legislation [Box below Para 2.24].

COMMITMENTS AND PLANS IN CWP1	PROGRESS/NEW INITIATIVES/ FURTHER ACTION
	The Government is commissioning work on a computer-based system to help new businesses save time and understand their obligations in starting up [Box below Para 15.12].
	The Government intends to ease the burden of financial reporting on small firms [Para 15.31].
	The Government hopes to increase the number of Bills published in draft in advance of introduction in Parliament, allowing more consultation [Para 15.42].

BUSINESS OF GOVERNMENT

COMMITMENTS AND PLANS IN CWP1	PROGRESS/NEW INITIATIVES/ FURTHER ACTION
Box in para 14.5 - An Efficiency Scrutiny of Government Research Establishments sector by sector. It will identify those where privatisation is feasible and desirable, and will make recommendations in other cases.	The Government is considering the recommendations of the scrutiny and will make an announcement shortly.
Box following 14.6 - Compulsory Competitive Tendering extended to local authority professional services.	Statutory framework for implementing CCT for legal services, construction and property services and several manual services in place. Tendering to be completed by April 1996 in first authorities. Further statutory instruments extending CCT to Finance, IT and Personnel services brought forward in May 1995.
Para 14.11 - Unitary authorities may be created in many areas depending upon the individual recommendations of the Local Government Commission.	The Local Government Commission recommended new all-unitary structures in ten of the 39 shire counties. The Isle of Wight unitary authority was established on 1 April 1995, to be followed by those in Cleveland, Avon, Humberside and York on 1 April 1996. Twenty-four more unitary authorities proposed for 1 April 1997. Local Government Commission to be asked to carry out fresh reviews of a small number of individual districts. Unitary authorities resulting from these reviews will be set up in 1997 or 1998. In Scotland and Wales, a new unitary structure for local authorities will be established on 1 April 1996.
Para 14.11 - Reforms to the Police Service including major restructuring of pay and conditions of service, including the use of performance related pay.	Reforms for all ranks fully implemented on 1 April 1995. In Scotland changes in the structures of authorities take place from 1 April 1996.
Para 14.12 - Any pay increase for public sector employees to be offset by improvements in productivity.	Public expenditure programmes set on the basis that pay increases will be covered by efficiencies and other economies.
Para 14.12 - Substantial delegations of pay bargaining processes to be extended.	Within the Civil Service, delegation for all staff below senior levels to be completed by 1 April 1996.
Para 14.12 - Introduction of accruals accounting in the rest of central Government.	Green Paper published in July 1994. All Departments aim to implement accruals accounting by 1 April 1998.
Para 14.12 - Initiative to increase interchange through more non-executive opportunities in private sector for senior civil servants.	366 Civil Servants were were seconded to the private sector [Para 10.14].
Box after 14.12 - The number of civil servants will continue to fall.	Nearly 524,000 Civil Servants were in post in January 1995. Departments plan to employ 477,000 civil servants by April 1998.
Para 14.14 - White Paper on the Civil Service.	White Paper "The Civil Service: Continuity and Change" published 13 July 1994. Further Command Paper "The Civil Service: Taking Forward Continuity and Change" published 26 January 1995, following consultation and Select Committee Report. Policies being implemented across the Civil Service.
Para 14.14 - Evaluation of the Competing for Quality Initiative to see how far its objectives have been met and how best it can be developed in future years, including making greater use of innovative ideas from the private sector.	Evaluation underway, and scheduled to report in autumn 1995.

COMMITMENTS AND PLANS IN CWP1	PROGRESS/NEW INITIATIVES/ FURTHER ACTION
Para 14.14 - Announcements of the timing and terms for the full reviews of proposed or existing agencies, as well as large executive Non-Departmental Public Bodies.	Reviews of all Bodies are now publicised as they fall due.
Para 14.14 - Review of management planning control systems in Departments.	Report published. Ministers taking forward recommendations.
	The Government will continue to privatise services which need not be the responsibility of Government [Para 10.4].
	Where privatisation is not practicable, the Government will, where possible, introduce private sector management to organisations likely to benefit [Para 10.7].
	The CSO plans to expand the range of statistics available on services, and is encouraging data sharing and best practice among data collectors [Para 10.14].
	A further 65 executive agencies are in the pipeline. When in place, three-quarters of civil servants will be working in Next Steps organisations [Para 10.20].
	The 1995 Next Steps Review will include trends, reporting on executive agencies' performance against their targets over three financial years [Para 10.22].
	Departments and Agencies will be encouraged to adopt best practice from both private and public sectors in their three year efficiency plans [Para 10.28].
	The Government aims to complete its programme of fundamental expenditure reviews during the course of this Parliament [Para 10.28].
	The Government will reduce the burden of surveys and strengthen survey control through a programme to cut out duplication and reduce random sample surveys sent to the same firm; publish best practice guides on administrative and survey forms; use more electronic collection of data; and consider more business representation on the CSO Board [Box in Para 10.28].
	Decisions on implementing proposals for removing unnecessary burdens from local government will be taken as soon as practicable, in the light of DOE's consultation document "Deregulating Local Government - the First Steps" [Para 10.35].
	Local authority associations intend to produce this summer a Good Practice Guide on how they carry out enforcement. A package of other measures will be announced shortly [Para 10.36].

PUBLIC PURCHASING

COMMITMENTS AND PLANS IN CWP1	PROGRESS/NEW INITIATIVES/ FURTHER ACTION
Para 15.6 - Government aims to secure agreements under which UK suppliers can gain access to public sector markets abroad, and to ensure the effective implementation of these agreements.	Action continues to extend the Government procurement agreement and other international agreements and to monitor their implementation.
Para 15.9 - Sixty-nine PURSUIT-based systems planned.	Nineteen Departments have implemented fully or partially PURSUIT-compatible systems.
Para 15.9 - Introduction of standardised Electronic Data Interchange systems involving 20 Departments.	User Group established. EDI implementation guide to be published by July 1995. Full implementation for completion by April 1998. Six Departments so far have full operational EDI systems implemented.
Para 15.13 - Government to continue to encourage the Commission to improve its monitoring of public procurement rules, the transparency of these rules, and its effectiveness in handling complaints.	Action plan agreed by Ministers and relevant issues raised with the Commission. Commission has announced mid-term impact assessment for report in 1996.
Para 15.15 - Development of a strategy to improve value for money and the competitiveness of suppliers and encouragement to all Departments to develop further and better performance indicators.	The strategy is published in the White Paper "Setting New Standards" on 22 May 1995. All Departments are preparing to implement the White Paper. Improvements will be published in Departmental Reports [Para 10.38].

COMMITMENTS AND PLANS IN CWP1	PROGRESS/NEW INITIATIVES/ FURTHER ACTION
Para 15.15 - Development of effective benchmarking systems on purchasing.	Trial with the Chartered Institute of Purchasing and Supply underway. The results will be available later in 1995 [Para 10.39].
Para 15.15 - 75 per cent of staff in key procurement posts in central Government should either have professional qualifications, or have completed two years professional training programme.	64 per cent have either qualified or are studying for the qualification. Target to be achieved by 31 December 1996.
Para 15.15 - Continued examination of ways of making it easier and simpler for companies of all sizes to bid for public contracts.	Survey completed. Departments are addressing weaknesses in their performance flagged up by suppliers [Para 10.40].
Para 15.15 - Review of the help currently provided to SMEs in bidding for public (and private) sector contracts to see whether more can be done to encourage SME participation.	Review completed December 1994. Follow-up work will establish best practice in publications for SMEs and help small firms gain access to Government contracts [Para 10.41].
Para 15.15 - Monitoring impact of new EU legislation to ensure that it increases opportunities for competitive suppliers.	Inter-departmental group convened in 1995. **The Government will consult widely on Commission review of purchasing Directives [Para 10.43].**

GLOSSARY

ABCC	Association of British Chambers of Commerce
AEA	Atomic Energy Authority
ACBE	Advisory Committee on Business and the Environment
ADAS	Formerly known as Agriculture Development and Advisory Service
AS	Advanced supplementary level
Basic Skills Agency (formerly ALBSU)	This Government-funded agency is the central development agency for basic skills in England and Wales
BBC	British Broadcasting Corporation
BSI	British Standards Institution
Business Links	A network of independent local business information and advice centres offering a wide range of services to the business community, designed to enhance the competitiveness of local companies. They are run by partnerships which include Chambers of Commerce, TECs, Local Authorities, Enterprise Agencies and DTI.
CAA	Civil Aviation Authority
Cadbury Committee	A committee chaired by Sir Adrian Cadbury that recommended changes to corporate governance in the UK
CAP	Common Agricultural Policy
CBI	Confederation of British Industry
CCT	Compulsory Competitive Tendering
CCTV	Close circuit television
CDL	Career Development Loans - private sector loans to individuals (with Government funded interest 'holiday') to fund training
CNC	Computer Numerical Control
CONTACT	Consortium for Advanced Continuing Education and Training
CRINE	Cost Reduction Initiatives for the New Era - offshore oil & gas industry
CSO	Central Statistical Office
CTC	City Technology College
DERA (formerly DRA)	Defence Evaluation and Research Agency

DFE	Department for Education
DGXXIII	Directorate General XXIII of the European Commission, responsible for telecommunications, information market and exploitation of research
DH	Department of Health
DNH	Department of National Heritage
DOE	Department of the Environment
DTI	Department of Trade and Industry
DoT	Department of Transport
EASDAQ	European Association of Share Dealers - Automated Quotation
ED	Employment Department
EDI	Electronic Data Interchange
ECGD	Export Credits Guarantee Department
EEA	European Economic Area - a free trade zone covering the countries of the European Union, Iceland, Norway and Liechtenstein
EEF	Engineering Employers' Federation
EFTA	European Free Trade Area - a grouping composed of Iceland, Switzerland, Norway and Liechtenstein
Enterprise Networks	Scottish Enterprise, Highlands and Islands Enterprise (H&IE) and their networks of LECs
ERDF	European Regional Development Fund - an EU Structural Fund which co-finances activities such as infrastructure investment and business support measures
ESI	Electronic Share Information
ESRC	Economic and Social Research Council
EU	European Union, formerly European Community, composed of Austria, Belgium, Denmark, Germany, Greece, Spain, Finland, France, the Republic of Ireland, Italy, Luxembourg, the Netherlands, Portugal, Sweden and the United Kingdom (in the charts, unless otherwise stated, figures for the EU include figures for the UK)
EUREKA	An initiative to encourage and assist market-driven collaborative research and development projects by organisations across Europe.

	Members include the EU countries, Hungary, Iceland, Norway, Russia, Slovenia, Switzerland, Turkey and the European Commission	**HEFCs**	Higher Education Funding Councils
Eurostat	Statistical Office of the European Commission	**HEIs**	Higher Education Institutions
FCO	Foreign and Commonwealth Office	**HMI**	Her Majesty's Inspectorate of Schools
FDI	Foreign direct investment	**HMIP**	Her Majesty's Inspectorate of Pollution
FE	Further Education (provided mainly by FE, sixth form and some specialist colleges)	**HMT**	Her Majesty's Treasury
		IBB	Invest in Britain Bureau
FEDA	Further Education Development Agency	**IFI**	Industrial Finance Initiative
FEFC	Further Education Funding Council	**Information Superhighways**	Broadband communication networks capable of transferring large amounts of information quickly, usually in both directions
FEFCW	Further Education Funding Council for Wales	**Internet**	The Internet is a collection of thousands of networks linked by a common set of technical protocols which make it possible for users of any one of the networks to communicate with or use the services located on any of the other networks
FEI	Federation of Electronic Industries		
G7 countries	Canada, France, Germany, Italy, Japan, the UK and the United States		
GATE	Guaranteed Accommodation and Training for Employment		
GATT	General Agreement on Tariffs and Trade	**Intrastat**	EU-wide collection of trade statistics
GCE	General Certificate of Education	**Investors in People**	The national quality standard for investment in training and development to achieve business goals
GCSE	General Certificate of Secondary Education		
GDP	Gross Domestic Product - the total value of goods and services produced during a period of time	**IoD**	Institute of Directors
		IRTU	Industrial Research and Technology Unit (Northern Ireland)
Germany	Unless stated otherwise, figures in the charts for Germany refer to the territory of the Federal Republic before October 1990	**IT**	Information Technology
		ITCs	Innovation and Technology Counsellors
GEST	Grants for Education Support and Training	**ITOs**	Industrial Training Organisations - mainly independent industry training bodies that set sector training strategy
GNVQ	General National Vocational Qualifications (see box below)	**JSA**	Job Seeker's Allowance
GO-L	Government Office for London - one of the Government Offices for the English regions established in April 1994 to bring together the regional operations of DOE, DoT, DTI and the Training Enterprise and Education Directorate of ED	**LECs**	Local enterprise companies in Scotland which combine business development and training responsibilities and have some functions in common with TECs in England and Wales
		LINC	Local Investment Networking Company
GSVQ	General Scottish Vocational Qualifications (see box below)	**LINK**	A Government-sponsored scheme that encourages collaboration between industry and the science base in over 30 priority areas of research
HE	Higher Education (provided by universities and in some FE colleges)		

MAFF	Ministry of Agriculture Fisheries and Food
MBA	Master of Business Administration
MCI	Management Charter Initiative - an employer-led organisation which promotes the development of managers and has lead responsibility for developing national standards of performance for managers and supervisors within the NVQ framework
MOD	Ministry of Defence
MTTA	Machine Tool Technologies Association
multimedia	multimedia denotes the combination of the different media of voice, text, still and moving pictures. The word is also commonly used to describe the process of convergence between the telecommunication, broadcasting and publishing sectors
NACETT	National Advisory Council for Education and Training Targets
NAFTA	North American Free Trade Agreement
NASDAQ	North American Association of Share Dealers - Automated Quotation
NATO	North Atlantic Treaty Organisation
National Curriculum	The framework for teaching and learning across a range of subjects and the associated assessment arrangements, laid down by Statute for all pupils of compulsory school age (5-16) attending state schools
NCVQ	National Council for Vocational Qualifications
NEARNET	Networks of local contacts across the UK to enable local sources of innovation support to be brought together in a coherent way.
NICEC	National Institute of Careers and Education Counselling
NICs	National Insurance Contributions
NIESR	National Institute of Economic and Social Research
NVQ	National Vocational Qualifications
ODA	Overseas Development Administration
OECD	Organisation for Economic Cooperation and Development
OFSTED	Office for Standards in Education
OPSS	Office of Public Service and Science
OST	Office of Science and Technology
OTIS	Overseas Technology Information Service
OTS	Overseas Trade Services - a joint operation of the DTI and the FCO and the Government's main deliverer of export promotion services
PFI	Private Finance Initiative - it is designed to encourage private-sector involvement and finance in capital projects
PPP	Purchasing Power Parity - modified exchange rates which adjust for differences in price levels between countries
PSBR	Public Sector Borrowing Requirement
PTP	Postgraduate Training Partnership scheme
R&D	Research and Development
RDOs	Regional Development Organisations - local authority and private sector partnership bodies that promote inward investment in the English regions
RPI	Retail Prices Index
RSA	Regional Selective Assistance in the assisted areas - a job related assistance scheme operated under Section 7 of the Industrial Development Act 1982
RTOs	Research and Technology Organisations - private companies that provide research and associated services on behalf of particular groups of companies which use similar technologies or are in the same sector
S&T	Science and Technology
S,E&T	Science, Engineering and Technology
SBAC	Society of British Aerospace Companies
SCAA	School Curriculum Assessment Authority
SCOTVEC	Scottish Vocational Education Council

SHEFC	Scottish Higher Education Funding Council	**TCS**	Teaching Company Scheme - places high quality recent graduates with companies to carry out supervised projects to encourage technology transfer
SIC	Standard Industrial Classification		
SRB	Single Regeneration Budget. Created in 1994, the SRB brought together 20 of the existing regeneration programmes into a single, flexible budget to regenerate local areas in England	**TECs**	Training and Enterprise Councils - industry-led bodies that set local strategies for training and economic development in England and Wales
SMART	Small Firms Merit Award for Research and Technology: a scheme to support firms with up to 50 employees in highly innovative areas of technology	**TENs**	Trans-European Networks - a range of transport, energy and telecoms networks in the EU which may be financed by EU grants, European Investment Bank loans and private sector finance
SMEs	Small and Medium-sized Enterprises	**TVEI**	Technical and Vocational Education Initiative
SMMT	Society of Motor Manufacturers and Traders Ltd	**UCAS**	University and Colleges Administration System
SPUR	Support for Products Under Research: a scheme to help firms with up to 250 employees improve product and process development	**UKCS**	United Kingdom Continental Shelf
		UNICE	Union of Industrial and Employers' Confederations of Europe
SRAMA	The Spring Research and Manufacturers' Association	**US BoL**	US Bureau of Labor Statistics
Structural Funds	EU Funds which make grants to a range of economic regeneration measures and projects particularly in specially designated geographical areas	**WWW**	World Wide Web. A search technique for the Internet which links related information.
		WTO	World Trade Organisation - inter-governmental body set up as part of the Uruguay Round to administer multi-lateral trade agreements, including GATT
SuperJANET	Development of JANET - the Joint Academic NETwork which links academic institutions across the UK		
SUPERNET	Services from centres of technological excellence.	**YT**	Youth Training - Government-sponsored work-based training available for all 16 and 17 year old school leavers
SVQ	Scottish Vocational Qualifications		

VOCATIONAL QUALIFICATIONS AND THEIR EQUIVALENTS

APPROXIMATE DESCRIPTION IN EMPLOYERS' TERMS	VOCATIONAL QUALIFICATIONS		ACADEMIC QUALIFICATIONS
	GNVQ/GSVQ	NVQ/SVQ	
Professional Qualifications /Middle Managers	5	–	)
Higher Technician /Junior Manager	4	–	) Higher) Education)
Technician	3	Advanced	2 A Levels or 3 Highers
Craftsman	2	Intermediate	5 GCSEs (A-C) or SCE Standard Grades
Pre-vocational	1	Foundation	4 GCSEs (D-G) - no equivalent in Scotland

Printed in the United Kingdom for HMSO
Dd 5064128   5/95   C140   51-8424   48003   Ord 322313